MY BELOVED COUNTRY MADE ME CRY

MY BELOVED COUNTRY MADE ME CRY

CRIME | COMPASSION | HOPE

Debby Thomson

Copyright © 2019 by Debby Thomson

All rights reserved. This book or any portion thereof
may not be reproduced or used in any manner whatsoever
without the express written permission of the author or publisher
except for the use of brief quotations in a book review.

Project Manager: Fred van der Linde
Design and Layout: Ronel Niemand
Cover Design: Bjorn van der Linde
Editor: Jacques de Villiers

Printed in South Africa
First Printing, 2019

ISBN: 978-0-6398354-4-0

WoodRock Publishing
South Africa
www.woodrockpublishing.com

The author and the publisher believe on the strength of due diligence
exercised that this work does not contain any material that is the subject
of copyright held by another person.

CRY THE BELOVED COUNTRY

"Who indeed knows the secret of the earthly pilgrimage? Who knows for what we live, and struggle, and die? Who knows what keeps us living and struggling, while all things break about us? Who knows why the warm flesh of a child is such comfort, when one's own child is lost and cannot be recovered? Wise men write many books, in words too hard to understand. But this, the purpose of our lives, the end of all our struggle, is beyond all human wisdom."

Alan Paton, Cry the Beloved Country

Hailed as one of the greatest South African novels, Cry the Beloved Country was first published in the United States in 1948 bringing international attention to South Africa's tragic history.

This all-time classic highlights issues such as the importance of family and the unification of family; re-uniting the nation; moral values of kindness, compassion and understanding; tensions between different societies within South Africa and the impact government decisions have on the many citizens of this country.

The sad reality is that 71 years later, very little has changed. Although present in different formats and different guises, the same issues and problems still abound and the government and all its systems are still letting the citizens down on a daily basis.

This book looks at these issues within the context of South African living today and how the citizens of today are crying within our beloved country.

For my Family

For my Community

For my Country

For my Brother

Acknowledgements

This has most certainly been a long and emotional journey, not just for myself but my entire family.

Thank you to each one of you for standing together along the way, and not letting this tragedy destroy us or pull us apart in any way.

To Mom and Dad, thank you for all the support and love you have always given us all. We have watched how this tragedy has broken you down, but you have both found a way to pull together and rise above it all. Your love for your children and grandchildren is like a beacon in the dark.

Lorna, how do I even begin to express my admiration for you and all you have done for Megs, Nick and Annie-Rose. One of the first things Mike ever said to us was that he had found the perfect person to be the mother of his children and you have shown the world that he was 100% spot on. You have brought up your children to be the most loving, gentle, caring and understanding individuals I know. Mike without doubt looks down on you all daily with pride and love.

To Allan and Sarah, thank you for all unquestioning support to the entire family from the minute we got that first phone call. You opened up your home and your hearts to allow us all to be together as a family and to tread those first few difficult days together as a united family of souls. You have continued to be a support to Lorna and helped her with all the difficult processes and decisions she has had to face on her own thereafter.

To my sister Cally and to my long-standing friend Helen, thank you both for all the support and caring you have given to Mom and Dad through this all. You have both been there for them whenever they have needed that extra support, love and understanding.

To all my nieces and nephews, Shanny Debs, Megs, Nick, Annie-Rose, D-Man and Boysie – you are all the shining lights in our lives and your enthusiasm and successes are a pride to us all. You keep us young, you keep us laughing and you keep us loving. You are the kind of citizens of the future that can take this wonderful land to where it needs to be.

To Rich and Lou – thank you for everything you have done since that first morning and for the continual support and strength you have been for Lorna and the children along the way. Rich, thank you for stepping in and, specifically in more recent years, for being the fatherly figure and support that they have needed, when they have needed it, and to both of you for being the home base, and security base they are so in need of.

To Bruce, our Hero Cop. Thank you for all you did not just for us and for the other Razor Gang victims, but thank you for all your years of dedication to the force and for your commitment to protecting and aiding your fellow countrymen. We are ever grateful for the day you stepped into our lives.

Thank you to Stan Lorge and your team at Computershare. Your vision and hard work assisted us in ensuring that Mike would never be just another statistic and you assisted us in making something positive out of his tragic demise.

Since that tragic night, my life has taken a drastic turn and from originally heading into a life of conservation and biodiversity management, I suddenly found myself heading into a direction of trauma support, safety of my community and fighting crime. Through this, I have had the privilege of working alongside some of the most committed, hardworking, compassionate and caring citizens this country has the honour to be home to.

To my fellow "bestuur's groepie" members within Hoedspruit Farmwatch, Mike, Jane, Lafras, Jaco, Courtney, Sieg, Dawie and Ramon. Thank you for all the many hours that you put in to making this a safer community for all. Thank you for all the hard work and difficult decisions we need to face when addressing the fears and threats in our community and the steadfast and clear headed manner in which you face them.

Together with the rest of the Farmwatch Reaction unit, thank you for all the many nights you leave your families behind and head out in the night, to take on the criminals within our communities and to keeping our community safe. You are all heroes in my eyes and it is an absolute privilege and pleasure to work with you all.

To my Victim Support Unit crew, we have grown from the small little group of five initial volunteers, to fifteen caring hearts who are willing to go out late at night to assist and support our community in need. Specifically to Christine and Rita – you were part of the first little group of 5 that saw the value in the vision of a VSU and you have stood by me all these years. Thank you for your continued care and compassion to your fellow man.

To all the outstanding SAPS members that we work with, whether locally at our station, or whether part of the specialist units we work with. The hours, commitments and expectations that are put upon you are extreme. You work in some of the most challenging situations anyone could ever imagine and your continued commitment to your calling is beyond remarkable. I honour you all and I thank you

In focusing on the goal to bring this book to fruition, I thank everyone along the way that has assisted me and supported me in this goal.

To Jamie and Bronwyn Paterson, thank you for your openness and willingness to share your journeys with me. You have handled your experience with such strength and honour and I am amazed at the grace and strength that you continue to shoulder in the face of it all.

To all the helpful police officers that have assisted me in sourcing the case files, dockets and information I have needed to substantiate everything written within and to all the different individuals I have reached out to along the way for further documents, facts or evidence.

And most importantly, to the team behind making the actual book a reality – Fred, Ronel and Jacques. Thank you for your support, your guidance and your kind words. It is greatly appreciated and hopefully this book is a reflection of your commitment and input to bringing it to fruition.

To all my friends, that have supported me and encouraged me along the way and to all those that have helped with proofreading and initial thoughts and inputs. Thank you for your eternal patience and support. You all make my life so much richer.

To The Jam Donut and The Fine Doctor. You know who you are and you know what you have done. I thank you from the bottom of my heart. Thank you for the support, the love and the many laughs.

And lastly to each and every South African that is contributing towards making this a better country and taking us forward from the darkness we are in. To each and every person that assists another and does all they can to make a difference in their community or in someone else's life. This book is dedicated to you all.

"I see only one hope for our country, and that is when white men and black men, desiring neither power nor money, but desiring only the good for their country, come together to work for it.
I have one great fear in my heart, that one day when they are turned to loving, they will find we are turned to hating."

Alan Paton, Cry the Beloved Country

Contents

Prologue	19

Introducing The Men Who Would Irrevocably Change Our Lives Forever

Raymond "Razor" Bheki Zulu aka "The Nasty One"	25
George Vincent Nyembe aka "The Wet One"	29

The Start Of The Nightmare

The Night It All Happened	33
The Greatest Theft Of All	39
The Family Arrives	43
The First Disillusion	47
Doing What Has To Be Done	53
A Broken Boy	61
The First Step To Fighting Back	65
The Evidence Of Crime	69
The Violence Increases	75

It doesn't Stop	85
The Peaks And Troughs Of The Paterson Aftermath	93
A Man Born For Blue	99
Our Hero In Blue	107
Communities Fight Back	115
Taking A First Step	123
Newsprint Or Not …	129
The Infrastructure Reflects …	137
Changing The Law	141
Moving Forward	151
The Phoenix From The Fire	157

The Policing System And Judicial/Legal Systems And All Their Failings

The Flaws Of Lady Justice	167
The Search For Court Records	173
The Paterson Case	175
Lives On Hold	189
The Wrong Courthouse And A Rush Across Town	193
Missing Paperwork	197
"Courts daydream" – Nick's memory of that day	209
And Again …	211
The Final Court Case	217

Finding The Humanity Within The Nightmare And The Aftermath Of It All

Taking A Gamble At Sun City	227
Looking Beyond The Bars	245
A Different Kind Of Rat	253
Even A Hero Suffers Defeat	261

Against The System	261
Causes And Origins	269
Filling In The Gaps	285
The Magic Words; VOD. Just What Does It Entail?	289
Heading Back To Sun City	293
Music of the Past – Annie-Rose Thomson - Aug 2016	315
Life Changing In The Lowveld	319
Where To From Here	325
Epilogue – Final Thoughts	337
References & Additional Reading	353

Prologue

In honour of my brother - 27 September 2017

Today here I sit and reflect on it all
On everything that's transpired, since the last day you stood tall
27 September, 10 years ago,
A day we'll never forget, but wish we could so
The day a knife and a bullet, made your heartbeat one last time
Another South African statistic, another casualty of crime
When those four men left your home with all your belongings in tow,
I wonder if they realised and if they really know
That in fact what they stole was more than money could install
For stealing your life that night was the greatest theft of all.
And so here I sit; 10 years on; deep in thought
On what their murderous actions have in fact bought
I look at your family with admiration and admire
All they've become…. And continue to inspire
Your heartbroken wife has faced the odds at her feet;
And still brought up your children to be caring, loving and sweet.

No hatred or revenge do they harbour at all
Neither "lets get them back," do they ever call.
Though their hurt and their heartache, is always so clear
They choose to live in love and light and not give into hatred and fear.
The shock of your murder and the depth of your parting
Has resulted in other initiatives starting
Mom wrote a book on her loss and her pain
And through this has helped others deal with the same
The now well-established, Mike Thomson Change-a-Life Trust
Is something remarkable and something I must
Honour today, and say thank you Computershare
For establishing this and enabling South African's to care
Over R30-million has been raised in your light
To fight crime in this country and to try put right
The social issues that contribute to and feed
The ills in this country and where there is need.
Laws have been changed to help fight crime
Lives have been changed throughout this time.
And on a personal note and in my own way,
I have taken to the task today and every day
To support and help others who are victims of crime
To help guide them through this terrible time
And where I can and where I might
I am also involved in the now daily fight
Against this scourge that just seems to grow and expand
And every day is taking control of more of this land.
But each time I help another in the dark of night
Mike, I do so in your name, your honour and in your light.
And I hope I bring to them a little of you to your core
Of the amazing person you were and all you stood for

And I hope that your strength comes through me each day
And helps someone else in some little way
And so today I sit here, and reflect on it all
The day a knife and a bullet made a great man fall
But like the phoenix from the fire, from the ashes we arise
And try to create positive from your early demise
And although we've come far, and much has been succeeded
There is still far too much to do and much that is needed.
10 years ago, in all our hurt and our pain
We made a promise that your murder would never be in vain
And my reflections reveal that this may have been done
We've each done our best, each and every one
But there is just one last thing I must say
Just one last thing that I continue to pray
That somehow soon, our government will come right
And commit themselves to ending this plight
To lead with ethics and with morals to which we can relate
And stop looking for blame or someone else to slate.
To lead with honour and show that crime is not right
To take us out of this darkness and lead us into the light
I honour you Mike and all the families who have lost
To crime and violence and paid the highest cost.
You have paid the highest price anyone could comprehend
Let's stop crime in this country and bring it to an end

A poem written and dedicated to the 10-year anniversary of his death - published on Facebook

27 September 2007 at 21h00: I had just climbed into bed when I received a phone call and on screen, I saw that it was my sister-in-law, Sarah. I immediately thought that something had happened to my parents. I answered with trepidation.

"Hi Debs, I'm sorry to call so late, but I've got bad news. Mike and Lorna were attacked tonight, Mike has been shot".

"But he's Ok, isn't he, he is in hospital? "That was the full extent I could allow my brain to think and I immediately envisioned him lying in the hospital bed but smiling - as any other vision was too much for me to construe on my own at present.

"No, he is dead," she managed to say. "I'm Sorry." The words echoed around and around my head, the smiling, hospital bed vision exploded in my brain. "Dead, dead, my brother is dead!" My knees buckled and I suddenly found myself sitting on the floor.

As with the rest of my family, these few words were to change my life irrevocably.

This one phone call was to change the direction of my life forever.

My family and I didn't choose this journey, who in their right mind would? We have, however, picked up the shattered fragments of our lives and have done everything possible to create positivity out of all the heartache we were engulfed in and to bring optimistic change into a journey of darkness and tears.

It took a 10-year uphill battle to get the murderers convicted. This story reveals all the phenomenal South Africans who are doing their utmost to fight the scourge of crime, violence and murder that is endemic in this country. This story is a shocking revelation that South Africa's systems are failing its citizens every day, why crime is what it is and is as violent as it is and, why our policing and judicial systems, as well as our government, aren't getting on top of the problem.

Whilst this is a story of tragedy, sorrow, incompetence, frustration and bitterness. It's also a story of hope, healing and heroism.

PART I:

Introducing The Men Who Would Irrevocably Change Our Lives Forever

"It is not permissible for us to go on destroying the family life when we know that we are destroying it"

Alan Paton, Cry the Beloved Country

Raymond "Razor" Bheki Zulu aka "The Nasty One"

"How much more grievous are the consequences of anger than the causes of it."

Marcus Aurelius

Raymond Bheki Zulu, who was later to be known as Razor to his friends, was born in the dusty hills of the Eastern Cape. He was born in a rural community where his mother lived with her family in a close and connected village-based culture. He recalls that as a young boy, even though life was simple, he lacked for nothing and his life was good. The only responsibility required of him and his two younger brothers, was to go to school.

After completing four years of schooling, Razor's mother decided to move to Natal to stay with the children's father. Packing up the young children and her meagre possessions, she readied herself for the long trek to the neighbouring province. As they were about to leave her brother asked her to stay. She refused and an argument ensued. The children watched in horror as their uncle pulled a gun on her and threatened to shoot her if she tried to leave. He told her that if she did leave, none of them would ever be welcome in the village again. Fearing for their lives, she locked herself and her children inside her room.

Later that night, while everyone slept, she woke up the children, picked up all she could carry and they fled into the dark of night, knowing that they would never be welcome back there again.

They made their way to Natal using any form of transport they could find. When they arrived at the family homestead of their father, little did they know what a turning point this would be. He wasn't at all happy to see them as they'd hoped. On the first night, whilst they were trying to fall asleep, he came into their one-roomed hut and beat their mother with a knob-kierie (a heavy wooden stick with a large rounded end to it). The children were horrified to hear that he was angry because he did not want the children around because they were extra mouths to feed. He wanted her to send them away. The more she refused, the more he beat her.

Early the next morning, beaten and broken, she wrapped up her children once again and this time, headed to the only place she could think of where she might be able to find some way to look after her family; Johannesburg, the city of gold.

Unfortunately, like most people who come to Johannesburg with the hope of finding work, she realised that the city is not paved on gold but on the bones of the destitute and hopeless. She was met with hopelessness, hardship and impoverishment. The family had no choice but to join the thousands living on the streets. As time progressed, Razor's mother managed to find herself a room on the side of a shack in Alexandra Township. But, by then, the 10-year-old Razor had quit school and joined young street gangs learning a new set of skills to help him survive his new life. By the time he was 13 he was stealing bicycles and car radios so that he could buy food and fund his drug habit. He smoked a mix of Mandrax and marijuana and would ultimately progress to Crack Cocaine.

From 13 to 28 his crimes progressed to shoplifting, burglary, housebreaking and armed robbery. He claims that during this time that he dreamt of his days in the Eastern Cape. He missed the safety, security and sense of belonging he once felt there. He blamed all his misfortune on his uncle and dreamt of killing him. With no adult guidance and moral mentorship, he continued to make one wrong choice after the other.

At 26 he was arrested for assault and while awaiting trial he found himself sharing a cell with a man by the name of Thabang Maxwell Kheza. They hit it off immediately and became firm friends. They both had their cases dismissed around the same time and ended up back on the street together. They decided to form a team. Thabang introduced Razor to some of his criminal cohorts. They included, Bongani Masumpa, Mzilowo Tofele (known as Mzi) and George Nyembe. Razor in turn, introduced them to two of his cohorts; Sibusiso Mashinine and Armando Makamo as well as two others that were not to come onto our radar at all, Elvis Mabuza and Sifiso Manyoni.

This cohort of criminals became known as the Razor Gang.

George Vincent Nyembe aka "The Wet One"

"I have often wondered how it is that every man loves himself more than all the rest of men, but yet sets less value on his own opinion of himself than on the opinion of others."

Marcus Aurelius

George Vincent Nyembe's early life was less erratic than Raymond Zulu's. But because it was entrenched heavily in poverty, it had the same affect and impact on him and the future choices he made.

George was born in a shack in Alexandra Township and was one of six children. His mother was unemployed and battled daily to find work and feed her children. George remembers many evenings where the children were forced to go to bed hungry or after having shared a single slice of bread. From a young age, George and his six siblings would look for any opportunity to find something to steal so that they could feed themselves.

George never knew his father and couldn't say if he was dead or alive. He had only ever been brought up by his mother. George's mother was a caring lady who loved her children but was weighed down heavily with the pressures and stress of poverty.

Living deep in the maelstrom that is Alexandra Township, it was only natural for George and his siblings to join street gangs and to turn to crime. By the time he was 25, four out of his six siblings had been killed.

George became friends with Thabang Maxwell Kheza, Bongani Masumpa and Mzilowo Tofele. In time, Thabang introduced him to Raymond "Razor" Bheki Zulu, and they were to form a team, a team that was to change our lives forever. As a natural progression in their career of crime, they turned their hand to aggravated and aggressive house robbery, threatening their victims with guns and weapons and ultimately culminating in rape, armed robbery and murder.

By the time the Razor Gang shattered our lives, they'd reportedly been involved in at least 16 cases, followed with another three or four thereafter.

PART II:

The Start Of The Nightmare

Who knows for what we live, and struggle, and die? Wise men write many books, in words too hard to understand. But this, the purpose of our lives, the end of all our struggle, is beyond all human wisdom.

Alan Paton, Cry the Beloved Country

The Night It All Happened

"What broke in a man when he could bring himself to kill another? What broke when he could bring himself to thrust down the knife into the warm flesh, to bring down the axe on the living head, to cleave down between the seeing eyes, to shoot the gun that would drive death into the beating heart?"

Alan Paton, Cry the Beloved Country

It was another humid Johannesburg evening in Craighall Park. The Thomson family had just finished dinner and the children were telling their dad about their fun and games in the rain that day. Putting the dirty dishes into the kitchen, mom Lorna took their youngest daughter, seven-year-old, Annie-Rose to bed. Her sister, Megs was 11 and her brother, Nick was nine years old.

With Annie-Rose in bed and asleep, the rest of the family headed off to the master bedroom to watch television. This was one of the rituals they cherished as a family - mom and dad on either side of their king-size bed with the children cuddled between them. It was a perfect moment.

Because the air was humidly warm after the rains, Mike had opened the bedroom doors leading onto the pool and adjacent courtyard. With the doors open and the safety gate barring the doorway, the family felt safe as they were flicking through the television channels and chatting about the day's activities.

Finally, Nick went to bed and as he moved out of the room, Mike cast his eyes to the pool outside and noticed that the day's rainfall had caused it to flood.

Mike decided to go outside and backwash the pool, an action that on any other night may have taken 10 minutes and he could be back on the bed cuddling with his children and his wife, but on this particular night, it was a decision that was about to have devastating consequences. For hidden in the depth of the shadows lay more than the usual menagerie of millipedes and garden fauna, instead, on this particular evening, there loomed those monsters that all South Africans dread. Those menaces that lurk in the blackened night.

Mike unlocked the security gate and stepped outside. As he stood beside the pool to start the backwashing process, he moved towards the shrubbery on the side to throw out the unwanted contents from the leaf litter basket. Two shadows rushed at him. The first, brandishing a gun and the second, a screwdriver.

Mike's first reaction was to shout, "Hey, what do you want?"

He was answered with a shot, straight into his right lung, the bullet coming to rest between his ribs and his trapezius muscle. Mike felt nothing and instead, his 20 years of martial arts training kicked in and he attacked.

The one that had shot him had already run past him and together with an accomplice, entered the house. The remaining two stood in front of him. One cocked his gun at Mike, but it jammed. This gave Mike an opening to land a punch that sent him flying and knocked him out. Mike grabbed the other and threw him into the pool. He jumped in after him and attempted to drown him. Whilst Mike held his head under water, the intruder used the screwdriver in his hand to stab Mike again and again, 14 times in total. Yet, Mike didn't flinch and carried on holding his head under water bringing his attacker close to unconsciousness and drowning.

Coming to his senses after being knocked out, but still not having success with his weapon, the now conscious gang member shouted to his friends for help. This brought the initial invader back outside and seeing Mike was about to drown his fellow criminal in the pool, he coldly let off another shot, this time directly towards Mike's head, a shot that no amount of training nor martial art skills can withstand, a shot that killed him instantly.

In that moment a great man fell, and many lives were changed forever.

Coughing and spluttering from his near drowning, the gang member managed to pull himself out of the pool, leaving Mike behind in the bloody waters. The three of them entered the house and joined their friend who had already tied up Lorna, Megs and Nick, and all of them now turned their hands to the thieving and plundering actions to follow.

∽

Lorna's first realisation that something was wrong, was the sudden image of two dark faces bursting through the courtyard door and grabbing both her and Megs as they still lay on the bed.

They were at once ushered down the passage to Nick's room where he was still awake and getting ready for bed and where they were all tied up using Nick's various socks and school ties. The one given this task seemed to show an extraordinary amount of gentleness, care and concern for them all, considering the heinous act they were invoking. Thus it was, that Lorna was thereafter to refer to him as "The Nice One" in her later statements to the police.

Lorna immediately asked "The Nice One" if she could fetch Annie-Rose as the thought of her alone in her room with the thugs moving through the house was too much for her to bear.

The leader of the gang walked back into the room and gruffly barked at her that Annie-Rose was to stay where she was. His aggressive and frightening demeanour throughout the ordeal caused her to dub him "The Nasty One".

For the next hour or so, the gang ransacked the house, while Lorna, Megs and Nick were tied up in Nick's room and Annie-Rose lay in her bed fast asleep, totally unaware of the horror unfolding around her.

Every so often "The Nasty One" would come and grab one of them, yanking them out of the room and parade them around the house asking to be shown where the money, jewellery and any other secreted belongings may be hidden. Nick was given a particularly hard time. Mike had put up music system speakers in the top corners against the ceiling in Nick's room.

The gang mistakenly thought that the speakers were CCTV cameras and dragged Nick around the house demanding to be shown the recording base. They threatened to shoot his mom and sisters. The nine-year-old had no idea what a CCTV was and fearing for their lives, all he could reply with was a wailing, desperate and confused, "I don't know."

He was shown a particular amount of aggression before they realised he could not help them and they returned him back to the room with Lorna and Megs.

At this time, Lorna kept on asking, "Where's my husband?" "Don't worry, he's just sleeping," was the answer she received. She presumed, and deep in her heart hoped, that meant he had possibly been knocked unconscious and was lying on the ground somewhere. It would only be two hours later that she would find out just how wrong that thought was.

∽

After climbing out of the pool, the last gang member entered the house. On seeing the wet footprints on the floor, this instantly brought the realisation to Lorna that Mike was outside near the pool, and with immediate effect, she started praying that if they had knocked him out, please God, make sure that he had not fallen in the pool and be left to drown. The thought of it was too frightening to think of, so instead, for now, she chose to hold onto their statement that he was "only sleeping" and held onto a vision of him lying on the paving next to the pool possibly only injured or unconscious. She would go and look for him and wake him up as soon as she was able to and she knew that when she did, all would be well in her world again. If only that were so …

In her recalling of events, she dubbed the last member "The Wet One".

The Greatest Theft Of All

"For who can stop the heart from breaking?"

Alan Paton, Cry the Beloved Country

After the last ransack through the house, "The Nasty One" barged into Nick's room again to check that they were still tied up. He grunted at them that they were leaving now and they were taking Mike's car but they would be leaving someone behind and if Lorna tried to call for help, or if Mike's car turned out to have a tracking device in it, the remaining person's task was to kill them. With that, they walked out of the once happy Buckingham Avenue home, seemingly unfazed by the colossal heartache and destruction they left in their wake.

Still reeling under the last hour or so from fear and terror, there was nothing in Lorna's make-up that allowed her to doubt the last threat that was thrown at them. She made the children sit quietly with her, listening to every sound outside the door in fear that it would be the person left behind, coming to finish them off. She had remembered that Mike's car did have a tracker in it, and so expected nothing less than the realisation of that last departing threat.

However, being the nurturing mother and loving wife that she is, the situation was too much for her to ignore. She knew that Nick and Megs were safely with her in the room and physically, they were relatively unharmed. However, Annie was still in her own room and she had no idea if anything had befallen her, and of course, she still needed to go outside, find Mike and wake him up from where she had chosen to believe he was still "sleeping" on the paving next to the pool.

Eventually her love took control of her fear and she could not sit there terrified any longer. She had to go and find Annie-Rose and Mike and bring her family back together again. She needed Mike's strength and guidance to remind them that all would be well in their world once more.

After untying one another, they took their first faltering and frightened steps into the corridor, heading for Annie-Rose's room. It was with great relief that they found her asleep, untouched and unharmed. Lorna woke her up and told her that there had been some bad men in the house that had robbed them, and they all need to go outside together to call for help and to look for Daddy.

As Lorna left the bedroom and headed into the night outside, she cast a cursory glance around the pool, and her heart went cold as she could not see Mike lying anywhere that she had spent the last hour or so envisioning him to be. She decided to first call for help from her neighbours next door and then she would look for Mike. She walked past the pool and climbed onto a table against the wall. With her head over the wall, she shouted for help. Nobody answered. She decided to turn to the neighbours on the other side of the property.

As she turned around to climb off the table, she could not help but look into the pool and suddenly she recognised the cold and fear that had been gnawing at her since she first heard the words, "Don't worry he's sleeping."

She could not help but see him. There lay Mike, at the bottom of the pool, his life's blood swirling around him. In that instant, the full force of the situation hit her and just how much those thugs had stolen from her, Megs, Nick and from Annie-Rose that night. They had taken a husband and a father. Her rock, her anchor and the love of her life. This theft was incomprehensible. This was the greatest theft of all.

She screamed at the children not to look at the pool as she rushed them to the gate on the other side of the garden.

Perry and Ronel Hutton had been sitting in their living room watching television, unaware of the nightmare that had just occurred mere metres from them.

Perry was showering before retiring to bed when he heard what he thought were children screaming. For a moment he thought that Ronel had put the television back on. He turned off the tap so that he could hear more clearly. There was no doubt that there were children screaming hysterically. He dressed frantically and as he passed the bedroom window, he saw Lorna and her three children standing in his garden. They were crying and screaming. He heard the muffled words, "Please help." Somewhere in the hysterical pleas, he thought he heard the words Mike, dead, shot and pool.

He ushered them into the warmth and safety of his home, where he then heard an unimaginably horrifying tale. Now the mixed-up jumble of words started falling into place and he was mortified. He sprang into action and phoned the police, the neighbourhood security company and the call we all dread … the call to the rest of our family.

The Family Arrives

"The tragedy is not that things are broken. The tragedy is that things are not mended again."

Alan Paton, Cry the Beloved Country

Perry first called Mike's older brother, Allan. After hearing the news Allan had to make the hardest phone call he would ever have to make; to his parents. With his wife Sarah supporting him, he made the call.

"Mom, I'm coming to pick you and Dad up, we need to go to Mike and Lorna. They've been attacked by an armed gang. Mike has been shot, he's dead," he said.

How else do you tell your parents this kind of news?

Mike's parents, Brian and Di Thomson, could not move. They sat in their bedroom in disbelief. Their brains trying to comprehend the words they had just heard and their hearts holding onto the remaining presence of their son.

Slowly, they got dressed and in a numb, robotic state, headed to their townhouse complex security gates to wait for Allan to arrive.

On the way over, Allan turned to Sarah and tremulously said, "What are we going to do?" Calmly and thoughtfully, Sarah replied, "We'll just do whatever we have to do, take one day at a time, and just do what we have to." Little did we know then, just how long "one day at a time" was going to take and for how many years we would just be doing "whatever we had to do".

They arrived to a home awash with blue and red flashing lights and droves of policemen, paramedics and security guards.

Brain, Di and Sarah rushed to Lorna and the children while Allan was taken by a police constable to the swimming pool.

Taking in the scene, Allan was alarmed. Based on American crime scene movies and television series, he was expecting a controlled scene where forensics personnel professionally went about their business. What he saw horrified him. There were 20 to 30 people constantly walking in and out of the house, seemingly with no purpose, order or control, potentially destroying any possible evidence.

The constable led him through the house, through the throngs of first responders, and out to the pool at the back, where Mike lay, still at the bottom of his watery grave. Allan was devastated when he saw his younger brother's body. It's a sight that would never be erased from his mind and one that would plague him for many years to come.

The forensics team, known as LCRC officers (Local Criminal Record Centre officers), were last to arrive on the scene. It was only once they had taken all the photos and picked up whatever forensic evidence they may have been able to collect after twenty or thirty other feet had paraded through the house, only then could they actually take Mike out of his watery tomb.

They placed him in a body bag on a low gurney and wheeled him out to the forensics van. As the family watched him being taken away, Lorna felt a gentle hand on her shoulder and an angel called Jade, from the

Parkview Victim Support Unit, gently took her hand and placed Mike's wedding band and his watch in her hand.

Lorna held Mike's wedding band to her chest, as close to her heart as she could. She immediately placed it on a chain around her neck, so that it could remain as close to her heart as possible. It still hangs around her neck to this day. Lorna gave Mike's watch to my mother who put it on immediately. This watch was to become a vital tool for my mother in dealing with her own heartache and in finding a path through the quagmire of hurt she had been thrown into.[1]

Watching the van drive away with Mike's lifeless body within, was more than the family could bear. Now that Mike was gone, they needed to leave too. They needed to get away from all these people, the flashing lights, the cold procedures and this now terrifying house.

Bundling Lorna, the children and their 3 dogs into their car, the 8 broken hearts made their way back to Allan and Sarah's house. Arriving at their home, away from the mayhem that was continuing at Buckingham, Lorna and the children just melted and had a total breakdown.

---

[1] In her book "Soul Connections" by Diana Thomson, she talks extensively about the watch and how this helped navigate her through her own path of hurt and heartache.

The First Disillusion

"Deep down the fear of a man who lives in a world not made for him, whose own world is slipping away, dying, being destroyed, beyond any recall."

Alan Paton, Cry the Beloved Country

After receiving that fateful call from Sarah and hearing those words, "No, he is Dead." My knees buckled and I found myself sitting on the floor.

I don't remember much else of the conversation at all. I only remember Sarah saying to me that Mom didn't want me to drive through the night as she wouldn't be able to cope with the worry and stress. It's a five-hour journey from Hoedspruit to Johannesburg and it's too taxing to undertake at night on my own in the current state I was in. I put the phone down, pulled myself back up onto my feet and suddenly felt lost and minute in my little home and couldn't think what I should do next.

Robotically, I climbed into bed. I knew that there was absolutely no way I would sleep tonight, but I also knew that I was in no state mentally to take the long drive through the night, in order to get to the family.

I thought, the only option would be to read and keep myself occupied and distracted for the next eight hours until it was light enough to drive. I picked up my book and proceeded to do what I thought was to read, however 10 minutes later I realised that not one word had been absorbed. My mind was in a million shattered pieces and most certainly was not in a state to focus or concentrate on any one thing. This was definitely not going to work, nor get me through the long night ahead. I realised, I had to leave now, I had to get to Johannesburg, I had to help, I had to do something, and I had to be with my family now.

I suddenly remembered my long-time friend Helen had mentioned that she was planning a Johannesburg business trip soon.

I reached out to her and suddenly found myself having to mention those life-altering words that I had only just heard myself. "Mike has been shot. He is dead."

Without hesitation, Helen offered to take me to Johannesburg immediately.

It was about 23h00 by the time I met up with Helen and Derek (her ex-husband) on the side of the road and Helen and I started the long drive up to Johannesburg. Driving extra cautiously and extremely slowly, we arrived in Johannesburg at around 05h00 the following morning.

Immediately on our arrival into the city, we had received a call that Mike's car had already been found abandoned in Alexandra Township and was now at the Sandton Police Station. The police needed someone in the family to come through to confirm that it was indeed his, so that forensics could process the vehicle. Helen and I changed course and drove straight to the police station, to go and start the process of doing "whatever we had to do".

When I saw Mike's car, my knees buckled, and my heart broke yet again.

Mike ever the family man, chose a car that could fit his entire family, friends and the dogs into. Seeing the Volkswagen Touran standing in the police courtyard, I had a vision of one of the last times I had seen Mike and his family in my hometown of Hoedspruit.

They were on their way up to our holiday home on the game reserve N'tsiri. On their arrival at the restaurant where we were meeting, I watched in amusement as four adults and four children piled out of a five-seater vehicle. That was Mike, with his family, his father-in-law, as well as Lorna's brother and his daughter, all in one car; he could not be happier, nor think of a better family experience.

After the holiday, when little Annie-Rose was asked by her uncle, how the holiday had been, she had only one word in response, "Squishy."

Annie's little voice and the merth of laughter it brought from us all was all I could think of as I now looked at this vehicle that somehow itself looked heartbroken, and looked as if it has had all it's happy family memories ripped from within, and in the half-hour of being in the forced "ownership" of those deviants, now oozed out a grey and heavy energy instead.

Forensics were busy with the car when we arrived, and I was introduced to my first horrifying realisation of just how different and back-to-front the South African system was to the rest of the world. The first of many reasons in the earlier years, why crime has been allowed to grow so rampant in this beloved country of ours.

I moved slowly towards Mike's car, my heart hating every thought of who and what had recently been within. "Look," says the man in blue in front of me, with a smile on his face, "Here's a good fingerprint, we should definitely be able to get something from this."

"Great," I respond. "So how long will it take us to process this and see who it belongs to?" I ask.

He looks at me and laughs, "No, that is not how it works."

"What do you mean, 'That's not how it works?'" I ask in confusion. "Surely that's how fingerprints work?"

We have all watched television shows and we have seen the speed that a suspect is identified when a clear fingerprint is found. We take the fingerprint, put it into the computer, the computer compares it to all fingerprints taken when we apply for any kind of legal document and hopefully, finds a match. Surely that is how it works?

"Not in South Africa," he says. "Come upstairs to my office and let me show you how it works here." There he introduces me to the previous South African concept of the "Criminal Database".

"In South Africa when fingerprints are taken, we cannot just go and see to whom they belong as that is considered to be against their constitutional right,[1]" he says.

"Instead, they're loaded into what is termed the 'Criminal Database' to say that this person has been involved in a criminal incident.

"Anyone who is arrested thereafter has their fingerprints compared to the Criminal Database to see if they have been involved in any additional incidents prior to their arrest," he says.

My head starts spinning at this news. "You've got to be kidding," I say. "Somewhere out there, this man's fingerprints should be on record if he has an identity book or a driver's licence, yet we are not allowed to find out who this murdering thug is because it's against his constitutional right?

"How many more people will this thug have to kill before you might arrest him and be able to link him to this particular incident?" I ask. Shrugging his shoulders with either indifference or shame, he mutters "Yebo, it's difficult, they kill too many first."

Feeling even more despondent and horrified at all the new feelings and realisations I am quickly being introduced to in the last eight or nine hours, we finally head home to see the family, to see Lorna and the

---

[1] It needs to be added at this point that this is no longer the case and as of 2010, thanks to the DNA project, the fingerprint law has now been changed to allow for this immediate identification of suspects

children and to start the long process of "taking one day at a time" and just doing "whatever we have to do".

Doing What Has To Be Done

"You ask yourself not if this or that is expedient, but if it is right."

Alan Paton, Cry the Beloved Country

The first week after a traumatic incident and leading up to a funeral or memorial service is always one of the hardest for family and friends. There's so much to be done logistically, legally and emotionally. This all needs to be done on the back of your own crashing feelings and uncomprehending brain, as well as in between the droves of family and friends coming around to show their support and share in your heartache.

For us it was no different!

After Helen and I finished up at the police station, we finally made our way to the family.

Seeing just how broken Lorna and the children were and how distraught and lost my parents were, brought up the feelings that I was to become very familiar with and get to know on an intimate basis. For the second time in just a few hours, I felt a rush of anger and disgust at what these deviants had done and all for their own self-serving and extremely limited needs.

By the time I arrived at Allan's home, the news of the home invasion and Mike's death had spread like wildfire and the phone was constantly ringing with one call of shock and support after the next. The extent of heartache and outpouring of love and compassion was totally overwhelming for us all.

Amidst all of this, we had to make two heartbreakingly difficult phone calls. Allan made the first phone call to Mike's boss, Stan Lorge from Computershare, who has turned out to be the most incredible man and a support to the family still to this day. Stan was horrified at what Allan had to tell him and before the end of the day, was sitting with us in the lounge sharing condolences as well as planning means to honour Mike, and to take on and tackle this fight against crime on a national basis. Something that he and his team have done to the most exceptional level and ability in the years to follow.

I made the next emotional phone call to Lorna's now-late dad, Neil Shields who lived in Scotland. A wonderful quiet man, he had loved Mike like a son from the day he had met him. For him, it was such a joy that his daughter had found a loving and committed husband, the perfect father to his grandchildren. I now had to tell this gentle soul of the horrors that his daughter had experienced the previous evening and that in her very early 40s she was now a widow.

Allan had immediately offered to pay for Neil to fly out here as soon as possible so at least, when sharing with him this great heartache, I was able to tell Neil, that we would be arranging a plane ticket to South Africa that day or the next, so he could focus on coming out here to be with his daughter, and I did not have to leave him floundering alone, in his own heartache, thousands of kilometres away. One of Lorna's friends then took on the responsibility of arranging a flight for Neil and to get him out here as soon as possible and within a day or two he had arrived.

One of the first people to show up at the house, almost before dawn itself, was Mike's long-time school friend, Richard Moss. Mike and Richard had met in Standard Six (now known as Grade Eight) at Bryanston High School and were inseparable ever since. They played sports together, got up to pranks together, chased girls together, went on double dates together, humorously even tried their hand at acting in the school play together, studied at WITS University together and started their married lives together. It was no surprise that Mike asked Richard to be the godfather to his first-born child, Megs.

When Richard arrived at the house he was as broken as we were. Richard had contact with a private detective, Ollie (Gert Olivier), who had a sterling reputation in solving cases such as ours. It turned out that Ollie's efforts went a long way in assisting us in getting the case through the defunct court system and successfully prosecuting the Razor Gang.

Richard called Ollie immediately and a few hours later we were sitting around a table with him to discuss what little bits we knew at the time, and what options were available to him to start a search for the murderers. We knew that timing was crucial and that the earlier one starts, the greater the chances of success are. Stan offered that Computershare would foot Ollie's bill and with that, Ollie immediately started working on the case.

As this first day continued, we started making lists of all the things that needed to be done to prevent anything falling through the cracks within our scattered brains and shattered souls, and so we could allocate tasks to appropriate friends and family. Helen had designated herself as chief tea-maker and found herself, together with my sister Carol, making copious cups of tea and coffee as one friend after another arrived.

In an unexpected turn, we managed to sneak Lorna and the children out of the house as soon as the shops were open. The reason was two-fold. Firstly, Lorna was not yet ready to face the droves of people that were starting to arrive and secondly, we needed to buy the children something to wear. They had fled Buckingham Avenue in nothing but their pyjamas and were still too afraid to go back to the house.

I also needed to buy clothes because in my shocked, confused and frozen state and when looking to see what I could loan the children, I found I only packed a selection of long pants and underwear. I had no tops, no skirts, or pyjamas.

With the children then temporarily swimming in oversized shirts and shorts from their aunts, uncles and elder cousin, we went straight to Woolworths in Rivonia and arrived as they were opening their doors. Whilst milling aimlessly around the aisles, involved in more of an escape from the realities back at home, than a conscious shopping trip, I received a call from Richard Moss's younger brother Pete. On the back of Richard and Mike's great friendship, Pete and I had become firm friends from the day we met in Standard Three (Grade Five) and apart from a bit of secretive handholding in primary school days, we had a great supportive, platonic friendship throughout high school.

The minute Pete had heard, he called me instantly, but by the time I had answered the phone, he was so distraught and was sobbing so much on the other end that he could not get two words out. After trying again and again to say something to me, he somehow managed a very muffled, "I'll have to call you later. I'm sorry."

Until this very moment, I had been running on automatic and concentrating on being strong, not getting overly emotional yet and simply doing what needed to be done. Yet standing here in the middle of Woolworths with Lorna and the children aimlessly wondering around trying their hand at a simple chore of shopping, yet finding themselves lost in the task, and hearing the extent of emotion in my friend Pete, and just how distraught he was at the news, was all it took for my own emotions to come rumbling to the surface.

For the first time since receiving the ominous call the night before, the tears came. The next thing I knew, I found myself sitting on a bench somewhere in between sandals and summer pumps on special, sobbing my eyes out and succumbing to the emotions I had been working so hard on controlling since I had first received Sarah's phone call.

∾

By the time we arrived back at Allan's home, the droves of caring friends and family, colleagues and well-wishers were gathering en masse. From that moment on, for the next six or seven days, until the funeral, we had so many people coming and going, that we were needing to cater for as many as twenty or thirty people at each meal. For the first day or so, when everyone would call, they would all offer "what can we do for you, how can we help?"

Our initial response of "Thank you so much but there is not much anyone can do at present," was very quickly replaced with "send food and drinks please". With constant streams of people in and out the house from the very first morning and most of them remaining or arriving over mealtimes, it was not long before we had cleaned out Allan's fridge trying to keep the comforting well-wisher's fed.

The food started arriving in copious amounts and supplying meals to everyone became an easy chore for the friends and family that had been tasked with kitchen duty.

∾

One of the most difficult tasks a family has to go through is to identify the body of a loved one. State mortuaries are cold, heartless centres and the majority of the staff within, are apathetic and hardened to the tasks at hand, and any depth of emotion you may be arriving with. I have seen some of the most horrifying indifference at state mortuaries in the years to follow, with the voluntary work I have taken on in honour of Mike.

For us it was no different. As this task was definitely not something we wanted our parents to do, or something Lorna should be further exposed to, Allan and I elected to do it. The support of a family member or friend in this activity, is vital and something I would highly recommend for anyone who has to face this gruesome task.

Allan and I arrived at the Braamfontein Mortuary nervous and unsure, as we had no idea what needed to be done or what to expect. They took Mike's identity book from us to process and showed us through to the tiny waiting room. Sitting there nervously and totally unsure of what was to come, we noticed a list on the wall. It was an inventory of what was expected to be in the room. We observed that only about a third of what was listed still remained. Amongst the items missing were couches, pot plants, coffee tables and curtains. To relieve our tension, we giggled nervously when we found ourselves creating amusing scenarios of how the missing items had made it out of the room.

Once again, the perceptions and visions that the movie-world has created about similar scenarios could not have been more misleading and wrong. There were no caring people coming to comfort us and guide us through the process, no prepping of the body to make the deceased look as decent as possible for the family to see, and no professional processing of what was to come.

Instead, after waiting for what seemed like an eternity, another automated employee told us to follow him. We moved a short way down the corridor and were then taken into a small room, no bigger than a dishwasher. The walls were stark and bare with absolutely nothing within, apart from a cheap curtain hanging directly in front of us. The man shut the door behind us and with the three of us jammed into this tiny space, he asked if we were ready for him to open the curtain. It was only at that stage that we realised Mike was lying behind it. Holding onto each other for support, we nodded.

Behind the curtain was a glass window looking into a room that was even smaller than the one we were in, and in the middle of this room stood a gurney covered in a grey "dog's blanket" and under it, lay Mike. He looked so small and so unlike the large, strong confident man he had been. My big, strong, older brother reduced to this.

They hadn't covered his head properly and in trying to look at his face to make sure there was peace behind his closed eyes, we noticed the crisscross of surgical cuts and rough stitching where they had to cut his head open to document the final bullet through his brain. Seeing this was more than we could handle, and in that moment brought home the realities of the situation. Mike was dead, they had stabbed him, they had shot him in the chest and again in the head and he was dead. Our brother was gone! And within that second, both Allan and I had to get out of there as quickly as we could. We climbed into the car and drove the emotional distance home in silence, each of us ruminating on the finality of seeing our brother lying there inert and lifeless in that cold heartless establishment. As the reality set in that Mike was really gone, we headed home to continue with the laborious tasks required in sorting out the life of a loved one, once they are taken away so quickly and so dramatically, leaving a gaping hole in your heart and a mound of paperwork and legalities to sort through.

A Broken Boy

"Cry, the beloved country, these things are not yet at an end. The sun pours down on the earth, on the lovely land that man cannot enjoy. He knows only the fear of his heart."

Alan Paton, Cry the Beloved Country

The rest of the week continued in a haze while throngs of family, friends and caring hearts continued to pour in and out of the door on a daily basis and Helen and my sister Carol found themselves making one cup of tea after another.

Allan and I started sorting out Mike's affairs, insurance and paperwork. Every evening we would all come together as a family, collectively with whomever was visiting at the time, and discuss what had been done that day, any new information received on what had happened that night at Buckingham Avenue, or what tasks needed seeing to the following day and who was going to see to them.

On one of these evenings, Allan's first girlfriend from school, Nikki Bush (née Bennet) was with us and shared a few ideas on some different and memorable options to include in the funeral that would honour

Mike in every special way possible. Little did Nikki know at the time, that ten years later, on 18 November 2017, she would find herself sitting in the same heartbroken situation, after the shocking murder of her own husband during a break-in at their family home in Bryanston.

During her visit, the family decided on what we all wanted for Mike's funeral and everyone then took on their allotted tasks to make sure we could not only say goodbye, but also honour Mike to the full, for the remarkable man he had always been; as well as finding a way to show that we wanted to take a stand against this scourge that is affecting far too many in this beloved country.

And so, the week moved past in a confusion of heartache, logistics, comforting support and funeral planning. There were so many people around at any given time that there was always someone there to assist with a task or to look after someone that was battling for the day. While Allan and I dealt with the logistics and the paperwork and the hard, cold facts of what had to be done, my younger sister focused on our parents. She made sure that they had the extra support they needed. They appeared to have aged dramatically overnight.

Somewhere in the middle of that week, a close family friend of Lorna's, Janie Green, who had originally brought her out to South Africa as an au pair, together with her ex sister-in-law, Rosie Deans, offered to get the children out of the house for the day and take them away from the continuous depth of emotions that lay over the house like a suffocating cloud at times.

As the children were in need of anything to do with comfort and support, Janie and Rosie took them off to the new "Build-a-Bear" factory in Sandton City. There the children could choose, build and dress any soft toy they wanted. Megs chose a giraffe, Annie-Rose a bunny and Nick a monkey. The monkey immediately received the name Mike and then became an important indicator as to just how well Nick was coping each day. Mike the Monkey was never allowed to be put down, and was held by Nick 24/7, but depending on his level of coping for the day, was either gripped tightly to his chest, or allowed to hang loosely in his hand. Without being too intrusive or obvious, it was a great help to us all to be able to see just how much extra support Nick may have needed at any given time.

Mike's funeral was on Friday, 5 October. Once again, the level of Mike's popularity and impact on other people's lives was evident in the attendance at his funeral. Expecting a little over 300 mourners, we were totally overwhelmed when we arrived to find well over 700 filling the church and even standing in the aisles and out the doors. There were friends and colleagues from all the stages of his life. If only these thugs could see the extent of the hurt and heartache they have caused, and the value of the life they have taken away from us all. For what? The value of a few electrical items, with less value than they were worth, on the black market?

At the end of the service, the pallbearers moved up to walk Mike's coffin out of the church. Mike's father, his brother Allan, his father-in-law Neil, and his closest friends from school and university had been allocated the heavy duty and grim honour.

Because Nick was only a child, nobody thought to include him in this difficult task. Seeing all the men in his life heading towards the coffin, Nick couldn't bear to see his father being walked out the church without him. He rushed to the front to join the other men and took his place alongside Mike's coffin. Holding his head high and Mike the Monkey tightly against his chest, he bravely walked at his father's side for the last time!

Holding all his feelings within and putting on a brave face for the rest of the day, could only last so long for a little boy of Nick's age and gentle heart!

When we all awoke the following morning, the depth of Nick's shattered emotions became evident. Presumably in a desperate attempt to cling onto anything remaining of his dad, he had woken up in the early hours of the morning, had put on his funeral outfit, had come downstairs to the television room alone. He was lying in a foetal position, in a near-comatose state, clutching Mike the Monkey tightly to his chest. He didn't respond to anything we did or said. He was truly broken. All the emotions over the last week and the realisation that his dad was actually gone, was just too much for him. All his little heart, mind and body could do was effect a total shut down.

In absolute desperation, I went running up to a child psychology centre we had noticed in Bryanston Drive, not far from Allan's house. Close to tears, I explained to them what Nick had been through in the last week, and how we had found him this morning and I begged them to please assist.

On hearing the story, these wonderful people immediately reshuffled their appointments and told me to bring him in as soon as possible. An hour later we had carried a comatose and totally unresponsive broken boy into the rooms, only to see him re-emerge later on, not only on his own two feet, but with the ability to talk to us again.

We have never truly ascertained what happened in that room nor what was said to him that morning, but we are forever grateful for the expedient response and clearly successful impact on that broken little heart. Whatever was said to him or shared with him in that moment definitely helped in the initial healing and helped him take the first steps out of the dark hell those deviants had thrown him into. It helped him become the phenomenal young man he is today.

The First Step To Fighting Back

"Sorrow is better than fear. Fear is a journey, a terrible journey, but sorrow is at least an arrival.
When the storm threatens, a man is afraid for his house. But when the house is destroyed, there is something to do. About a storm he can do nothing, but he can rebuild a house."

Alan Paton, Cry the Beloved Country

Every South African is extremely aware of the constant threat of crime but somehow, until it actually happens to you, you manage to live in a bubble, aware of its ever-looming presence, but thinking that it only happens to others. But when it actually happens to you, it's only natural to find oneself questioning your own future and questioning life in this country.

A number of the Razor Gang victims felt that there was no option but to flee South Africa. We were also now considering emigration as an option.

However, after due consideration, we concluded, that despite the threat to life and the lawless and violent side to the South African lifestyle, South Africa still offered us the best way of life and quality of life for us as a family.

In truth, we just could not see ourselves living anywhere removed from the African soil and where we could not be awash in the warm glow of an African sunset.

Looking back at our ancestry, my brothers, my sister and I, are 5th generation on one side and 11th generation on the other, our initial ancestors arriving here in the very early 1700s. With a distant combination of German, French and Scottish blood in the mix, we do not affiliate ourselves with any one country, nor any country other than South Africa.

We are African, I am African! And this is where we choose to stay!

And with that thought, we decided that no group of selfish thugs were going to chase us from our homeland. We are here to stay, and we are going to fight back. This country is crying, and we would rather stay and do what we can to help stem the tears.

Together, we made a commitment that Mike would not be just another statistic, we would make his death and our loss, mean something and ensure that it has an impact in our country.

Sitting on the couch in Allan's lounge the very first afternoon after the murder (28 September 2007), in amongst all the comforting well-wishers, was a man who was about to provide us with the platform and means to make this decision a reality. Mike's boss Stan Lorge made a decision that was to have consequences far greater than initially envisioned.

Stan was already in the process of initiating a trust in combination with Computershare in Australia for the purposes of community investment. Altering this slightly, he subsequently opened this trust in Mike's name to raise funds to fight against crime and the causes of crime, and to ensure that we do not continue to lose valuable citizens and people of Mike's calibre. With that decision, The Mike Thomson Change-a-Life Trust was born! It is dedicated to the peaceful future for all South Africans. It supports effective grassroots programmes that aim to address the causes and symptoms of crime.

Within the following two days, the newly envisioned trust, had its first beneficiary identified and confirmed, and one that would make an exceptional impact on the crime fighting ability of South Africa in general. The first hero to join this team as a beneficiary, was a remarkable lady, a school friend of ours, a visionary and passionately driven individual, who personally is responsible for a gigantic step in the crime fighting ability of South Africa – the DNA Project is the brainchild of Vanessa Lynch.

With a beneficiary on the books, the Trust now needed to put some money in the coffers - In order to raise funds to enable the visions identified, a fund raising activity needed to be created. This has been done most successfully.

The main fundraiser for the trust is the annual Change-a-Life Cycle Tour. It's a leading activity on the South African road-cycling calendar and open to a limited, and elite family of cyclists, most of whom are CEOs or leaders in their industries. At the time of initial writing, the Change-a-Life Cycle Tour has successfully raised close on R35-million to support its beneficiaries.

Initial beneficiaries supported by the trust include, the DNA Project, the Martin Dreyer Change-a-Life Academy; Nemato Change-a-Life; Change-a-Life Karate Do and the Change-a-Life Rape Crisis Centre.

All of these are organisations that either prevent crime, deal with the symptoms of crime or offer support to South Africans giving them morals, guidelines and belief in themselves in order to hopefully prevent the need to turn to crime as a means of survival, due to peer pressures or simply the inability to make better life choices.

The Mike Thomson Change-a-Life Trust was a developing phoenix that in turn, was establishing itself into an entity well deserved to take flight.

The Evidence Of Crime

"One thing is about to be finished, but here is something that is only begun. And while I live it will continue"

Alan Paton, Cry the Beloved Country

Another important visitor to come and show her support that first morning after Mike's murder was Sue Lynch. Sue is the proud mother of Vanessa Lynch. Vanessa herself was at school with all of us and had matriculated the year after Mike.

Sue understood first-hand what we were going through as she had been in the same heart-broken position three years earlier, as a result of the murder of her husband, Johnny Lynch, during yet another senseless and violent attack in 2004. Not only could Sue share in our heartache, she also shared with us all that Vanessa had been up to since the murder of her father and all she had discovered thereafter.

Vanessa, who was a lawyer at the time, was horrified when she discovered what little was done to collect, protect and use evidence on the scene particularly as regards DNA, and subsequently discovered massive gaps in the legal background in South Africa as regards the use of DNA as is done around the rest of the world. In a country so beset with violent crime, we did not have laws allowing for the proper use of DNA, specifically through the development of an "Expanded DNA database" as is used globally.

At that moment in time, Vanessa, having noticed and discovered this huge glaring gap in the South African system, decided there and then that she wanted to be part of the solution and not just another person complaining of all the problems and faults that become more and more evident day-to-day in South Africa and the South African systems.

Working on this premise, Vanessa took to researching how crime scenes were treated around the rest of the world and how perpetuators were successfully convicted using evidence collected at the scene and compared it to what she found was the situation in South Africa. The one thing that became clear was that the use of DNA is not only crucial, but highly successful.

Further research showed that South Africa actually has a relatively small population of criminals perpetrating large numbers of crimes. Repeat offences, or recidivism, as it's known, is extremely prevalent in our country. On average, a criminal in South Africa will commit more than 100 crimes before being caught, as opposed to the United Kingdom where the proper use of DNA is employed and results in an average of 2 – 2½ crimes before a perpetrator is caught.

In addition to this, it has also been discovered that apart from improving the ability to identify and apprehend criminals through linking them to scenes, it has also been proven that 95% of criminals immediately plead guilty when presented with DNA evidence against them. This could save us months and years of wasted court appearance time and possibly help relieve the pressure on our excessively overloaded courts.

Vanessa discovered that although South Africa made use of DNA, it was not using it to its maximum potential and effectiveness. DNA was only being used on a prosecutorial basis and not as a criminal intelligence tool. This means that DNA was taken on a case-by-case basis to prove the potential guilt or innocence of a suspect and thereafter all records were destroyed. DNA was not being used to record suspects and evidence on all scenes, nor link various scenes and suspects together. This is successfully done through the development of an expanded DNA database.

Vanessa started putting a vision together. The gaps in the South Africa system were evident and Vanessa set to work to create solutions to close those gaps.

In the same year that Johnny had been killed, another violent crime was getting prime time in the South African media. The day before her 21st birthday, Leigh Matthews had been kidnapped from outside her college in Morningside and 12 days later, her abandoned body was found in an open veld near Walkerville. Her anguished parents, Rob and Sharon Matthews, had become media names overnight. With their shared heartache, Vanessa contacted Rob Matthews and discussed her vision for improving DNA applications in South Africa. Rob immediately saw the importance and benefit in this and in 2005, he came on board. With that first and initial partnership, The DNA Project was born.

> An excerpt from its website: *The DNA Project is a registered non-profit, public benefit organisation that recognises the critical importance of DNA evidence in the resolution of crime. It's committed to advancing justice through the expanded use of DNA evidence in conjunction with a national DNA criminal intelligence database, also known as a 'National DNA Database'. The DNA Project hopes that its efforts will translate into the comprehensive use of DNA analysis for crime detection and prevention in South Africa.*

Sitting in the lounge at Allan's home that first week, and hearing all that Sue had to share, it was directly evident to us, that Vanessa had the background, she had the drive, she had the solution and the project, but all she was missing was steady financing to help her achieve her goals. Only hours after the initial discussion with Stan around the formation of the Mike Thomson Change-a-Life Trust, we had our first beneficiary. The Mike Thomson Change-a-Life Trust was to become an initial core funder to the much needed and visionary DNA Project.

Allan joined the DNA Project team as a Trustee and Director, and further plans were extended to take the project into the future and work on a development and implementation plan. Vanessa suddenly found herself with the wind she needed under her ever-expanding wings.

༺

The first thing that the trust funded was a visit to South Africa by the United Kingdom Forensic Science Services (UKFSS), so that it could conduct a diagnostic review to help understand the current situation in South Africa, as well as the future of forensic DNA in this country. The UKFSS and its national database is considered the benchmark of DNA forensic practices and databasing, worldwide. Its database was the first of its kind in the world and has received widespread acknowledgement as the most important advancement since fingerprinting in the prevention and detection of crime.

The UKFSS was also requested to undertake a review of the Pretoria Laboratory Biology Unit to establish if anything could be done to improve the efficiency, as well as the capacity of the DNA analytical process, reduce the current backlog, improve the contributions of the unit to the detection, as well as conviction of offenders, and lastly make recommendations for the future development and expansion of a DNA database.

Outcomes of the report were submitted to the Pretoria Forensic Services Laboratory in July 2008. One of the first insights that came out of the report was that South Africa had a world-class laboratory; one of the best in the world. Unfortunately, South Africa didn't have an Expanded DNA database and the law had to change in order to make this a reality.

And so Vanessa set to work. She was not simply going to take the murder of her father lying down, she was going to fight back. In doing so, she chose to take on the South African criminal processes and legal systems.

The Violence Increases

"I have one great fear in my heart, that one day when they are turned to loving, they will find that we are turned to hating."

Alan Paton, Cry the Beloved Country

A mere five days after the murder of Mike, feeling nothing at all and bearing no effect on them whatsoever, the Razor Gang were at it again; and not just in a small way. With increased violence and aggression, they struck once more!

On 2 October 2007 at approximately 21h00, the Paterson family were doing just as they would on any normal weekday and school night. Ten-year-old Angus was already asleep, Jamie who was about to start writing her Grade 12 exams, had just put away her books and climbed into bed. Dad, Alan, was in the lounge watching television and mom, Bronwyn, had just headed off to the bathroom during an advertising break. As she was returning to the lounge, her heart went cold and her mind numb. Standing in front of her was the realisation of a man, a man who did not belong and should not be there. As she looked behind him, her horror grew even more as she saw a second one coming through the window, squeezing himself between the burglar bars.

Before she could react, she had a gun to her head and was being forced to the front door. She whispered to herself, "Whatever you do, don't panic."

They ordered her to open the front door. Seeing the panic button inches away, she hesitated, thinking about activating it. She assessed that she wouldn't make it out alive if she did. Instead, she placed her hand on the doorknob and gingerly opened the door. Four menacing bodies rushed past her into the house.

Still holding her in his grasp, the one with the gun growled at her, "Where is your husband? Where are your children?"

She croaked, "My husband is in the lounge watching television. Please leave the children, they're asleep in their rooms."

"Is there anyone else in the house?" he continued.

"Zodwa, our domestic worker and her boyfriend will be outside in her room." They marched her to Zodwa's room and demanded that she wake them up. She turned to the thugs and reasoned, "If I do that, she may press the panic button and you will then kill us all, I am not going to allow that." They accepted her explanation and left Zodwa alone.

Alan heard a noise and looked up to see Bronwyn enter the room in the grip of an extremely aggressive and dirty-looking man.

One of the gang grabbed Alan and threw him on the floor. "Please be careful," Bronwyn shrieked. "He's had a stroke."

Turning to Alan she softy said, "Don't fight them Alan, just do what they say."

They tied Alan's hand behind his back, ripping off his watch and wedding band. They threw Bronwyn on the ground alongside him, also ripping the rings off her fingers.

"Where is the fucking money, motherfucker?" one of the gang

members aggressively barked at Alan. "It's in the safe," Alan stuttered.

Bronwyn intervened, "Please talk to me. With his stroke he battles to find words sometimes and then gets angry. I don't want you to misunderstand his anger."

He yanked Bronwyn up and said, "Show me then."

While dragging her down the passage to the safe, he shouted, "Where are your fucking children?" She hesitantly headed towards Angus's room where the safe was hidden.

Jamie who had not yet fallen asleep realised something was wrong when the light in her room was switched on. She pretended to be asleep, peering through the slits of her half-open eyes. She saw a young black man in her room looking around. He walked out, leaving the light on and the door open.

Jamie continued to lie in bed pretending to be asleep, she heard the dog barking from somewhere in the house, followed by the aggressive demands from one of the gang to keep it quiet. She then heard her mother shouting at the dog. As soon as the dog was quiet, Jamie heard another gang member shout at her mother, "Where are your children? Get your children now."

Jamie froze with fear, waiting for the inevitable.

Bronwyn headed first to Angus's room and the thug dragging Bronwyn, headed into Angus's room with her. Bronwyn quietly woke Angus up before she was yanked away from his bed and taken back out into the passage, leaving Angus alone with the intruders. Still drowsy and rousing from a deep sleep, Angus opened his eyes to find a strange face staring at him. He suddenly noticed a foul smell accompanying the strange face mere centimetres from his. Suddenly he was wrenched him from his bed, and dragged out into the passage.

"Where is the fucking safe?" Still sleepy and trying to clear his head and comprehend what was going on around him, young Angus didn't answer.

They marched him down the passage towards the lounge.

Two men, together with Bronwyn, entered Jamie's room. Bronwyn headed over to Jamie's bed, gently roused her and quietly said, "Jamie wake up. We need to cooperate with these people and do whatever they want."

Jamie remained calm and quietly climbed out of bed. One of the thugs asked here where her cell phone was. Jamie pointed to it. He snatched it up from next to her bed. "Please can I just keep my SIM card," Jamie pleaded. "I want to see your missed calls first," he replied, presumably wanting to check if she had managed to make any calls for help. After checking the call log, he gave the SIM card to Jamie and pocketed the phone.

"Come with me bitch," he ordered.

"May I please get my dressing gown first, I'm cold," Jamie pleaded with him, feeling vulnerable and naked in her flimsy pyjamas. "No, just take the blanket," he replied, pointing to the duvet on her bed.

As she entered the passage, she saw young Angus being dragged from his room too. Jamie protectively grabbed Angus from the clutches of one of the gang and defensively put her arms around him as they trudged towards the lounge.

Still lying face down on the floor, with his hands tied behind his back, Alan managed to crane his neck and see the rest of his family being herded into the lounge. They were all made to kneel on the floor next to him. Jamie, still holding protectively onto Angus, told him to keep looking down and not to look at any of the gang. One of the thugs grabbed the duvet Jamie still had wrapped around her and threw it over all of them, partially obscuring their vision of what was going on in the room.

Once again, they demanded that Bronwyn show them the safe. She took them back to Angus's room and pointed towards a cupboard.

"It's in there."

One of them opened the cupboard. "You're fucking lying!" he screams and viciously starts beating her. "Move the boxes at the bottom," she cries. "The safe is behind them."

"Where is the fucking key?" "I don't know. You'll have to ask my husband," she cries.

"You lie motherfucker, you fucking white bitch, I'm gonna kill you," he screams, hitting her repeatedly. He drags her back to Alan so that she can ask him where the keys are. Alan tells her that they're in a tin in the passage. They find the keys, but it's a large bunch with many keys and this proves problematic for the gang. They battle to find the correct one to fit the safe. With every failed attempt, they swear at Bronwyn and continue to assault her. They eventually find the right key and empty the safe out.

Battered and bruised, Bronwyn's hands are tied behind her back once more.

Amongst a handful of cash and jewellery in the safe, they find a box of 9mm pistol rounds. This find ramps up the terror that Bronwyn is still to face. In fear, Bronwyn can almost see their drugged and addled gears in their brains at work … If there are bullets, there must be a gun! "Where's the fucking gun," they scream at her. "We sold it," Bronwyn sobs. "I hate guns."

Once again, they attack her repeatedly. "You are lying you fucking white bitch, where is the other safe?"

In response to the growth in violent crime in South Africa, some families had come up with the idea of two safes. The first is a ruse and is only there to house a few silly items that may look valuable. That's the first place you'd take home invaders to. The second safe is well-hidden and contains your real valuables. The idea being that hopefully the first safe will appease their demands and needs and the second safe can remain undetected. There are few situations where this has truly worked. Sadly, most home invaders now know of this ruse, too.

"There is no other safe," she whimpers. "We only have this one."

Still convinced that there's another safe, they drag her from room-to-room so that they can find it. They drag her to the kitchen, yelling constantly, "We're gonna kill you, you fucking white bitch, I've got HIV and I'm gonna fuck you!" Finding a pair of scissors in the kitchen, and still fully convinced there is a second safe, one of them stabs her twice in the neck. He screams at her, "Stop lying you fucking white bitch and tell me where the other safe is."

The rest of the family helplessly listens to Bronwyn's agony, not knowing what has befallen her. They're powerless to do anything. "There's no other safe, I promise," Bronwyn whimpers.

The beatings, terror and horror continue for Bronwyn taking her to the edge of survival and the edge of sanity. Finally, they give up and drag her back to the lounge.

The rest of the family are all still lying under the duvet, their hands bound behind them. Alan is partly able to see from under the duvet. He sees a barely-recognisable, blood-soaked, Bronwyn being dragged in.

Angus feels something fall on top of him and he thinks that they have dropped the television onto him that they had been dismantling to carry out. He managed to peek out from under the duvet and sees blood everywhere. Horrified, he realises that it was his mother on top of him … she's been beaten to a bloody pulp. He hears her whisper "I'm going to die. I'm going to die now." Angus is frozen with fear.

The gang then turns its attention to Alan and start asking him questions, "Where is the gun motherfucker?"

"We don't have one, we sold it," he says. "You are fucking lying," they shout at him and it's now his turn to receive the fury of their anger and frustration as they start hitting and kicking him. Someone shouts at him, "I'm going to kill you and kill your family motherfucker."

They drag Bronwyn back to the passage. She has no idea where they're taking her.

One of the thugs asks Jamie where the safe is. "We don't have another one," she calmly tells them. She's hit repetitively on the head. They're angry and frustrated. They insist that there must be a gun if there are bullets.

A less aggressive gang member approaches Jamie and Angus. He tells them that he doesn't want to hurt them and that he and God loves them all. In his wisdom, Angus replies, "We know and understand that you come from poverty and that you need to steal to make a living, but please, just don't hurt us."

"Yes, this is just for money, that is all," the gang member explains. "I don't want to hurt you, but if you don't co-operate with my friends, they will kill you."

Jamie can see that he's a little calmer and possibly someone she can reason and negotiate with. She starts trying to bargain with him and convince him of other items of value that they may have, such as her pure silver flute, in the hope of turning their attention elsewhere.

Suddenly, another gang member enters the lounge, grabs Jamie around the waist and drags her down the passage towards her room. "I'm going to fuck you," he says.

Through her swollen, battered and bruised eyelids, Bronwyn sees Jamie being dragged down the passage. Another member of the gang meets him in the passage, and they start arguing in Zulu. She believes they're fighting over who is going to rape Jamie. She's horrified. The gang member that initially laid claim on Jamie wins the argument and drags her into her bedroom, closing the door behind him.

Bronwyn is dragged into the master bedroom where one of the gang finds a skipping rope. He gloats, "Hey you lying fucking white bitch, I'm gonna strangle you," holding the rope in front of her face. He loops the rope around her neck and pulls at it as if he's going to tie it into a knot, while grinning at her with malice.

Bronwyn does the only thing she feels she can do in the situation.

She starts praying! "Please God, please God, we have no more valuables, please, please let them believe me and make this all stop! They can kill me if they must, but please just make this all stop. I don't want to wake up tomorrow in a world like this" she continued in prayer. Voicing out her prayer aloud, Bronwyn start pleading with the deviant. "You have hurt me so much already, how can you still hurt me more, please, please stop," she begs.

Turning back to prayer she once more offers the supplication, "Please God just make this stop. I ask you in Jesus name, just make it stop." And almost within that instant, the thug drops the rope and turns his attention elsewhere.

Bronwyn is stunned for the slightest of moments but quickly regaining her thoughts, she quietly kicks the skipping rope under the bed, hoping if they cannot see it, they won't use it.

The dog starts barking again, and they pull Bronwyn up and shout at her to shut it up. Bronwyn manages to part her swollen and split lips to shout at the dog and tell it to keep quite. They throw her onto the floor again. They're shouting at her, shouting at the dog and shouting at each other. It's a scene of total anger, aggression and chaos.

They take her to the lounge where they throw her next to her Alan. They cover her with the duvet as well and she hears one of them shout, "Get the cushion!" Someone puts a cushion on top of her head, and she fears that she's going to be smothered. "Not on top of her head, put it under her head," she hears the same person say. One of the others then puts the pillow under her head and puts the duvet over her in a surprising show of gentleness and concern. She manages to feel for Alan's hand and gives it a squeeze to see if he's okay. He squeezes back. She feels a small sense of relief that he's okay and still alive.

In the meantime, Jamie's nightmare continues. The gang member throws one question after the other at her. "Where's the fucking gold, where's the jewellery and where's the cash?" She gives him all the jewellery she has, but he's still not happy. "I'm HIV positive and I'll give it to you if you don't stop lying and give me everything," he threatens. She remains calm and gives him what she can to appease him.

He grabs her and takes her to the bathroom where he locks the door. He puts a gun to her head and tells her to take off her clothes. There, in the bathroom, Jamie endures what so many dread. He rapes her.

When he was done with his malicious deed, he wiped himself with her T-shirt, and leaving her in the shower, shut the shower door behind him. Further to his despicable character, he nonchalantly whistles away while he washes his hands at the basin.

Digging deep into the resolute inner-strength within her, Jamie sits quietly in the shower, listening to this "couldn't-care-less" attitude and hears this thug climbing out the bathroom window to leave, taking the key to the bathroom door with him. Entombed in what has now become a room of hatred, Jamie sits for ages huddled up in the shower, trying to find herself and find her inner strength once again.

A few minutes later one of the gang bangs on the bathroom door and asks her if she was still inside. She answers him. He then asks her where the other man is and she tells him that he has climbed out through the bathroom window, taking the key with him. In yet another surprising turn, he suddenly sounds very concerned for Jamie and quietly asks, "What did he do to you?" "He raped me," she replies.

Jamie hears one of the others shouting "Humba" (let us go) to them all and she then hears the man moving away with the rest of them, leaving her alone and locked in the bathroom.

The gang had loaded all of the plundered possessions into the Patersons' vehicles. And with keys in hand, they left, leaving behind a home and a family that would never be the same physically or emotionally again.

Bronwyn had massive bruising, her one eye was swollen shut, part of her ear was ripped off, her ribs were broken, and her neck bled profusely. She remained in ICU for three days whereafter she was transferred to a trauma ward. It would be ten days before she was allowed home once more.

Jamie is transferred to Sunninghill Hospital where she receives trauma counselling for rape and is put onto anti-retrovirals to prevent her from getting HIV. She goes into anaphylactic shock when they enter her system.

A week later, Jamie shows the world just what a remarkable young woman she is.

Not only does she open up to the world, including the media about her ordeal, she also sits down to write her Grade 12 final exams and passes them with seven distinctions.

Considering the depths of the trauma experienced, all that they went through as a family and all she went through as an individual that horrifying night, as well as the continual negative affect that anti-retrovirals have on a person and how you feel day-on-day, this is a truly remarkable achievement. Jamie has my utmost respect and admiration.

It doesn't Stop

Sadly, before the Razor Gang was apprehended, they still had one or two more vicious attacks lined up.

> ***Author's Note:*** *Please note that all names in the following story have been changed as those involved have fled the country and have opted for no further contact in this regard. As I have not been able to get hold of them to get their co-operation in all that has been stated, I have opted to change their names. Please note, however, that all information has been taken from their official statements given at the time and currently within the docket representing this case and thus all aspects listed within are correct and factual.*

Pastor Tom Redmond and his wife Jenny lived in Buccleuch in Amy Place. They had two cottages in their yard, one housed Tom's ageing parents, Neville and Sue Redmond, and the other, they rented to a young woman, Mbali Ngwena, who worked in Sunninghill.

On Monday evening, 17 December 2007, just as we were preparing for our first and emotional Christmas without Mike, the Razor Gang was about to inflict another life-changing event on everyone residing at the cottages in Amy Place.

At around 21h00, Tom's 74-year-old mother, Sue, popped outside their cottage to smoke a cigarette when she found herself standing face-to-face with six dirty and aggressive black men.

They pushed Sue back into the cottage, where her 78-year-old husband, Neville, was engrossed in the latest episode of his favourite television show. They pounced on him and forced him to the ground, making him lie on his stomach. As an elderly man with failing health, this was a risky position for him to be in. Sue reacted immediately and pleaded with the gun-wielding gang to allow him to sit up as lying down could affect him badly. In a rare moment of understanding, they pulled him up again and allowed both of them to sit on the couch. Sue started talking to them again. "Shut the fuck up," they barked at her.

Holding guns against their heads, Sue and Neville were then forced through to the bedroom where both their hands and their feet were bound. With the bedroom door shut behind them, the gang moved off to ransack the rest of the house. Some of the gang headed for the adjacent cottage.

It was 19-year-old Mbali's cottage. She was enjoying the evening with her friend Patience and her boyfriend Thabo, as well as another mutual friend, Vusi. They were listening to music and enjoying a few drinks. Thabo headed into the bathroom to relieve himself, shutting the door behind him. At that exact moment, one of the gang burst into Mbali's cottage brandishing a gun in front of him.

He shouted that they need to get out of the cottage. The three friends immediately obeyed and headed towards Neville and Sue's cottage. With their hands and feet bound, they were all made to lie down on the floor in the lounge.

Finishing up in the bathroom, Thabo was surprised to discover that his friends had gone. He heard voices outside and headed out to investigate. He sees a man that Mbali had introduced to him before as the property owner. He's talking to two men. One of the two men notices Thabo and calls him over. As he approaches them, he asks them if they've seen his friends (still blissfully unaware that anything was untoward). They point him to Sue and Tom's cottage. Thabo heads off in that direction. As he enters the cottage, he has a gun shoved into his face. "Lie the fuck down," says the face behind the gun. He immediately complies and is tied up.

The two men outside the cottage with Tom had by then successfully relieved Tom of his watch and rings and thereafter manhandled him into the cottage to join the others already rounded up in the lounge. As Tom was forced in through the door, he noticed all the others already tied up and lying face down on the floor.

"Lie down" growled the deviant closest to him, pointing to the floor next to the others, "And don't fucking look at us" he snarled. As with the others, they tied Tom's hands behind his back and using stockings, secured his feet as well.

With everyone apart from Tom's wife Jenny, now tied up and lying on the floor in Sue and Neville's cottage, the men began ransacking all three dwellings.

Jenny was asleep in the main house. "Wake up bitch. Wake the fuck up," she heard, as if from a dream. She woke with a start and her brain spinning at the speed of light, Jenny immediately knew that something was wrong, something was very, very wrong

The face behind the gun barked "Where is your jewellery?" and simultaneously ripped off the necklace from her neck and the bracelets from her arms. "Give me your rings," he said. She struggled to get her rings off and he shouted at her "I'll cut your fucking fingers off if you don't take them off now." Not wanting to anger him further, she opted to use her teeth to pry the rings off and thankfully was successful.

"Where the fuck is your other jewellery?" he demanded.

Jenny showed him her jewellery box. He snatched it up and he tipped the contents into his pockets throwing the empty box onto the floor.

Swearing and cursing at her, the deviant drags her out the house and takes her down to the cottage where they have managed to round up everyone on the property. Just like the others, she too is made to lie down face first on the ground and her hands are summarily bound behind her back.

When everyone was in the room, the demands came fast and furious. The gang asked about cash, cell phones, laptops, guns and bullets.

The gang was aggressive and looking to vent their anger. One of them noticed that the ropes around Vusi's wrists were too loose around his hands. Thinking that he had tried to untie himself and escape, they viciously attacked him … pistol-whipping, kicking, punching, screaming, shouting, swearing … a non-stop harangue of anger, aggression and violence.

"Kill the fucker!" one of the gang shouts. "He thinks he's so clever, just kill him."

"Ja, shouts another, teach the clever fucker a lesson. Kill him."

"No," shouts the third, "We cannot kill him," as he continues to kick Vusi.

When they got tired of attacking Vusi, they started raging again asking for cellphones, laptops, cash and guns. Tom told Jenny where he had left the laptops and she is dragged by one of the gang to show him where they were. The thug hands the laptops to one of the other gangsters currently emptying out the house and he grabs Jenny once again and directs her out of the house and back towards the cottage. As he exits the house, he changes his mind and takes her around the house to enter back in through the front door.

"Where are you taking me now?" Jenny asks. "You are scaring me." "Shut up bitch," is the single response she gets as he pushes the barrel of the gun deep into her ribs.

Jenny is terrified and her imagination is running wild with the possibilities of what is going to happen next. She does the only thing that she has the power to do. She slows down and almost stops walking. It may have been the only option available to her, but it was not a wise one. The gangster immediately pistol-whips her across the back of her head. He throws her onto the steps in front of them, and with the gun waving in front of her face, he spits profanities at her. He grabs her arm again, hauling her off the stairs and marches her inside. He drags her towards the master bedroom. Jenny is overcome with fear; she can only imagine what is to come next.

"Don't do this," she sobs, "please don't do this."

"Take your clothes off bitch. I'm gonna fuck you."

"No, please. You don't have to do this. Don't you know God loves you, Jesus loves you?" she pleads.

"Shut the fuck up and take your clothes off or I'm going to kill you," he shouts at her.

Jenny was left with no option and had to obey. In what was once the safety of her bedroom, the deviant raped her.

When he was done, he threw her clothes back at her and simply told her to "Hurry up." He dragged her back to the cottage and just before forcing her back inside the door, he whispered roughly in her ear, "If you tell your husband, I'm going to fucking kill you all."

One of the other deviants inside the cottage told her to lie down again on the floor next to her husband. Quietly sobbing to herself, she once more did as she was told. As she was doing so, she noticed that there were only men in the room. Mbali and her friend Patience were missing.

Patience is dragged through to Mbali's cottage first with demands to look for their cell phones. She locates them all, except for Mbali's. Just as she thinks they're going to drag her back to the others, the thug accompanying her pushes her into the bathroom instead and with her hands still bound behind her back, he viciously rapes her. Before he was even done, another deviant entered the bathroom, told the first it was his turn and then covering her face with a towel first, he too then raped poor Patience as she lay there, hands still bound behind her back. Just when she thought this ordeal was over, yet a third entered the bathroom and he too raped her. By the time the third deviant was done, poor Patience lay on the floor in a pool of her own blood. Each of them had beaten her, using excessive force and aggression throughout.

Mbali is then dragged back with demands to find her phone, the only one not yet located. On entering her cottage Mbali sees Patience on the bathroom floor, with one of the deviants kneeling over her and blood all over the room. Mbali starts sobbing, she can only imagine what is coming next.

"Shut the fuck up," the deviant behind her growls and shoving her in the ribs he tells her to switch off the light to the main room. She does as she is told, and no sooner had she flipped the switch, than she found herself being forcefully thrown to the ground and the deviant jumped on top of her.

A few minutes is all it took, and she too become another excessive rape statistic in South Africa.

Yet another deviant enters her cottage and says to his friend "Hurry up, we are going," he says in Zulu. The deviant on top of Mbali nonchalantly pulls himself off and they all leave the cottage.

Mbali and Patience manage to find each other in the darkness and sit on the floor hugging each other and sobbing.

Back in the parent's cottage, one thug had been left behind standing guard over the rest of the group still bound with their hands behind their backs and lying face down on the floor. Tom heard both his and Jenny's vehicles doors slamming shut and the vehicles reversing down the driveway before being driven off, loaded to the hilt, with what was once their worldly possessions.

About 10 minutes later the deviant remaining received a call on his cellphone, presumably from his despicable cohorts, and in response, and without another word, he immediately walks out the door and disappears into the dark of the night beyond, just as the others had done minutes before.

Suddenly, the cottage and everything around them was deathly quiet. Tom gingerly pulled himself up off the floor. Vusi helps Jenny to untie her hands and she then fetches a knife to cut everyone else's hands free. They all head into the bedroom to check on Neville and Sue who have been isolated from everyone throughout the entire night.

Thabo heads off to find Patience and Mbali. He finds both of them sitting on the floor of the bathroom, holding onto each other and crying. Patience is badly injured, and he knows that he needs to get her to a hospital as soon as possible. He heads off to find Tom and to see how they can get help.

Tom heads straight up to the house and presses the panic button and before long the neighbourhood security company and the police arrive. For the first time that evening, Jenny is able to break down and tell her husband what had happened and what had been done to her when she was dragged back into the house. Tom is horrified and can do nothing but hold and console his devastated wife.

Paramedics whisk Vusi and the three women off to Sunninghill Hospital. Vusi to tend to his repetitive beatings and open wounds and the women to undergo the all-intrusive, and just as traumatic rape test procedures. Patience was also treated for the beatings and wounds sustained through her horrific three-time ordeal.

By the time they were all allowed to return home, the realisation was still to hit each one of them - the night may be over, but the nightmare would remain with them all forever. Razor Zulu and his misdirected friends had irrevocably changed lives once again and re-created dynamics in families, forever creating a "before" and an "after" point in all that had been and would be to come.

The Peaks And Troughs Of The Paterson Aftermath

"The one thing that has power completely is love, because when a man loves, he seeks no power, and therefore he has power."

Alan Paton, Cry the Beloved Country

Understandably, the Patersons didn't want to go home after the horror that they had now been exposed to.

With Bronwyn still in hospital, Alan, Jamie and Angus moved from one family of friends to another. Just before Bronwyn was to be discharged, a very close family friend saw the concern and worry of the family as to where they were going to stay once Bronwyn was out of the hospital, as they just could not return back to the same house. After making a few well connected calls to some friends of hers, the Westcliffe Hotel, with the concern and generosity that South Africans can be known for, suddenly opened their doors and welcomed the Paterson family into the hotel where they stayed for a week, while trying to make other plans.

Little did they know, another generous gift was about to unfold and present itself to them.

While trying to sort out what they were going to do next, Bronwyn receives a phone call from one of the most well-known South African families that are synonymous with not just financial success, but philanthropy and a generous spirit beyond note. This occasion was to be no different. "Are you sitting Bronwyn?" the voice on the other end of the phone asks her as she introduces herself and tells Bronwyn who it is on the phone. "We've just converted some stables on one of our properties in Inanda into a lovely home and we'd like to offer it to your family as a place of safety for as long as you need it."

Soon, the Patersons were settled into the property. A few weeks later their generous benefactors arrived at the house for the first time. They'd been in the United Kingdom and had only just returned home.

After warm hugs and words, and hearing the full story on all that had occurred and all they had all been through, "Mrs Benefactor" turned to Jamie and said, "You haul ass my girl, you haul ass in matric and we will sponsor you at any university anywhere in the world that you would like to go to".

Knocked off their feet once again, Bronwyn turned to them and asked the only thing she could think of…. "Why?" she asked, "Why would you do this for us?" "Because we can" was the reply she got "and just leave it at that please" Mr Benefactor requested with a large grin on his face.

There was just one request put to the Paterson's in conclusion of this offering – they would like to remain anonymous and to please keep it out of the media as to who they are that are making these fantastically generous gestures to them. Bronwyn was more than happy to comply.

As we have already ascertained, Jaime sure did kick ass with her 7 distinctions in matric and with that she headed off to the UK to study law at Cambridge University. Since 2 or 3 years old, Jamie had always thought that she would work with animals and wanted to be a wildlife vet, but after all that they had been through, she was filled with a new burning desire to fight this crime and to right all wrongs and thus went to study law instead.

∽

During these first few weeks and months, as so many South African's do, and just as we had done within the first weeks after Mike's attack, the Patersons too sat down to ponder that common consideration. To leave or not to leave!

Everyone around them was saying: go. Get your family and your children out of this country. It's rotten!

There were strong reasons to leave and the United Kingdom was on their radar. After careful consideration, the family realised it would be too financially prohibitive to uproot their lives. There was something deeper too. Bronwyn realised that she was African, and this was her home. She was here to stay!

After Jamie completed her law degree in the United Kingdom, she returned to South Africa, her true home. This is where her roots are, this is the land and the soil that she loves, and the passion for Africa's wildlife she had built up since she was two years old, bit her once again. She found herself heading into a direction with wildlife and African Sunsets as a host and guide on an online safari experience.

She has truly made this world her oyster and became a celebrity in her own right as one of the lead-rangers and presenters who offered on-line safaris where over a million viewers from around the world, tuned in each day as Jamie, her fiancé and a number of other rangers would take them on live game drives in South Africa and Kenya, all while in the comfort of their own homes scattered across the globe. Jamie has proven that she's one with this land and that there is no way that someone like Razor Zulu is going to scare her away from all that she loves.[1]

Bronwyn herself truly felt that South Africa had far too many positives still to offer and the negatives involved in relocating them all to the UK could not outnumber the positives in staying. And so it was that she made one of the hardest decisions of her life and thus they stayed.

∽

Their belief in South Africans and the potential of South Africa as a nation, was well founded.

As so often happens in our darkest times, we often get to experience the most astonishing kindness. Apart from the incredible generosity of 'Mr and Mrs Generous Benefactor', the Patersons were also to be blown away by the generosity of another group of South Africans, this time on completely the opposite side of the spectrum to 'Mr and Mrs Generous Benefactors'.

Bronwyn received a call from someone who introduced himself as the pastor of the Grace Bible Church in Pimville, Soweto. The congregation had read about the attack in the newspapers and they were horrified that South Africans could do this to each other. They invited the Patersons to their church one Sunday as the congregation wanted to honour them and to award Jamie for her bravery while also apologising to them on behalf of all those that had wronged them.

The Patersons were truly humbled and inspired by this gesture and were blown away at the kind thoughts that were coming from this community.

This was a clear indication of the true nature of most South Africans and the true desire that most of us have to live together, to work together,

---

[1] Subsequent to writing the book and at the time of publication, Jamie is about to go to Onderstepoort in 2020, to achieve her childhood dream to study veterinary sciences and become a wildlife vet.

to understand and to support each other. However, despite this incredible gesture, the Patersons were still very shaken up and not yet strong enough emotionally to travel into unknown areas and communities on the other side of town and specifically into what is traditionally a black township area. Gently explaining this to the Pastor, he replied that they understood and would see what they could do in return.

A few days later, with a knock on the door, the Pastor and his wife, had made the journey across to the Patersons themselves, and on behalf of the congregation, they presented to Jamie a crystal trophy with an angel on top, bearing the words ... "For your Brave Spirit" and this poor and destitute community had put together an amount of R5000 which they gave to Jamie as this was the only way they could think of, in trying to make up for all that their fellow countrymen had done to her and taken from her. This was the only way that they could show that they disassociate themselves from the actions of their fellow countrymen and to show us all that they too abhor and despair at all that we are as a country and all that is being done to the citizens within.

This is another, of many examples of the generosity of spirit that makes South Africa great. Thank you to the congregation of that church in Pimville. Thank you for your humble and compassionate spirit and for reminding us what true South African nature is all about. With citizens like you, we can take this country to where it needs to be. You are the future of this country.

A Man Born For Blue

"In a land of fear... incorruptibility is like a lamp set upon a stand, giving light to all in the house."

Alan Paton, Cry the Beloved Country

Sitting at the Sandton Police station was a detective Warrant Officer Bruce Mac Intosh. Bruce was one of the rare gems that, although still in existence, we seldom find in the policing system in recent days. He's an old-fashioned policeman, totally committed to his job, to solving crimes and to helping the South African public. With his job taking first priority in his life, and the most extremely supportive and understanding wife beside him, Bruce Mac Intosh puts his heart and soul into every case he could. Because of his dedication and hard work, he can claim the credit for arresting most of the Razor Gang, together with other well-known gangs and gangsters. He's both feared and respected in the criminal underworld. So much so, that anyone who ends up in prison as a result of Bruce's efforts, is given senior status in the prison system.

All Bruce ever wanted to be was a policeman. The day he left school he committed himself to the police college and before long he found himself proudly dressed in blue. Bruce was in his element and couldn't wait every morning to hit the streets searching for criminals, searching for clues, putting various puzzle pieces together and working out all that may have occurred on different crime scenes.

In 1992 he was allowed to join the detectives branch as an investigator. His primary focus was wanted criminals (still-at-large). With his complete drive and passion together with his unwavering focus on what he wanted to achieve, combined with his natural skills and abilities, Bruce, together with his fellow team members, proved to be a force to be reckoned with and started notching up one successful arrest after another.

With the increase in home invasions and house robberies, Bruce was seconded to a special unit set up to deal with this scourge. Together with his field team colleagues, Bruce realised that in order to get on top of this new wave of crime, which now had a very personal aspect to it, where the criminals actually sought out direct contact and conflict with their victims, and naturally in turn, the violent nature of these crimes started increasing, Bruce and his colleagues in turn would have to step up their game.

To achieve this, the unit increased its presence and penetration into the townships, they expanded their intelligence network and their informant base, they spent hours combing through crime scenes to pick up the smallest trace of evidence that could help point them in the right direction. They continued notching up arrests well into 1996 and became a feared unit amongst the criminal fraternity.

In response, the criminals started fighting back and started targeting members of Bruce's unit. Nkosinathi Mgwaba was driving a recovered stolen vehicle back to the station when he was ambushed in Alexandra Township as he slowed to stop at a stop street. A group of thugs rushed at the vehicles from the side and at point blank range, shot him through the head.

A message was sent!

On the other side of the game, the message was received, loud and clear!

Sadly, as a result, an executive decision was made at senior levels to disband the unit. Bruce once again found himself back in the detective branch as an investigator.

Shortly thereafter, Bruce was asked to start a motorbike unit in the Sandton jurisdiction. The idea was to increase the movability and speed of the police in this area. This new task created an interesting new challenge for Bruce. His job now wasn't to try and solve crimes, but to try and prevent them. This new skill set was to make him an even more outstanding policeman.

The next move for Bruce in about 1999, was to see him returning back to action in a field team. The previous provincial commissioner Perumal Naidoo, put together a specialist cluster unit to deal with the increase in hijacking in the North Eastern Region. This meant that Bruce was now pulled from the Sandton Police Station and as part of this new unit, was now to function at a cluster level that covered six different police stations in the north-east section of Gauteng.

Although initially set up to deal with hijackings, the unit ended up focusing on all kinds of violent crime. Their main task was profiling suspects as well as profiling scenes and building subsequent intelligence on all aspects gained therefrom. The specialist unit consisted of a team of ten highly dedicated and committed policemen. It was not long before they too started racking up one success after the other.

In 2002, tragedy struck, one of the unit members, and Bruce's closest friend, Pine Pienaar, was murdered by one of his employees.

Pine ran a successful security company on the side. One of his security guards had been involved in questionable activities and Pine was to meet with him to question him and pay him his final salary. Bruce had a bad feeling about the meeting and had begged Pine not to go on his own. However, Pine didn't believe it would be a problem and went ahead with the meeting. He had arranged for two other senior staff members to be present as well. When he arrived for the meeting the staff member pulled out a gun and shot Pine and his colleagues before turning the gun on himself. There was not a living soul left in the room.

It was at this stage that Bruce had his first really negative experience with the new South African Police Service. Pine had been a highly respected and passionately dedicated policeman his entire life. He had committed himself to the police prior to 1994 and was a dedicated servant of the people right to the end. However, Bruce and the rest of the team had to fight tooth and nail in order to get authorisation for Pine to be buried with full police honours, as well as for the entire unit to attend his funeral in full police uniform; a marked sign of respect and honour for the fallen.

The new senior members seemed keen to disregard all the years of commitment and dedication, let alone his successes and achievements in blue, but rather were of the opinion that his demise occurred in his own time and off duty, therefore, he wasn't worth the honour. Bruce and the rest of the unit fought vociferously and eventually were given the unwilling permission to give Pine the honourable send-off he deserved.

This internal fight, together with the loss of his greatest friend and colleague, lit a fire in Bruce that could not be stopped. Bruce went ballistic on the streets and no criminal was safe anywhere. He took out all his inner turmoil and his emotions on catching criminals and putting them behind bars.

With the continual successes of their unit, another executive decision was made and three of the successful specialist units, including Bruce's, were combined and transferred to Johannesburg Central. Bruce was about to enter the most frustrating time in his career.

Not only did he discover that the person put in charge of this new unit showed high levels of incompetence and ineptitude, but, for the first time, Bruce came face-to-face with intense levels of corruption and ineffectiveness. The only benefit to him during this time he recalls is that he was involved in intelligence and thus was able to further hone and improve his profiling skills. However, not being one to suffer fools lightly and being totally abhorrent to the presence of corruption, Bruce found himself bumping heads with his senior staff on a daily basis.

Bruce could no longer handle it. He called his previous supervisor, and current station commander of the Sandton Police Station, and requested to return immediately. Colonel Kemp jumped at the opportunity to have a policeman of Bruce's calibre working at his station. Bruce was immediately transferred back to Sandton.

Within a few months a new crime scene profiling unit was formed called the Robbery Reaction Unit of which Bruce became a member.

Bruce and his colleagues' newest challenge was a new scourge called "driveway robberies".

As it was ascertained that most people carried a certain amount of valuable items with them at any time, and as many homes had become veritable fortresses, gangs began attacking people in their driveways as they came from or left for work. Vehicles were hijacked and personal jewellery, to handbags and laptops were targeted. Anything you carried with you was vulnerable to theft, and in turn, made you vulnerable as a potential victim. Bruce and his colleagues had a new type of crime to familiarise themselves with and to try to get on top of.

At this stage, the South African Police Services starts going through some major changes on all levels that start niggling at Bruce and causing levels of concern. Where previously specialised units were composed 100% of committed and dedicated individuals, who lived for the job and gave of their lives to it, more recently, Bruce found himself working in amongst a new breed of Blue. For many it was just a job and was not accompanied or initiated by that passionate drive to "right the wrong" and to "protect and serve". Many had been put into positions to fulfil quotas or to reflect representivity, and thus were severely lacking in the passion, the deep will and the conviction towards the job that is truly required to be a committed police officer and face all that one has to face on a daily basis in this kind of job, for it was just that – a job and an income, and this is as far as the motivation extended.

Regardless of his commitment and his successful track record in the field, Bruce was continuously overlooked and pushed aside when it came to promotions and benefits. Bruce had to sit back on many occasions and watch young members of the new breed of blue who weren't as committed as he, who didn't have the extensive experience as he and who without doubt lacked his track record within their careers, yet time and again, rank and promotion were bestowed upon them one after the other as part of the new BEE processes required in the new South Africa. Although there was always a niggle at the back of Bruce's mind, as long as he still had the opportunity to take criminals off the street, he was happy to keep doing what he was doing. Bruce put his head down and just kept on working.

Shortly thereafter, Bruce was moved to the Sandton Tracing Team. Its main focus was to track down wanted criminals as well as follow up on fingerprint connected cases. Just because he couldn't get it out of his system, while busy with that, he would also take on additional work and still visit as many crime scenes as he could, in order to assist with in-depth profiling of each.

Once again, built on the success of this unit, it was soon amalgamated into the Trio Task Team, dealing with what are termed "Trio Crimes": car hijacking, house robbery and business robbery.

It was in his role as a Trio Task Team member, that Bruce Mac Intosh entered our lives.

Our Hero In Blue

"But when that dawn will come, of our emancipation, from the fear of bondage and the bondage of fear, why, that is a secret."

Alan Paton, Cry the Beloved Country

One cannot talk about Bruce without talking about his wife, Larha! A man as dedicated to his oath to "Serve and Protect" as Bruce was, can only be successful if he has the backing of a loving, supportive and totally understanding wife. Larha Mac Intosh is just such a wife. Having coffee with Larha, she tells me of their eternal inability to commit to anything. "Criminals don't care if it's your birthday, or if it's Christmas, or if you have booked tickets for a play," she tells me with a wry smile playing at the corners of her mouth. No matter what plans they had made, Bruce would invariably receive a call just before, and would speed out the door in pursuit of some information or to profile a crime scene or a criminal itself. But no matter what the plan, nor what the incident was, Larha never begrudged him at all. He had taken an oath for this job, he was 100% committed to his job and to his oath, and instead she did everything she could to support him in it. She recognised that this was an integral part of the man that she had married, and she knew that this is what inspired him, this was what made him wake up each day and this is what made him the passionate man he is.

They had in fact met many years earlier when he responded to a break-in at her own home where she lived with her parents, and deep down she knew, she had met him on the job and subsequently had acknowledged that she had had to marry the job as well. Instead of resenting him or any part of it, Larha set her sights on supporting him in all he did.

In order to help buoy him up after each incident, she established a routine between them. Whenever Bruce had to rush out to an incident, regardless of the time of day or night or of how disruptive on their personal lives, Larha would sit up and wait on his return, and she would immediately have a cup of hot tea waiting for him. Together they would sit in the kitchen and he would tell her all he had had to witness or experience that night. She became his soft place to fall and his unofficial debriefer after each and every episode. Sometimes she would be horrified at what he had to tell her, sometimes she would laugh and sometimes she would return to bed and cry herself to sleep over an incident he shared. More times than she can remember, she would find herself asking him, how on earth families manage to carry on and rebuild their lives after a murder, a traumatic robbery or the rape of a loved one. She heard many of the worst stories that occur in this beloved land of ours, she knew her husband had to come face-to-face with them daily and all she could do was support him in it, and silently at night send out prayers and heartfelt thoughts to all those affected. She prayed nightly for all those crying in our beloved country.

It was during one of their kitchen tea moments that Bruce shared with Larha his current findings. He told her of this gang of thugs that have been involved in one incident after another with increasing levels of violence and sexual assault. The informants had all reported that those linked and suspected to be in the gang were of no standing or relevance in the townships of Alexandra, they seemed to have no official documentation – no ID books, no driver's licenses, they had no fixed addresses, no status, and thus were very difficult to track, hiding in different "nooks and crannies" they could find, they slunk around like sewer rats and thus became dubbed as "The Sewer Rats" by Bruce and his colleagues.

Over a hot cup of tea, Larha was once again hearing about the sewer rats and how this time, they had murdered a man in Craighall Park and left him in the bottom of the pool. They had tied up his wife and his two little children and traumatised them for hours, before finding their father and husband's body in the swimming pool an hour or two later. This was one of the occasions that Larha recalls going back to bed and crying herself to sleep thinking of Lorna and thinking of the children and asking Bruce again and again, how people manage to put their lives back together after such an incident.

Bruce was even more determined than ever to put a stop to this gang and to these sewer rats from Alexandra.

∽

Arriving at Buckingham Avenue after Mike's murder, Bruce immediately suspected that this was the work of his gang of sewer rats.

It is a researched fact the world over that no criminal starts with serious crime initially. Every criminal has a similar "career path" starting with minor crime incidents and working their way up to major and violent crime – the trick is to catch them early on and halt the natural progression as the crime increases. Bruce spent hours looking through previous records, trying to link them to previous crimes, but battled to find much on them, and it was only through his superior detective skills that he was able to deduce what in fact had occurred. None of the individuals involved seemed to have any official records of who they were – no ID books, or ID numbers, no fixed addresses, no jobs, no bank accounts. There was no official record anywhere of their existence or the presence in this world. Bruce was fast learning just what "sewer rats" he was in fact dealing with. He then worked out that as a result, each and every time they had been arrested for anything in the past, the wily thugs had all given different names and different birthdates on the arrest records so there was very little to tie them together and to link them from one incident to another.

Bruce truly has his task cut out for him. But somehow he perseveres.

While the systems are clearly not in our favour, fate seems to be doing what it can to assist.

Somewhere in the chaos that is Alexandra Township, George Nyembe, one of the prominent members of the Razor Gang, had just moved into a shack with a cousin of his, Rueben Nenzehlele.

Each and every time, George came and went from the shack, Reuben noticed George elusively hiding a gun and trying not to let Reuben see that he always carried it with him. Eventually Reuben plucked up the courage to broach the subject with George and he asked him "Do you have a firearm with you," he asked.

"Not a firearm" George replied, "Firearms!" he added, expressing the presence of numerous weapons. This information intrigued Reuben and he was fascinated with his cousin and the presence of such "power" in the form of numerous firearms.

On 12 December 2007, as we as a family were preparing to face our first Christmas without Mike, fate played her first card.

Reuben, clearly impressed with his cousin and wanting to emulate him, snuck into George's room and found one of the hidden guns. He slid it under his shirt and went to visit his girlfriend. On arriving at his girlfriend's house, he discovered another man sitting in her room. In a jealous rage he brandished the gun. His girlfriend and her visitor managed to overpower him and remove it from him. They called the police who arrested Reuben for illegal possession of a firearm. Putting the details and serial number of the weapon into the system, it immediately came up with a red flag and a match. The gun was registered to its previous owner: Michael Roy Thomson.

Reuben was automatically queried as they thought he may then be linked to Mike's murder. However, he informed the police that he had got the weapon from his friend and cousin, one George Nyembe.

Suddenly George was a man Bruce wanted to find … needed to find, and Bruce set his sights to finding this first sewer rat.

Bruce had received hot information on George's whereabouts and had built up a considerable profile on him. It turns out that George was responsible for stabbing Mike and ending up in the pool with him at Buckingham Avenue, for beating Bronwyn Patterson to a pulp in Bramley and for raping Jenny Redmond in Buccleuch. George was also out on bail for a previous conviction at the time that all three of these incidents occurred.

Bruce had been informed that George was hiding out in a shack on 14th Street in Alexandra Township. Moving quietly into position, Bruce and other members of the Tracing Team burst in. Bruce noticed that George hid something under the pillow behind him, before leaping off the bed in fright.

The team arrested George. Bruce lifted up the pillow to see what George was hiding. He found a Nokia 6230i cell phone and an 80Gig iPod; spoils from one or other robbery. Whilst the team was questioning George, Bruce's quick eye spied George surreptitiously fiddling behind his back. Bruce spun him around and found him trying to slip off a men's Tag Heuer watch and a gold wedding band with a black onyx stone set in it.

"Where did you get these?" Bruce asked him. George refused to speak.

George was taken to the Sandton Police Station where he was booked and charged for house robbery, rape and murder.

The arrest of George Nyembe was the beginning of the end for the Razor Gang.

Over the next two days, Bruce spent considerable time with George, questioning and re-questioning him, pushing him for answers and filling in any remaining troublesome gaps and before long, George was singing like a bird.

He spared no detail about the Buckingham Avenue attack, the attack on the Patersons and the attack on the Redmonds. He told Bruce and his team about each and every person who participated in the Razor Gang, who they were, the names they went by and where they were hiding out at the time. He even agreed to show Bruce where each of these locations were.

George took them to one of Sibusiso Mashinine's shacks first. Although Sibusiso could not be linked to Mike's attack, Bruce was convinced he was present. He was, however, definitely linked to the Paterson and Redmond attacks, as well as other Razor Gang attacks.

Sibusiso realised he was about to be arrested and managed to launch himself out of the small window at the back of the shack. The team gave chase, but Sibusiso fled over the rooftops of his neighbours shacks and managed to evade them. The team returned to the shack and conducted a full search. A large quantity of brand-name clothing was found, as well as expensive jewellery, watches, audio and visual equipment, camera equipment and cellphones. Wrapped up in a green canvas bag, hidden under the bed, Bruce pulled out a Walther P38 9mm Parabellum Semi-Automatic Pistol together with copious amounts of different live rounds

George then guided the team to another gang member known as "Serge" but later identified at Armando Makamo, a Shangaan-speaking man from Mozambique. After refusing to let them into his shack, the team broke down the door and arrested Armando.

At around 04h00 on 1 February 2008, after searching for him in two different hideouts, Sibusiso Mashinine was finally arrested.

Shortly after Sibusiso's arrest, Bongani Masumpa and Mzilowo Tofile, both of whom were present at Buckingham Avenue that fateful night, were arrested.

This left only two sewer rats remaining - Razor Zulu and Maxwell Kheza (aka Thabang).

On the 29 April 2008, Bruce once again received hot information on the whereabouts of one of the last remaining rats, Raymond "Razor" Bheki Zulu, also using the alias's "Mandla Skosana" and "Moses Zwane". The informant called Bruce and told him that Razor was currently sitting and socialising in the street in the area around 3rd Ave in Alex. Bruce headed off to the identified area and surreptitiously made his way down the street to where Razor was supposed to be sitting. As he cautiously rounded the corner, he saw Razor sitting out in the open. Bruce crept up on this remaining rat and the leader of this despicable gang who had spent years causing chaos and trauma around Gauteng, and most certainly had changed the lives of the Thomsons, the Patersons, the Redmonds and other victims of the Razor Gang.

At 14h00 on 29 April 2008, and with little fuss and not much ado, Bruce effectively arrested Razor, leaving one single known member of the Razor Gang, known as Thabang, still at large.

Shortly after that, Thabang and a number of other friends attempted to rob a business in Fourways. The police pursued them in a high-speed car chase and in the mayhem, Thabang was shot dead.

Bruce called Bronwyn Paterson and he called my mom to let them know that all seven of the identified members are now accounted for. Six were now arrested and safely behind bars and one was deceased. We could all finally take a breath. All we had to do now is wait for the judicial system to do its duty and to ensure that these sewer rats could never hurt another soul again … or so we thought!

Little did we know at this stage, what a fight and uphill battle we still had ahead of us and little did we know what lessons we were going to learn about the state of our legal system, and its blatant inefficiencies. Little did we know that another failure of the system would result in yet another obstacle that would have Bruce having to start over again with more searches, more informants and more arrests.

But learn we would … a long and arduous nine year lesson until we could eventually put this entire scenario behind us and try to move on instead of living one day to the next just doing "whatever we had to do".

Communities Fight Back

"We do not work for men. We work for the land and the people. We do not even work for money."

Alan Paton, Cry the Beloved Country

Once everyone started to settle down into some sort of altered normalcy, and we had sorted out all the legalities and paperwork around Mike's life and the abrupt ending of it, it was time for me to start thinking of heading home and sorting out my own life.

Just over two months, after hastily packing my bags and meeting Helen on the side of the road in the middle of the night, I packed my bags and my dog into my car once again, and headed back to Hoedspruit.

Adjusting to life back home wasn't easy. After living on top of family, always having someone to do something with, always having someone else to focus on and always having someone else to share in the ever-present sorrow, it was now very difficult to come home and adjust to the solitude of what was once my own haven of peace.

I battled to focus on my work again. I battled to find the enthusiasm and passion required in all I did at the time and then of course, there was also … "that memory thing".

Supposedly as a protective measure, to help deal with all one has to accept and comprehend with the onset of a traumatic situation, the brain has a way of partially switching off and shutting down non-necessary functions, and interestingly, short term memory is one of them. And this does not just mean short-term memory as regards remembering the incident itself, it also affects remembering anything that may occur thereafter. Anyone who has been through a very traumatic experience will suddenly notice that their short-term memory will desert them entirely. Many think it is their own fault and chastise themselves for allowing their minds to remain so scattered, but I have seen this happen time and again lasting up to six months after an incident.

The physical impact of trauma on the body is immense and is something that many people are not aware of or are prepared for. Sure, we all know and expect the usual seesaw of emotions, but little details such as a change in the activity of the brain or any other part of the body is not openly spoken about.

During Nick's schooling years, many of his teachers were left confused and unsure as to Nick's abilities in exams. During the year and in class he showed exceptional abilities with his work and included comprehensive understanding and at times above-average intelligence However, when it would come to exams, Nick was seldom able to complete an entire exam paper. It seemed that he was reading at a slightly slower pace than the rest of his peers. Lorna took him to the usual gauntlet of practitioners, therapists and counsellors to see if they could assess what the problem might be and eventually, she was recommended to a therapist in Mossel Bay. Not thinking for a minute that there might be a direct connection to the trauma he experienced, it was a real eye-opener for her (excuse the pun, as you will understand shortly) as to what the problem was.

This particular therapist had worked with a large number of children in her practise that had been exposed to severe forms of trauma at one or another stage in their lives. Through this work, she had discovered that many children exposed to such extensive levels of trauma, develop a breakdown or disconnection between the eye and the brain, almost as if they brain cannot comprehend what the eye has seen and simply attempts to break the connection, and as such there is a continued halt in communication between the two vital body parts. Thus, as was initially suspected, Nick did in fact read slower than his peers during his exams as a direct result of this continually interrupted communication between his eyes and his brain.

The interesting flip side to this is that Nick is in fact an avid reader. Like his dad before him, he loves nothing more than losing himself in amongst the pages of a good book.

In the first four days following Mike's incident, and apart from the initial support received from Jade (Parkview Victim Support Unit) on the scene itself, we received daily visits from two young women, Paula and Lulu, who were also part of the Parkview Victim Support Unit. Their support, advice and general presence were such a phenomenal help and blessing to all of us; specifically, Lorna and the children. I was so impressed by the impact the Victim Support Unit (VSU) had made on all of us that I decided that it was a service that was needed in Hoedspruit. It was also something I could do to honour Mike.

Every person or victim I could assist thereafter would be for him, in honour of the remarkable man he had been, and equally in honour of the country I believe South Africa can be. In my own small way, I could then do something to counteract the hurt and the tears that criminals, rapists and murderers are spreading around this passionate land we all belong to. I would do what I could to thwart additional crying in this beloved country.

After a few months of finding my feet and getting myself back into day-to-day life at home, I contacted Paula from the Parkview VSU and asked her to send me all the information she had on how to start something similar in Hoedspruit.

After receiving all the information, I put together a plan on how I was going to get this off the ground and started acting on it immediately. The first person I went to see was the station commander at our local police station, as theoretically, all VSUs (or Victim Empowerment Programme as they're also known) should work under, and in conjunction, with the police. The station commander was super excited at the concept. He immediately set up a meeting with various policemen at the station to introduce me and let them know that Hoedspruit was about to get its own VSU.

I put out a notice looking for volunteers and within a month, I had our first little group of five willing souls who were prepared to help others in traumatic situations. We all underwent a series of courses and training in basic Trauma Counselling as well as the concept of Emotional Diffusion, which is largely what we do on any given scene. All my volunteers bought their own 'Hi-Viz" jackets and I had them printed with Hoedspruit Support Unit on the back and following that, we purchased a stock of rescue remedy and other items that would be helpful in dealing with such situations. We were all set and ready for action … and then we waited … and we waited … and we waited!

Six months down the line and the police had not called us in for a single incident yet. We knew they were happening; we would hear about them, or at least a dramatised version thereof, the following day on the insidious local "grapevine", but yet, we were not being called to action.

I became increasingly frustrated. I really wanted to help victims and in the process to honour Mike.

Sitting down to strategise, I realised that I was going to have to come up with some other ingenious plan if I wanted to get the unit functioning and operating. It was then that tragedy struck our little town!

∼

Farm murders are an epidemic in South Africa and in many quarters are called genocide in disguise. In 2019 alone, there had already been more than 180 farm attacks in which 20 people had been murdered.

Hoedspruit, as a rural farming town had been fortunate enough to have not succumbed to this just yet and was an exceptionally safe place to live. However, in February 2010, we had our first farm murder; an event that sent fear through everyone living in the region and brought Hoedspruit to the realisation that we too lived in the criminal state of South Africa.

This murder resulted in the formalisation of the Hoedspruit Farmwatch.

With crime having become so prevalent, communities countrywide have banded together to take the safety and security of their region into their own hands and to work together with police to ensure a safer community.

A few short months after the murder, Hoedspruit constituted its own official Farmwatch organisation and was exceptionally privileged to have been developed under the leadership of a farmer, who not only is passionate about the safety of the region, but also is endowed with patience, foresight, discipline and the ability to see the bigger picture. Mike Scott brought to the table his ability to truly understand a situation for what it is, the passion to deal with the status quo and the patience and aptitude to do so with discipline and vision. Under his leadership and passion, and later added to by the phenomenal compassion and commitment of Lafras Tremper, the head of the Reaction Unit, Hoedspruit Farmwatch has become a real force to be reckoned with and an organisation that has gained the respect, confidence and support of every citizen in the region, regardless of their status, colour or creed.

One of the first realisations that Hoedspruit Farmwatch took on board was that despite coming to being as a result of increasing crime in the area, they recognised the importance of working in cooperation with the police and in working together as a unified resource; and to not see themselves as functioning instead-of, or in-spite-of the police. As a result, Hoedspruit Farmwatch and Hoedspruit police services have formed a strong and very successful partnership over the years and we have been able to see a remarkable increase in the ability, commitment and effectiveness of our police amongst themselves.

The formation of Hoedspruit Farmwatch was the perfect platform for me to get the VSU off the ground. After meeting with the initial management team and teaming up with the growing Farmwatch Reaction Unit, my small group of volunteers finally found themselves very active in all manner of support and assistance within the community.

Eventually I was able to establish and initiate the activities I so badly wanted to be available in our area, and finally I was personally able to initiate and implement something that would not only contribute towards the mitigation of crime and assisting the symptoms of crime, but also be able to honour Mike and the man and brother that he was. Still to this day, every incident I assist with and every victim I support, is in honour of him and the memory of all he used to be.

In addition to coordinating the VSU, I have also become more and more entrenched within Farmwatch itself. Presently, I'm part of its management team and the core of many of the activities undertaken. In recent years and as dynamics and the threat of crime is increasing further in our area, I have also started adapting a data collection platform that can be used to assist and support intelligence. Any information that is obtained and analysed is then shared with specialised and identified high level police officers that are then able to enact on anything shared with them. This new strategy has taken our effectiveness to a whole new level.

Over the years, both the VSU and Hoedspruit Farmwatch have grown from strength-to-strength and are greatly respected and appreciated by the greater community. Farmwatch now has the reputation of being one of the most organised and most effective crime-fighting units in the country. As a result, it is often requested to assist other communities in establishing a similar operation within their own areas. It has equipped itself with resources and technology that take the ability of crime fighting in the region to a level never previously possible through the police alone. This has had an incredible impact on general crime, armed robberies, hijackings, cash-in-transit heists, and of course, our most renown challenge; poaching.

The involvement of communities in their own safety is a matter of necessity in South Africa. It's impossible for the police to handle it all on their own, specifically with the current man-power and resources alone. I encourage all communities to team up with their local police and work hand-in-hand with them. There is far more that can be achieved by working together, rather than working "in-spite-of".

For myself personally, it has been of valuable assistance to get personally and effectively involved in the fight against crime, albeit on a very local level, and to be able to contribute towards the mitigation of the scourge that created such a gaping wound in our lives, while hopefully prevent others from experiencing the same.

The Hoedspruit story is not unique in its success. There are many other towns and communities where similar volunteer organisations are proving extremely successful and effective. It has become a way of life that communities have to get involved in their own safety and security, attending to their paid jobs during the day and donning bullet proof vests, kissing their wives and children goodnight and heading out to take on the thugs lurking in the shadows around us once the darkness has set in.

Every one of these men and women are heroes in my eyes and are indicative of the indomitable South African spirit. South Africans don't give up and always make a plan. South Africans of all races value the land we live in, the African essence, the way of life and the spirit that abounds in this land. South Africans the country over, will fight to protect it at all costs against those that wish to do others harm, and to destroy all that we are, regardless of culture, colour or creed. This is our Beloved Country!

Taking A First Step

"For it is the dawn that has come, as it has come for a thousand centuries, never failing."

Alan Paton, Cry the Beloved Country

Within the first few months after the arrest of Raymond Zulu (aka Razor aka "The Nasty One"), George Nyembe (aka "The Wet One"), Bongani Masumpa (aka "The Nice One") as well as their colleague Mzilowo Tofile (aka Mzi), Lorna and the children were called in for the first identity parade at the Hillbrow Police Station.

The investigating officer, Captain Kgabiso ran one of the most professional identity parades I have heard of to date.

He took exceptionally good care of Lorna and the children. On their arrival he immediately walked them through the situation and explained what was going to happen. He took them to the room and showed them where the identity parade would happen and that the glass between them was all one-way, so they could feel safe and protected.

He also ensured that Lorna could go first so that she could support

Megs and Nick after they had their turn. Annie-Rose was not needed as she had been asleep through the whole incident.

Both Lorna and Nick managed to identify Razor Zulu and Mzilowo Tofile (Mzi). Megs could not confidently identify anyone and had to admit this to the detectives.

Both Nick and Megs handled the experience with maturity and strength. But it was a harrowing and traumatic experience for a ten and twelve-year-old to go through.

About six months later Lorna, Megs and Nick were called in again for yet another identity parade. However, this one was to be a totally different experience for them and where their extensive fear was comforted and supported by Captain Kgabiso and decent infrastructure to allow for the safe activation of the process, this next one was everything that nightmares could be made of.

They were directed to one of the offices and left to wait there alone. Shortly thereafter, a police officer arrived and called one of the children to go through with him. Lorna requested that she go first so that she could wait for each of the children after they had gone through the process. She did not want them to sit on their own in a room after facing the fear and reality of seeing the deviants again. She was rudely told that it was impossible and that children were to go first. Lorna was very unhappy. It increased her angst and panic with the entire situation.

When Lorna's turn came, she was led from one room into another not far down the passage. Her fear was so great that she had a feeling that she was not standing behind one-way glass and that in fact she was in the same room as them. She was not able to confirm what the exact situation was as the lighting in the room was exceptionally poor and she was so gripped by fear she was not able to fully comprehend her surroundings. No one explained to her what is to come, no one talked to her to ensure that she was calm and relaxed so that she could do this properly. This only increases the fear she was already feeling.

Looking at the suspects lined up on the other side of the room, she noticed that the light behind them put their faces into shadow and created silhouettes rather than a clear vision of the individuals standing before her.

"Can they please step forward?" she asks. "I can't see them properly because the light is bad."

"No," is the answer she gets, "They are not allowed to move, you have to look at them where they are."

She also is not properly briefed on what she needs to do or what they want from her. She's told in broken English that there are three of them in the mix of the lineup and she does not understand properly and thinks that she has to select three individuals and is put under extensive pressure in trying to identify three individuals from amongst the mix.

Lorna tries her hardest to see enough to make an identification. In the end she had to give up because the lighting was so poor.

With that Lorna is led out the room and into a third room where both Megs and Nick are waiting for her. They too were very upset and traumatised in that they were not able to see properly and were too frightened to say anything to the policemen present. They were very aware of the pressure and the importance of what they were doing but instead were left feeling like they were at fault as they could not see properly, or make a proper identification.

As they're being escorted out, Lorna notices that the suspects are exiting their side of the room at the same time and into the same corridor.

"Wait," Lorna says urgently, "If we go out now, won't we bump into them in the passage?" The policeman pops his head out of the door and replies, "Oh yes, just wait a few minutes." Lorna stood shaking in fear at the realisation that she had almost been forced to bump into the substance of her nightmares.

Once again, we had been fooled by television shows on how professional identity parades were. The reality in South Africa is horrifyingly different and I hate to think how many violent criminals have slipped through the cracks as a result.

I've had to respond to two victims in Hoedspruit who went through a similar experience to Lorna and the children. Due to the lack of a room with one-way glass, victims in Hoedspruit are made to walk up to their attackers in a closed dark cell and physically touch them on the shoulder to confirm identification. They're then required to stand directly next to their attacker so that photographic evidence can be taken of the two together.

In both situations the victims immediately recognised their attackers. However, they were so terrified at what they had been told to do, that both of them pretended to not recognise anyone so they could get away from the situation as quickly as possible. They called me immediately, now re-traumatised and needing support once again to deal with this new experience thrown upon them.

On questioning this with our police officers on both occasions I was informed that touching a suspect on the shoulder is a legal requirement in South Africa. However, knowing that it was not what Lorna and the children had been requested to do at the first line up, I suspected this not to be true. I immediately emailed a contact at the National Prosecuting Authority for clarification. She informed me that they are aware that there are many police in South Africa that believe this to be a legal requirement and they are not sure where this belief comes from, however, it is definitely NOT the case. The only legal requirement is that the method of identification needs to be unquestionable and very clear.

Sadly, however, a large number of identity parades in South Africa are still run on this basis and subsequently, I am sure there are many identifications that fail as a result of all-encompassing fear from the victims.

Similarly, Bronwyn Paterson had to go through four identity parades. The last two, she recalls, were very difficult as they were now a good year or two after the incident. The suspects had changed. They had lost weight in prison, grown facial hair or shaved their heads, and thus, it was now a lot trickier to identify them.

Bronwyn was the only one that was able to correctly identify three of the gang: Razor, George and Bongani. The rest of the family had either been forced to remain under the duvet or had done exactly as they were told and not looked up at the faces at all.

I'm told by a reliable source that the Redmonds too had an extremely traumatic experience during their identity parade. It was in fact an experience that was so difficult to handle that it was the last straw for them and as a result they emigrated. The process was handled so badly, that not only did they flee the country, but also made the emotional decision to cut ties totally, and as a result, wanted nothing to do with anyone or anything related to the case thereafter. I have it on good authority that it was the identity parade that was the last and final straw for them. Once they left, they would not return for any further court cases or any other important process required to help secure the gang's convictions and, in fact, refused to take any further calls from Bruce or any of his colleagues thereafter.

Identity parades the country over are clearly something that need to be investigated and worked on. It can be such a crucial prosecution tool but through such severe mismanagement is nothing but the contrary and I hate to think how many violent criminals have slipped through the gaps as a direct result of such mismanagement of a simple basic process.

Newsprint Or Not ...

"Is it the bodyguards around you
Is it the high walls where you live
Or is it the men with the guns around you
Twenty-four hours a day
That make you ignore the crying of the people
Farmers get killed everyday
And you say it is not that bad
Policemen get killed everyday
And you say it is not that bad
Maybe if you see it through the eyes
Of the victims
You will join us and fight this

Crime and corruption

Do you ever worry
About your house being broken into
Do you ever worry
About your car being taken away from you
In broad daylight
Down highway 54
Do you ever worry
About your wife becoming
The woman in black
Do you ever worry
About leaving home and
Coming back in a coffin
With a bullet through your head
So join us and fight this

Crime and corruption"

– Lyrics to Lucky Dube hit song

The reggae beat and prophetic words of Lucky Dube are singing over the airwaves on every radio channel I tune to. It is 19 October 2007 – only three weeks after Mike's death, and a mere three days after what should have been his 40th Birthday. Every single radio station is lamenting at the senseless death of this local celebrity and international reggae king.

The evening prior, on 18 October, at about 20h30, Lucky was dropping his son off at a friend's house in Rosettenville. His daughter was in the car with him too. Three thugs were on the prowl, looking for a Chrysler to hijack. Lucky happened to be the unlucky individual who was first to cross their path. As he pulled over and was about to drop off his son, the men pounced. They shot him immediately, apparently not recognising who it was they were shooting – all they saw was the car, a car that they wanted – oblivious to the souls within. Lucky tried to drive away and escape the blasting gun shots but crashed the car into a tree and died on the scene; his two young children still with him in the vehicle, clearly terrified and frightened. His young son managed to jump out of the vehicle and run for help, however, thereafter he was apparently so traumatised, he was not able to speak to, or assist the police in any way at all.

The story was all over the news – every newspaper we picked up was covered in pictures of Lucky, the story of his senseless death and the heartache of his children and the rest of the family. His fans and the country as a whole were in mourning.

It was so easy to relate to what they were feeling. We were in the midst of it ourselves. My heart went out to them all. Another victim of the South African criminal epidemic, another family of young children, who had to look upon the lifeless body of their father, senselessly taken in the desire for material possessions, another broken family!

With all the media attention, it was no surprise that it was only a matter of days or weeks before his murderers were not only identified, but arrested. In that moment, I suddenly realised how we, ourselves, had been seriously misguided.

～

Within the first week after Mike had been taken from us, and due to his connections within the business world and possibly with the added sensation that he had been left at the bottom of the swimming pool for his wife and children to find later, we had a daily repertoire of journalists and newspaper reporters contacting us wanting more information and wanting the scoop on the story.

However, the very first day following the incident, we had been approached by a representative from the Parkview Police Station, who requested that we please deter any advances from the media, and that we "keep the entire story as quiet as possible". It was suggested to us, that when there was large media coverage on a crime, the criminals tended to go "underground" and made it harder for them to be found.

As our primary desire at the time was to find these thugs who had done this to Mike, to Lorna and to the children, we blindly went along with this request and all that was suggested to us. I remember thinking at the time that surely this was counter-intuitive as one would think that the more people that were aware of what had happened, the more potential witnesses or informants you may have and the greater the chance of finding someone who may have seen something, heard something or know of something that can come forward.

However, one of the realities about a situation such as this, is that one's brain tends to collapse entirely, and you become very aware that you are unable to clearly think for yourself. As a result, you become wholly pliable to taking advice from those that are seemingly "in the know", and those that are offering advice and suggestions around you, supposedly from a position of experience and knowledge. So it was for us, and numbly, we went along with whatever was requested or suggested to us in this regard.

The Paterson attack further indicated that this may have been misguided advice. Young Jamie – with the wisdom of an old soul, felt no need to hold back on the horrors that had been exposed to them and she was exceptionally open in the media, about her rape, what they had said to her, done to her and the horrors inflicted on her entire family.

This went a long way into helping confirm identification of the Razor Gang and assisting Bruce Mac Intosh and his team in their subsequent arrest in the two to three months following.

Watching the media response around Lucky Dube, I somehow found the ability to think a little more clearly on the situation and for the first time in this regard, to think for myself. It had become very evident to me that the advice given to us, and the reasoning behind it, is in fact the direct opposite of what tends to happen in reality. I went to Allan to discuss this with him and my concern that we had possibly been given incorrect advice. He responded that he too had been thinking the same thing, and had just come to the same conclusion. We felt we had been duped. With Mike's story now clearly "old news" there was nothing we could do to correct it. We had lost the window for mass exposure and possible information.

It seemed to us, that the police would rather keep things hidden to possibly help sweep another statistic under the carpet or potentially, to take the pressure off having to solve a case immediately, that if openly in the media, would have people wanting and expecting results and outcomes. We could not think of any other feasible reason as to why they would suggest to us to keep this quiet and it is the one aspect in all that we did, that we regret to this day.

Further to that, with the realisation that there are so many hundreds and thousands of serious crimes that are not necessarily reported on in the media, whether it be for the same reasons as we experienced, or because the victims do not have the strength or resources to find a public voice, or because as a nation we have just become so numb to the reality of murder, that just another one no longer shocks us nor is newsworthy, I found myself deep in thought as to what this meant to us as a family as well as to us all as a nation of citizens exposed to this on a daily basis, and just how as a nation we had become so de-sensitised to stories and issues around murder and violence, let alone crime in general.

I have been reminded of this on a number of occasions in the years since through my work with the Hoedspruit Victim Support Unit. On one specific incident, I was requested to come through to a lodge that had been robbed while the guests were all in the 'boma' eating dinner. Two thugs had systematically moved through the camp and cleaned out one room after another, with the guests only discovering this as they returned back to their rooms to retire for the night.

On arriving at the lodge I met first with the lodge owner to get the full run down of the story and the situation. I was informed that the guests comprised two Italians, two Germans, four Belgians and two South Africans. On initially meeting the guests, who were all gathered together on the deck with a drink in hand to calm their nerves, my first question was, "Which of you are the South Africans?" The two South Africans sitting to my right were immediately in tune with what I was in fact asking, and they responded, "We are, so yes, you don't need to worry about us."

As South Africans, they also saw this situation as not "too traumatic" as no one had been attacked, nor injured, no one had had a gun in their face, no one had been tied up, traumatised or raped. This was "just" another robbery. Their personal space was invaded, and their personal belongings stolen, but their personal beings were untouched. Yet for the other nationalities, who had never been exposed directly to crime in their lives, this situation was for them the most traumatic thing they had ever experienced. It was a real lesson and an eye-opening experience to me, as to just how hardened we have become as South Africans.

Why should we be okay with our possessions being stolen - as long as we are not attacked? Why should we be okay with personal space being invaded – as long as we are not raped? Why should we be okay with our holiday experience being destroyed – as long as we are not shot? Our sense of judgement and what is acceptable or what is not acceptable has become skewed.

With seemingly so little support towards curbing crime on a national scale, we as citizens have had to change our thinking just to survive emotionally. We now consider ourselves "lucky" if we are exposed to a robbery, but are not hurt in any way.

I find myself years later going through the same process once again. In doing research for this book and getting all the in-depth detail on all of the Razor Gang attacks and catch myself as I sit here with the thoughts …. "Good heavens Lorna was lucky. Looking at the levels of violence and rape they have shown all their other victims!"

"Lucky, Really???" Let's look at all she went through again that night, and that she had had her husband and father of her children taken from her, yet here I sit using the term "lucky" because she had been spared direct and personal abuse and rape of which the other Razor Gang victims had been exposed to.

I realise within myself, just how screwed up this thinking and this sense of "right and wrong" is, and I chastise myself for getting caught up in this maniacal train of thought.

I think back again on how we as South Africans have got to this point and cannot help but reflect on the high numbers of criminal incidents as well as the seemingly lack of government support in this regard. I am left pondering on this and am in awe as to how correct Lucky Dube had got it with the lyrics to his song, all those years ago:

Farmers get killed everyday
And you say it is not that bad
Policemen get killed everyday
And you say it is not that bad
Maybe if you see it through the eyes
Of the victims
You will join us and fight this

I can only wonder in sorrow whether he had any prophetic inclination that he and his family would be victims of this epidemic themselves, and whether he knew that he was in fact singing his own story:

Do you ever worry
About your wife becoming
The woman in black
Do you ever worry
About leaving home and
Coming back in a coffin
With a bullet through your head
So join us and fight this

Crime and corruption

The Infrastructure Reflects ...

"Justice is truth in action."

Alan Paton, Cry the Beloved Country

The South African Judicial System is fraught with problems and inefficiencies, as we were to discover over the next nine years.

One of the most horrifying is not only the lack of efficiency in processes, but also the alarming physical conditions of our courts.

On 1 February 2012, The Star newspaper ran an article called, *The List of Problems at the Alexandra Magistrate Court:*

"... only three phones lines in the entire court building are working. Switchboard phones have not worked in three years. The switchboard operator appears to have nothing to do because none of the phones work. Microphones inside the courts don't work. Stenography machines often break down..." and the most worrying inclusion of all "Security is a problem with broken electric fencing and low walls."

Considering the court has to temporarily house some of the country's worst criminals, this is a disturbing statement indeed. Many courts across South Africa are in the same abysmal condition as the Alexandra Magistrate Court.

Prior to this article, starting from around 2001, newspapers were littered with stories of escapes of violent criminals from holding cells, while awaiting trial. In the majority of these cases, these escapes were as a result of some or other failure of the system or physical court structures themselves.

In September 2006, four members of the notorious Sandton Knife Gang, suspected of being linked to eighteen violent robberies in the Sandton area, made a daring escape from the Alexandra Magistrate Court. Shortly after appearing in court, six of the gang tried to make a run for freedom through the packed courtroom and past at least two court orderlies.

They are reported to have had leg irons clasped around their ankles and after being denied bail were seen heading down the steps to the holding cells. However, shortly thereafter, came bursting back up the stairs and hurtled through the courtroom. Two were caught, four escaped. Police and prosecutors were furious and questioned how they could escape if they supposedly still had leg irons on.

Bruce and his colleagues had been responsible for the arrest of the Sandton Knife Gang and once again had to hit the streets, putting their lives in danger, committing valuable man-hours to hunt them down. With their proven skill and determination, they were able to re-arrest all four within a week. Not trusting in the security at the Alexandra Magistrate Court, or the abilities of the court orderlies, or the Department of Correctional Services attendants, this time Bruce and the rest of his team gave the Sandton Knife Gang a personalised armed escort to and from the court to ensure no further escapes were possible.

As a direct result of this incident, as well as previous occurrences, numerous requests were made for security to be increased and restored at the courts. However, nothing seemed to be done.

In 2009, the unthinkable happened. Razor Zulu, Sibusiso Mashinine, and two other dangerous criminals, both additional members of the Sandton Knife Gang escaped from the Alexandra Magistrate Court whilst they were appearing for the Paterson and Redmond cases.

Following the break-out, Bruce had the difficult task of calling the victims, including Mom and letting them know of their escape. In doing so, he also promised profusely that he would not rest until he had caught them and had them back behind bars once again. He kept his promise.

Bruce turns his attention once again to focus on the two remaining Razor Gang members who had escaped and once more he had to go through the lengthy process to track them down and re-incarcerate them.

Bruce and the rest of the Trio Task Team immediately activated all their informants and other intelligence networks in search of the missing fugitives.

On the 12 November 2009, just over two months after the escape, Bruce received information from a source on the whereabouts of Razor, this time in Diepsloot, a township north of Johannesburg. Finding Razor inside a locked shack, they managed to barge their way in and arrested him as he lay asleep on his bed. Caught totally by surprise, Razor was not able to use the CZ 7,65mm semi-automatic weapon resting in the front of his pants. All Razor could do was to look at Bruce in shock and respond "Eish, you have me Mr Bruce."

Catching Sibusiso Mashinine proved more problematic. Bruce never gave up and searched for him for a further two-and-a-half months.

Finally, on 26 January 2010, as the world was preparing for the World Cup Soccer in South Africa, Bruce received information he could act on. Sibusiso had attempted another house robbery in the days prior and in doing so was shot in the abdomen and severely wounded. He still managed to flee the scene but was taken to Edenvale Hospital by his family. From there he had been transferred to the Johannesburg General Hospital (now named the Charlotte Maxeke Johannesburg Academic Hospital). He checked in under the false name of Sibusiso Majopele.

As Bruce walked up to the injured man's bedside, Sibusiso immediately recognised Bruce and the shock at being found was clearly evident on his face. Reportedly "he almost had a heart attack when he saw Detective Bruce arrive" a hospital orderly stated. However, Sibusiso regained his wits very quickly and tried to insist he was not Sibusiso Mashinine at all but was in fact Sibusiso Majopelo and that he had been shot at a tavern in 1st Avenue in Alexandra Township.

Knowing full well that Bruce had his man, he ordered the patient to roll up his left sleeve. As he did so, Bruce instantly saw the confirmation he was looking for – a small tattoo of Mickey Mouse, a recorded mark on the marked man. Rodent against rodent - the comical and well-known mouse, had given the game away and helped seal the deal on the last remaining "sewer rat".

Changing The Law

"The Judge does not make the law. It is people that make the law. Therefore, if a law is unjust, and if the Judge judges according to the law, that is justice, even if it is not just."

Alan Paton, Cry the Beloved Country

Mom calls me on a Sunday afternoon in 2008. "You need to watch *Carte Blanche* this evening" she says to me. Later in the conversation she explains "Vanessa is on, she is talking about the DNA Project."

I watched Vanessa with respect and with pride as she explained her vision and her work. We had promised to make Mike's death mean something and through funding from the Mike Thomson Change-a-Life Trust amongst others, Vanessa was helping us achieve that in a truly remarkable way.

Caroline Hancock, Genetics Professor at the University of Kwa-Zulu Natal, also watched *Carte Blanche* that night. Caroline, affectionately known as Coo, was impressed with Vanessa. She felt that with her background, she would be able to contribute to the DNA Project. Not long after reaching out and connecting with Vanessa, Coo handed in her resignation at the university and joined the DNA Project full time.

They had identified four main focus areas for the project to be successful

The first focus area was to confirm the laboratories were properly equipped with the latest equipment to ensure appropriate efficiency in processing DNA samples.

The second focus area, headed up largely by Coo, was to establish a post graduate honours course in forensics. Until that time, there had been no course that allowed one to specialise in the field of forensic studies or applications. Most laboratory technicians studied genetics or microbiology and then picked up forensic experience in the field.

The first university to come on board was the University of the Free State in 2010. A total of 80 students are selected each year for the undergraduate BSC in Forensic Sciences and thereafter only a total of 10 are selected to do BSC Hons in Forensic Sciences and 10 selected to do BSC Hons in Forensic Genetics. The courses are currently being rolled out to other universities across the country.

The third focus area was to create awareness and educate the public and first-responders on how to treat crime scenes and protect them to avoid loss or contamination of DNA evidence. For this purpose, a series of workshops were run (and are still currently run) with various security companies, paramedics, community policing forums, Farmwatch and neighbourhood watch groups, as well as various school students. I myself spent 2 years hosting training courses for the DNA project in Limpopo and Mpumalanga. By January 2017, a total of 869 workshops have been run countrywide, with an impressive total of 43640 first-responders having been addressed.

The fourth, and most important focus area, was to get the laws in South Africa amended to set up and establish an Expanded DNA Database to be used as a criminal intelligence tool and not just to allow DNA to be used on a prosecution basis only. And to simultaneously propose a change to the fingerprint law in order to allow for fingerprint processing to happen on a more immediate basis, as well as to centralise and link various national fingerprint databases.

All of these focus areas have successfully been implemented and achieved. However it was the changing of the DNA laws that proved to be the most challenging for the entire team.

Despite these challenges, Vanessa, being the driven and dedicated individual that she is, took every obstacle, every difficulty and every delay in stride and never gave up. She knocked on doors of those who needed to hear her plan, she pounded the halls of parliament, and kept the media in touch making sure that the right people heard her, as well as properly understood what was being presented to them. Sometimes the delays and hesitations were understandable and at other times due to nothing more than total incompetence and a seeming lack of desire to sort out crime in the country. But Vanessa and her team never gave up.

In the middle of this lengthy process an article called *Raped Again - By The System* was published in the *Sunday Argus* in the Western Cape on 5 June 2011. The article is written by Chris Asplen, a former prosecutor in the US, where he was the advisor to two US Attorney Generals on the use of forensic DNA technology and where he was the Executive Director of the US Department of Justice's National Commission on the Future of DNA Evidence. The article outlines Asplen's shock and horror at the lack of action from the South African Government in dealing with crime and specifically, DNA. The article outlines that we may have the best laboratories in the world, however, it all means nothing if we do not have the laws to support the maximum potential and use of DNA. He points out that this is in fact the situation in South Africa.

A section that he includes that is particularly concerning states:

I first traveled to South Africa 10 years ago. I left the Department of Justice less than a year earlier and had been invited to participate in a meeting of Interpol's DNA Expert Monitoring Group in Pretoria. It was my first trip to the continent so to say that I was excited, is an understatement. I did not, in all honesty though, harbour great expectations regarding what I would see from the standpoint of South Africa's use of DNA technology. But when I saw what the South African Police Service (SAPS) was doing, I was nothing short of astounded. The SAPS had an automated system for DNA analysis that was unique in the world. As we toured through the laboratory, I realised that it was, at that time, the most advanced forensic DNA testing robotics system I had ever seen. I was so impressed that I literally walked out of the lab, got on my phone and called my former colleagues at DOJ trying to convince them to bring Johann and his colleagues to the US so that they could explain what they were doing. South Africa was going to be a model, not only for Africa, but perhaps for the world. They had crime statistics that proved South Africa to be one of the most sexually violent places on the planet and they had the capacity and technical sophistication to hit back hard. South Africa was going to prove the power of DNA like nowhere else.

Boy was I wrong.

I have just returned from another trip to South Africa, a trip I have made many times since my first visit. And to be clear, it's not the police that have failed, nor is it the technology, nor is it the laboratory personnel. Rather, ten years after South Africa created one of the most important laboratory infrastructures in the world, the politicians in the South African Parliament have still failed to give police the legal authority to save literally thousands upon thousands of lives with DNA. Ten years later and South Africa, in contrast with more than 50 countries around the world, still has no legislation allowing for the establishment of a forensic DNA database. South Africa is a strikingly beautiful country from its coastline at the Cape of Good Hope to Kruger National Park to the wine regions of Stellenbosch. It is also the economic anchor for sub-Saharan Africa. It has a technology portfolio that includes a nuclear weapons program (and the wisdom to subsequently dismantle it), a 2002 Nobel Prize for work in microbiology and the first human-to-human heart transplant was performed in South Africa.

And most importantly, it is a country which engineered one of the most significant triumphs of human spirit and potential — the non-violent elimination of apartheid.

But South Africa is also a country that, according to the United Nations, ranks second for murder and first for assaults and rapes per capita. Fifty-two people are murdered every day there and the number of rapes reported in a year is around 55000. It's estimated that 500000 rapes are committed annually in South Africa (many of them aren't reported). In a 2009 survey, one in four South African men admitted to raping someone. Even more insidiously, South Africa has one of the highest incidences of child and baby rape in the world. It's a country where the belief exists that intercourse will cure or prevent HIV/AIDS and where child rape is used as a method of retaliation against someone else for a perceived wrong. Children are murdered and body parts used for "traditional" medicinal remedies. And in a country also cursed with epidemic rates of HIV/AIDS, rape takes on an exponentially tragic dimension.

The world holds no shortage of human tragedies. But most of those tragedies persist because there are no clear, identifiable fixes. Feeding entire starving countries from overworked, infertile land or generating clean, lifesaving water from dry, parched earth, are heavy lifts. Wars and the conflicts that lead to catastrophic loss of human life have been with us since the beginning of time. But when it comes to fighting back against serial rapists and pedophiles? I have examples from every corner of the planet of exactly what works and just how well. There is nothing better at getting rapists off the street, at protecting little girls and, by the way, at protecting those who would be wrongly accused and convicted of those serious crimes than DNA databases.

And what exacerbates the tragedy tenfold is the fact that, unlike many countries with the wisdom to implement DNA databases fully, South Africa has all the other components necessary to leverage the power of DNA technology: the laboratory system, the finances, the education and the commitment by the police. There are no other excuses, nowhere else to place responsibility.

He ends off the article with the following thoughts:

As someone who works regularly in other people's countries, I don't "call out" or criticise foreign officials easily or often. But on a scale unequalled anywhere else on earth, hundreds of thousands of children's lives are sacrificed because of the failure to act by politicians in South Africa. The Parliamentary Portfolio Committee responsible for the legislation that would give police the ability to immediately begin taking rapists off the street has avoided acting on the law for years. The legislation sits in Committee while the worst sexual violence statistics in the world continue to pile up. Except, they're not really statistics. They're terrified woman and little girls staring into the face of horrific violence and evil while they're likely infected with HIV — three more of them just in the time it took you to read this article.

Despite these challenges and obstacles along the way, Vanessa does not give up. She finds the right people to talk to, those that care, those that will help her achieve what she needs to achieve and she and her team keep working hard, and keep focusing on what needs to be achieved.

On 27 January 2014, 10 years after the death of her father, Johnny Lynch and seven years after Mike's death, the DNA Act is finally passed into law in South Africa.

The three directors, Vanessa, Coo and Allan, were all on different sides of the country on that day, so there were no major celebrations nor group clinking of champagne glasses. It had in fact been such a long, tedious and painstaking journey that it all felt like a bit of an anti-climax. They had been running on reserve energy for the last few years with the last of the pushing and pestering required, that their energy levels were depleted and all they could do was to sit back, sigh a huge sigh of relief and look ahead to the mountains of work yet to come. Vanessa knew at that moment, that this was not the end, this, was just the start!!!

Thinking of both Johnny and Mike at that moment as well as the many other victims who had lost their lives during the 10-year journey, it was clear that this was truly a bittersweet victory for all, and given the choice, they would rather have their loved ones back with them instead.

However, the sad realisation is that they are no longer with us, and nothing we do will ever bring them back, but in their honour and in their memory, as well as for all the many hundreds and thousands of other victims in South Africa, we now have a new law that should help bring those criminals in off the streets of our country. We now have an official and revised DNA Act in South Africa.

∽

This new DNA Act now makes it mandatory for specially trained police officers to take DNA samples from suspects at the time of arrest for any Schedule 8 offences. These include: treason, sedition, public violence, murder, culpable homicide, rape or compelled rape, sexual assault, Any sexual offence against a child or mentally disabled person, trafficking in persons for sexual purposes, robbery, kidnapping, child-stealing, assault (when a dangerous wound is inflicted), arson, breaking and entering, theft, escape from lawful custody, offences under the Fire-Arms Control Act, offences under the Explosives Act, offences related to the Protection of Constitutional Democracy against Terrorist and Related Activities Act and lastly offences of torture.

Anyone involved in the conspiracy of, involvement in or the attempt to commit any of the listed crimes will now automatically have their DNA taken through a buccal swab (mouth/saliva swab) and their DNA will forever be recorded on a Suspect DNA database. Similarly, any evidence found at a scene will undergo the same process and forever be listed on an Evidence Database. The two will continually be compared to each other in order to link suspects and crime scenes/evidence together. The larger and more complex each of the databases grow, the greater the chances of a link and successful prosecution of a suspect. This is now the future of crime fighting in South Africa.

Every criminal leaves DNA evidence on a crime scene; it is virtually impossible not to. DNA evidence can be found in sweat, in saliva, in semen, in hair, on clothes, DNA can even be found within a smudged and unreadable fingerprint. It can be found on cigarette butts, on bottles or glasses they may have drunk from, drops of blood, blobs of spit. There is always something they leave behind somewhere, and with the correct protection and processing of a scene, it can now successfully be collected, processed and the suspect identified. Where previously only fingerprints and visible, obvious evidence was collected, crime scenes would now have to be treated with far greater consideration and concern in order to protect the presence of any DNA on the scene.

The DNA Project has developed a brief little summary they use to aid first responders as to basic guidelines on what should be done when arriving at a crime scene using the acronym DNA CSI:

Do not Touch
Note, Record & Observe
Assist Police Officers

Comfort and support victims
Secure the crime scene
Insist NO-ONE interferes.

This simple list has been shared with many first responders over the years and hopefully, we will start seeing some remarkable changes in how a crime scene is treated, protected and processed and, subsequently see a marked increase in the arrest and conviction of criminals running rife in South Africa and of course – the obvious goal, see a marked reduction in the number of and occurrences of serious and violent crimes in South Africa. Working closely on crime scenes over the years since the inception of the new law and seeing what is happening on the ground, it can only be stated that a lot of work still needs to go into this process to ensure that it is effectively initiated on the ground and that all of Vanessa and her team's hard work comes to fruition. It's the vital tool we so badly need in this country to stem this continual growth of crime in this beloved land of ours.

Moving Forward

"Pain and suffering, they are a secret. Kindness and love, they are a secret. But I have learned that kindness and love can pay for pain and suffering."

Alan Paton, Cry the Beloved Country

As the first year without Mike crept by slowly, Lorna and the children were doing all they could to find healing and a way to move forward. Having come to the conclusion that life in Johannesburg was no longer an option for her or the children, she started looking around at smaller, more rural and quieter towns. Hoedspruit was initially flagged as an option and I revelled in the idea of having them living near me.

After giving it serious thought, Lorna decided that emotionally she was not ready to face Hoedspruit just yet. Hoedspruit was where she met Mike and where they spent the majority of their family holidays at N'tsiri, a private game reserve bordering the Kruger National Park. It's also where we finally scattered his ashes, under his favourite tree along the banks of the N'tsiri River. Her heart was not in a suitable space to face the past or bring the past into her future. It would in fact be another eight years before she would be able to face her emotions and spend some time sitting under Mike's tree, looking across the dry riverbed and the African Savannah.

And so she continued to look elsewhere.

Midway through the year, as the school holidays rolled around, Lorna took the children down to visit her friends, Paul and Rosie Deans who lived in a little village down on the coast near Plettenberg Bay. While there, not only were the children able to sleep in their own beds at night for the first time since the incident, but they fell in love with the sea salt air, the sandy beaches and the sunny way of life.

Suddenly Lorna felt more relaxed. This was an option that could work and one the children looked forward to adapting to. Here they could face the idea of starting a new life without Mike.

Lorna started looking at homes in the Plettenberg Bay area and found something that would suit them all. The Buckingham Avenue house had just been sold so she was able to immediately put in an offer-to-purchase and before the holiday was up, the foundations for their new lives had been laid. All they had to focus on now was getting through the rest of the year and on surviving the nights filled with fear in Gauteng, that so often ended with them all huddled in a small cupboard awaiting the mornings light to wash away the ever-present fear of what may be lurking in the dark.

At the end of the year, just before the close of school, I came up to Johannesburg once more to help with the last of the packing up of their lives. Piling all the boxed-up belongings and emotions into our two vehicles, Lorna, Megs, Nick, Annie-Rose and I drove the long distance down to the coast, to their new home, a new chapter, and a light at the end of the tunnel.

I then spent the next three weeks in their new home helping them unpack, sorting out their new lives and exploring their new world and community around them. It was a time filled with mixed emotions. The ever-present sorrow and gaping hole where Mike should have been, mixed with the optimistic hope of a new beginning and a more peaceful future where the children could grow, learn to cope, and find a way to love life once again.

The first night on the street, we noticed their neighbour arriving home in his work vehicle and it gave Lorna an extra level of peace to note that the car was emblazoned with the unmistakable blue and yellow stripes and insignia of the South African Police Services. She had a policeman living next door to her and this gave her that extra bit of security and contentment in her new home. It was a good start.

During all the unpacking and sorting out of the house, the children had decided there was one priority that needed seeing to first. While Lorna and I unpacked the cutlery and kitchen knives, the children busied themselves with the creation of a "Daddy Corner" in the lounge.

In this corner, a table was set up with photos of Mike, special items that each of the children had chosen to remember him by, a large white candle to light in his honour and a few other knick-knacks of emotional importance. We set up a Granny Clock that Mike had made as a woodwork project in Grade 12 on the wall above, together with an array of photos and portraits of the family that once was.

Mike's presence was established in their new home from that very first night and as soon as the children had completed their creativity around the "Daddy Corner", we all sat around it with lumps in our throats, tears in our eyes, but a drink in our hands raised to the future and to finding light in their lives once again.

∾

We were not the only ones raising a glass with hope towards the future. Just weeks after the Patersons' attack, they too sat together as a family and although still trying to place all that had been done to them and trying to comprehend how one human can do this to another, they too felt the need to dig into their resilience and to find the tiny spark in all they had been through. Sitting together as a family, they drank to the future, a future where they could move forward and find a way to put this all behind them, and they drank to survival!

They had been dragged to hell and back, but, they had all survived and were there alive and together, albeit as a family of broken souls. A toast not afforded to Lorna, Megs, Nick and Annie-Rose, but one the Patersons felt the deep-seated need to acknowledge.

∾

Sadly, for some of the other Razor Gang victims, finding that little tiny spark of hope was more challenging, and for them there were no glasses to be raised. The terror of their night in hell at the hands of Razor Zulu and his group of deviants, just added to their lack of faith in South Africa as a country, a home and a future.

They took the first opportunity they could, to pack their bags and move thousands of kilometres and oceans away. Away from their homes, away from their roots and away from the country that had let them down. The evacuation trend is something that extended South African families know only too well. South Africa is a country with citizens scattered in all corners of the globe. The majority of them, having left due to a lack of faith and belief in the country of their birth.

∾

With the Razor Gang re-arrested and securely behind bars, we now looked to the justice system to complete the process. For the Thomson and the Paterson families specifically, we had now thought that the final steps had started and it would only be a matter of a year or two before it would all be behind us. We all knew that the court case and trial itself would be an emotionally charged experience, however, once it was done, it was done. This challenge and obstacle that life had dealt would be behind us all and we could all then truly find closure and move forward. With the Razor Gang in jail, and evidence piling up, we all believed an average of two years was all we would be looking at. Two years of continuing to live through this, two years of continuing to just do "whatever we needed to do" and two years of just living "one day at a time". But oh, how wrong we were!

We did not realise at that stage, what a long fight we had ahead of us and just for how many years we would have to continue to do "whatever we needed to do" and for how many years we would still be taking "one day at a time" and just how much we as citizens would have to get involved to ensure their convictions and fight the failing systems to prevent these deviants from being returned to the streets to continue their vicious choices and way of life. We were about to learn the hard way.

The Phoenix From The Fire

"I have always found that actively loving saves one from a morbid preoccupation with the shortcomings of society."

Alan Paton, Cry the Beloved Country

It's always important to remember that no matter how dark the clouds are around you, so often within, one will find the beauty of a rainbow.

While we were unwittingly steeling ourselves for the long fight ahead, the phoenix that had emanated from this situation was rapidly growing and starting to take flight. The Mike Thomson Change-a-Life Trust continued to expand and to achieve remarkable accomplishments.

It was not long before the DNA Project was joined as a beneficiary by other well deserving projects. The next beneficiaries to join the ranks was the Martin Dreyer Change-a-Life Academy and the I-Choose-to-Change-a-Life project.

Seven Times Dusi Champion, as well as a South African multi-sport king, Martin Dreyer has committed himself to changing lives. Through his years of paddling down rivers, or pounding the footpaths and trail runs of the Valley of a Thousand Hills, Martin took note of how most of the youngsters lived in the rural villages scattered throughout. They were given so little direction on what their potential or prospects in life could be and generally were deprived of opportunities to forge ahead in life and make something of their lives. Some of them however, showed a definite interest in the mad world of canoeing that would pass through their valley once a year. After witnessing a group of young boys having rescued an abandoned and broken canoe, and patched it together as best they could, to then spend their days paddling and playing and imitating the canoeist that breeze past their pastoral playgrounds annually, Martin had a vision. He had a vision to change their lives.

In October 2008, Martin launched the Martin Dreyer Change-a-Life Academy. His goal was to groom at least 10 underprivileged youngsters to not only become leaders in their communities, but to also become sporting leaders in the Dusi Canoe Challenge. After only four short months of training, they took to their first Dusi Challenge and Martin was blown away. Eleven of his protégés completed the challenge within the top 50 and two of them were even in the top 10. From nothing to something ... and their lives were changed forever!

The Change-a-Life Academy team have gone from strength-to-strength. They are not only competing in, but frequently winning top canoeing, trail-running, mountain biking and multi-sports events. In 2011, they achieved 1st, 2nd and 3rd place in the Non-stop Dusi Canoe Challenge. Martin could not be more proud. Apart from the obvious successes that these youngsters have achieved, the benefits have been multi-pronged. As an important part of their training, nutrition is taken very seriously and to support this, Martin has arranged top sports nutritional supplements, as well as weekly food parcels to be received which also provide much needed support for their families. Some of the top performers have earned enough from their winnings to build proper homes in the valley and several of them have secured employment (many of them as coaches) as a direct result of the skills gained at the academy.

Even deeper than the obvious benefits, the successes achieved by the athletes has helped engender an understanding of "with hard work, comes reward" as well as helping the youngsters in the valley believe in themselves, and that with hard work, they too can achieve whatever they set their minds to. It has helped engender an understanding that they too are capable of success and of achieving something – all they need to do is put their minds, their heart and their souls towards it. This kind of mind-set and self-understanding is crucial in the drive to create a society that is less prone to turn to crime as an acceptable activity. Martin has changed many lives and continues to change many lives and many of the youngsters, who may have turned to crime, or whom felt they had no opportunities in life now have direction, goals and most importantly are strong ambassadors and representatives of that much needed entity … hope!

Following hot on the heels of the successes of Martin and his Change-a-Life Academy, is the iChoose-to-Change-a-Life | Valued Citizens Initiative. This initiative is aimed at providing guidance, training and leadership skills for children who have already been involved in crime. The children undergo six different leadership sessions that look at aspects such as:

- Understanding Leadership
- Committing to Self-Discipline
- Discovering the Leader within them
- How to be "Response-Able" and to Lead with Values
- Communicating through Openness
- Trusting in themselves and in their team.

Once they have been able to complete the programme, this is followed by a four-day leadership camp that sees the beneficiaries reflecting on the content covered as well as developing practical methods that will enable them to be effective leaders against crime in their spheres of influence, whether it be at their schools, in their homes, their communities or just on the playground.

Apart from developing self-confidence and a sense of responsibility in the youngsters, together with building consciousness and infusing constitutional values within them such as behaviour, the initiative also looks at improving the productive capacity and quality of many of the learning institutions that they interact with as well as developing dedicated educators, social workers, parents and ethical leaders as role models for children and youngsters in the communities. They have also created an active channel to ensure that at least 70% of the children exposed to the programme, are able to participate in the economic mainstream thereafter, by accessing tertiary education or getting exit opportunities after Grade 12, as well as assisted in creating an enabling environment to nurture entrepreneurial mind-sets within the youngsters. All of these objectives assist in contributing towards safer, and towards more sustainable communities as well as fostering social cohesion.

An additional project within the initiative, sponsored by the Change-a-Life Trust, is the iChoose Responsible Parenting Programme. This aims to enable family members to contribute effectively in leading children to become responsible adults and to live the values that bind family members together, developing healthy relationships, to enhance caring, nurturing, loving and supporting capabilities of families through parenting skills workshops.

The understanding behind this, is that the family is the pillar of society as it influences the way society is structured, is organised and how it functions. South Africa has a number of unique and problematic circumstances that affect this structure. These circumstances include the migrant labour system inherited from our historical past which undermined the African family and created conditions for its disintegration, as well as other circumstances such as poverty and the HIV/AIDS pandemic which has placed added burden onto children in communities. In 2012, statistics showed that only 35% of children were living with both their biological parents and as much as 23% were living with neither of their biological parents. It's this kind of dynamic that can seriously affect the socialisation of children.

International research as well as the Human Sciences Research Council have both claimed through studies that children growing up without fathers are more likely to experience emotional disturbances. And, more specifically, boys growing up within absent father households, are more likely to display "hyper-masculine" behaviour, including aggression and violence.

In a recent Green Paper on South African Families, it has been emphasised that it's now essential to promote family life and strengthen families to be able to effectively deal with conflict, stress and crisis, as well as to rise to their parental responsibilities and to provide a nurturing environment where traditions, rules and discipline are fostered for children to feel safe, cared for and appreciated.

I can't help but think about the Razor Gang, who all seem to have grown up without fathers present in their lives and definitely without the structure of a safe and nurturing family life. What would they have become and how would their lives have turned out if this basic necessity had been available to them? As much as they have been feared, and have chosen within themselves to spread violence and terror in all they did, are they too not victims of the systems and the society that they have grown up in? Have we as a collective country, not created our own evil?

As the Trust and the Change-a-Life Cycle Tour continued to grow, they were able to take on more beneficiaries and projects. An additional three projects were selected. These were:

- Nemato Change-a-Life is an organisation focused on giving hope, security, support and nourishment to impoverished children in the Nelson Mandela Bay Township, Port Elizabeth. Its primary intention is to teach them and actively demonstrate to them that by working hard, and positively grabbing any opportunity afforded to you, you can change your life and that for anyone and everyone, there is a bright future ahead
- The Change-a-Life Rape and Trauma Counselling Centre in Cape Town
- The Change-a-Life Karate-Do, a project initiated and run in honour of Mike by Allan

In 2010, Allan felt the need to do something that would not only link in with the trust but would also honour Mike and the remarkable Karate Sensei he had been. Allan and Mike had both run a dojo together for sixteen years. Allan had achieved the level of Fourth Dan Black Belt and Mike had reached Third Dan just prior to his death. Mike's passion had been to teach the children who came through the dojo. He had always been a man who enjoyed children and got great pleasure out of teaching them, supporting them and helping them grow.

In recognising on a deep level that many South African citizens are brought up in homes and communities where there is very little moral guidance, adult supervision and a basic establishment of discipline and belief in oneself and that children brought up in such a boundary-less society are very likely to end up making the kind of decisions and life-choices as those by Razor Zulu and his gang, Allan could clearly see how the discipline and benefits of Karate could help counteract this. It was on the back of this thought process that Allan decided to establish the Change-a-Life Karate-Do Programme.

The programme started with 15 students, aged between 11 and 20, who were recruited through church representatives in the squatter camps of Drummond, just north of Johannesburg. The aim of the programme is to inspire these children to grow in confidence and become well-balanced, productive members of society through the discipline and power of karate-do.

Despite being desperately poor, with few clothes and often little food to sustain them, the students all put their heart and soul into everything they were taught, and all passed their first official grading in August of 2010. The pride at receiving their first official karate belt and, for many, the first achievement ever in their lives, was clearly palpable. With the success of the Drummond students, a second batch of 15 students from Cosmo City was taken on as well in late 2010.

A minibus was purchased for the project and twice a week it's driven to each of the informal settlements to collect the children and bring them to the dojo now in the Petervale suburb of Bryanston. The children are also supplied with a balanced nutritional meal; for many of them the only proper meal they will receive all week. The children aren't only taught the practices of Karate-do. They're also encouraged to develop responsibility and leadership skills with many of them then encouraged to assist with teaching within the dojo themselves.

To date, 90 Students have passed through the dojo with four having reached black belt level.

All of these students are taught under the watchful eye of Mike whose image, gee and black belt adorn the walls of the dojo, looking down on all who practise within. We know he would be proud and thrilled at the introduction of these children into the disciplines and benefits of karate-do as well as the potential improvements and differences it can make for each one of them throughout their lives.

∾

We all know that Mike would be exceptionally proud in all the benefits that have transpired from his death. Mike had always been about supporting other people, assisting in their growth and creating positivity where there is none, and the projects taken on by the Trust in his name, are most certainly doing just that. The benefits achieved may only be affecting a relatively small portion of the greater population in South Africa, but we have been able to see how these benefits are multiplying exponentially. Each of the youngsters or adults touched by a Change-a-Life project are in turn sharing their knowledge and their experience with their peers, family and friends around them. They in turn are helping share and spread a sense of positive and well balanced thinking to help establish more nurturing families and a more secure society. A society that in turn can help produce more responsible and positively motivated citizens. The Mike Thomson Change-a-Life Trust is helping to develop the kind of South Africa that we all want to live in and that we all deserve to live in. With initiatives such as these, there is hope and there is light and South Africa can reclaim its compassion, its peace and its tranquillity back from the criminal element that has enveloped it in recent decades.

PART III:

The Policing Systems And Judicial/Legal Systems And All Their Failings

"Cry, the beloved country, for the unborn child that's the inheritor of our fear. Let him not love the earth too deeply. Let him not laugh too gladly when the water runs through his fingers, nor stand too silent when the setting sun makes red the veld with fire. Let him not be too moved when the birds of his land are singing. Nor give too much of his heart to a mountain or a valley. For fear will rob him if he gives too much."

Alan Paton, Cry the Beloved Country

The Flaws Of Lady Justice

"Let me not be afraid to defend the weak because of the anger of the strong, nor afraid to defend the poor because of the anger of the rich."

Alan Paton, Cry the Beloved Country

As we all know that life in South Africa is neither simple nor straightforward and is abound with complexities and juxtapositions. And so it was for us too. The Razor Gang were in jail once again, and so far managing to stay there. They had eventually been denied bail, bar one, Mzi (Mzilowo Tofile) who was apparently the getaway driver and not directly involved in any of the incidents. However, there was still the task of ensuring their final convictions.

~

It was late 2009, the Razor Gang, as mentioned, had been in jail once again and it was now over a year since their re-arrest. As a family, we weren't receiving communication as to what was going on or what the status of the trial was at. Mom would make regular calls to the investigating officer at the time only to be told that he was going to court on "Wednesday" and he would call mom back on "Friday". Needless to say, Wednesdays and Fridays would come and go without a phone call.

Mom was becoming desperate and was speaking to anyone she could. She wrote letter after letter to investigative journalists, television programmes, made regular calls to radio talk shows. She felt she was getting nowhere. Nothing seemed to be happening. In one of her more resilient days she was visiting a friend who had also lost a son in an armed robbery at their business in Broadacres. Her friend told mom of how they too had had the same experience but eventually they had taken on a retired prosecutor to assist with their court case in getting it to court firstly and secondly to actual trial. Her son's murder trial had been dealt with and wrapped up in three years, thanks entirely to this retired prosecutor. Mom asked for his phone number and reached out to him.

From the first time she met him, she felt that there may be light at the end of the tunnel. He seemed to know what he was talking about, and certainly seemed keen to assist. He also informed her as to what a shocking state our current courts and the entire judicial system is in.

"There are far too many violent criminals that slip through the gaps as a result," he said.

As, at that stage, we had been battling to get confirmation of the case actually being on the court role. He started there.

Heading over to the Alexandra Magistrate Court was his first plan of action. He phoned mom the next day to report. He mentioned how horrified he was at the number of cases that were still waiting to be heard. He said that Mike's case was not registered on the court role. In fact, Mike's file was one of hundreds of similar cases, simply lying on the floor in an office. It was possible for any member of the public to get access to the office and it would have been easy to remove any file.

After digging through the hundreds of files on the floor and locating Mike's file, he was then able to pull a few strings for us and at least get the case onto the court role. Maybe now we would get somewhere we thought, maybe now, we would start heading towards a courtroom?

We were wrong.

Some months passed by, and still nothing, no communications, no updates and no feedback.

Mom is listening to *Radio 702* as she usually does each day. Her ears prick up when she hears they're going to be discussing crime. She will use any platform and opportunity she has available to her, to tell her story and to try and get some movement on the case and the trial.

Mom listens as Bronwyn Paterson starts talking. Bronwyn tells of how they were attacked in their family home and how she was beaten, kicked, stabbed and left for dead. She spoke of the rape of her 17-year-old daughter. And following that, she continued with the frustrations they were experiencing with the police and the absolute lack of communication or feedback and the seeming lack of progress in getting the suspects to court and to trial.

It didn't take mom long to realise who was speaking. We had been informed by the detectives that the Razor Gang were also responsible for attacking a family and raping a young girl just a few nights after murdering Mike. Mom realised she was listening to the same woman the detectives had spoken to us about. This family had been victims of the Razor Gang too and like us, they too were experiencing frustration in their attempt to get justice.

Mom immediately called *Radio 702*. She wanted to talk to Bronwyn and to make contact with her but as is so often the case when a hot and emotional topic is discussed, the phone lines were jammed and totally tied up and mom was unable to get through at all. During the interview, mom felt she was listening to her own story – Bronwyn and the Paterson family were experiencing the exact same frustrations as we were. Mom started phoning around and did all she could to track down Bronwyn's contact details. Eventually she came right and she called. Bronwyn responded immediately and the very next day they met for coffee.

After numerous cups of coffee and shared emotions, they both sat in horror of each story and each feeling a small sense of relief in their own way. Mom feeling relieved that Lorna and the children had been spared the brutal beating and violence as well as the rape that the Patersons had experienced. Bronwyn feeling relieved that despite their beatings and the violence shown to them, they were all still alive to tell the tale. Each family's story was horrific in its own right.

Mom and Bronwyn became a formidable team and committed themselves to working together to bring the Razor Gang to trial and secure a conviction. They spoke regularly, they kept each other informed of anything they heard or did, they played tag-team with the detectives and both pushed them constantly for action and news and what was going on.

Maybe now we would start heading towards a courtroom we thought? But of course, once again, we were wrong.

The next we heard, there was another delay in that there had now been a decision to possibly lump all twenty-two cases that the police had been able to link the Razor Gang to, into one single case. This meant that should they be found guilty, they would only get one sentence for all the crimes. It would also mean that should there for any reason be a lack of evidence or should a single problem arise with the case, they could potentially get off the entire lot and not be convicted for any of it.

Mom is horrified and incensed at it all. She calls Bronwyn who had just found out the same thing and is just as horrified. They agree to fight this and to ensure that the cases are split. With greater focus now, mom and Bronwyn continue fighting, making one phone call after another, speaking to whoever may be able to assist. They hound the prosecutor, they hound the detectives, they call the media, they continue on and on.

It takes a few months but eventually they receive the news they have been waiting for. The prosecutor has now agreed to split the cases and try the Razor Gang for each and every single incident they have been involved in. One small victory and one small step forward. A small consolation that this obstacle is overcome and achieved, so maybe now, we can start moving towards the courtroom, so we thought? And of course, as usual, we were wrong.

Mike's case was originally opened at Parkview Police Station but then transferred to Sandton when all the cases were lumped into one. During this time it was also then sent to Bramley to be handled there and finally back to Sandton. This shuffling of the case between stations caused more complications, errors and delays.

We have never been able to get exact details on exactly what happened, but we are also informed, and I have received confirmation while researching in more recent years, that while Mike's docket was sitting at Bramley Police station – "someone interfered with the docket" and as a result some important aspects were missing, other evidence was corrupted and various other issues were incorporated into the docket. So much so, that the Sandton detectives apparently had to then re-do and re-build up a large amount of what they had originally included in the first compilation. As mentioned, no one has been willing to give me specifics on exactly what it was that went wrong, or who was responsible, however the process has been explained to me in no uncertain terms. Bronwyn is able to further support this information when she recalls a telephone call she received from a policeman, that wanted to stay anonymous but wanted to inform her that there was a Captain involved that was knowingly "covering things up" and "destroying" the case file.

With the docket now back at Sandton, and the detectives having built up the file once again, maybe now we will see some action? Perhaps now we would start heading towards a courtroom? We were wrong once again.

The Search For Court Records

"I have learned over the years that when one's mind is made up, this diminishes fear; knowing what must be done does away with fear."

Rosa Parks

The weeks continue and turn into months, the months continue and turn into years. Mom and Bronwyn do not stop or falter for a second. They continue to talk to newspapers, radio shows, investigative journalists, anyone they can think of. There is just no movement on the case.

In the last two years I have done everything in my power to get transcripts or any sort of record of all court appearances related to Mike's case and to the Razor Gang, so I can get to the bottom of this all and get an exact record of each and every appearance and each and every subsequent delay. However, I have been totally unsuccessful.

It was my intention to be able to draw up a detailed timeline that included every court appearance, details on what happened during each court appearance and the subsequent reason for the next delay thereafter, but clearly this is not to be.

I have contacted the final investigating officer to see if he can assist, and he's unable to. I contact the lawyers that we eventually hired to see the case through to court for us, as they should have records. However, due to various internal issues, a number of files have subsequently gone missing from their offices and Mike's file is one of them. I have been to the records office at the Palm Ridge Magistrate Court and trawled the passages and offices, spending hours looking for any sign of records, only to be told that they have no records of the case or the suspects and as it was in fact a High Court case and that I need to contact the South Gauteng High Court Case Department of DART (Digital Audio Recording Transcriptions). They apparently keep and store all transcriptions of court cases in High Court scenarios.

I am feeling positive and now maybe I should be able to get somewhere with this request. I contact them and am passed from person to person until I am eventually in contact with a very helpful lady by the name of Kate. I tell Kate my story and ask her to find me any records they have on Mike's case as well as the Razor Gang. I give her all the information and reference numbers I have. Five months later and after regular nagging from my side, Kate emails me most apologetically to inform me that she has not been able to find anything on this case or suspects at all and suggests I go back to the court itself and try with them.

This is when I gave up. Not living in Johannesburg, it was not easy for me to keep trying to chase up the same path and getting absolutely nowhere. To this day I have not been able to find or secure a single court record on anything to do with Mike's case or any of the cases related to the Razor Gang. It had been a six-month goose-chase. I guess that this is just another example of yet another system that is failing us as citizens.

The Paterson Case

"Never mistake law for justice; Justice is an ideal, and law is a tool."

LE Modesitt Jr

In 2010, three years after Mike's murder, we receive partial good news; the Paterson case is going to trial.

Of course, the Paterson case starts off with that usual error and incompetence as we have now come to understand and to expect.

The Patersons receive subpoenas to appear in court on the 9 September 2010. Bronwyn reads through the subpoenas. When she gets to the last one, the subpoena for Angus, her 10-year-old son, she becomes irate and refuses to sign for them.

Angus's subpoena has him listed as an adult female. How a prosecutor can confuse a 10-year-old boy with an adult female, with the name Angus, is beyond her.

Thankfully they're able to get a correct subpoena to them in time for the start of the trial and on 9 September, the Patersons head off to court.

The trial is set to start at 09h00 at the Alexandra Magistrate Court. My parents go along to support the Patersons.

They all arrive at the courthouse and, in a process as we would become very accustomed to years down the line, they head across to the courtroom allocated to their case and sit on the wooden benches outside the court in the long grey passages linking one courtroom to another.

While milling around in the corridors they see a police van arrive in the courtyard just below where they're sitting. Bronwyn is looking out of the window towards this van when every muscle in her body tenses as she recognises Razor and George climbing out of it. They look up towards the window and catch her eye. Razor sneers, at her and moves his hand across his throat in a threatening gesture, some of the others climbing out of the van give them the middle finger and show signs of threat and disrespect. Although unnerved, she takes a deep breath and steadies herself for all that is still to come.

As we would experience ourselves years, later, they were also made to wait for an age. Hours had passed since court was supposed to start and yet they were all still sitting outside waiting to be told what to do next. During this time, Bronwyn noticed a very sad old lady who had set herself apart from others. You could see from the way she dressed to the manner in which she held herself, she had been the victim of extreme poverty her entire life. Here she sat outside the courtroom and showed further signs of acute distress. Bronwyn had noticed this old lady, and in the depths of her compassion, despite the reasons she was sitting there in the first place, went to go and talk to her. From all indicators given, Bronwyn had presumed she was there for one of the prisoners but had no idea for whom.

Bronwyn sat down next to this old lady and gently put her hand on her shoulder and spoke to her asking her who she was and why she was there. The old lady looks at Bronwyn and with tears in her eyes, she starts talking in stilted English.

Bronwyn suddenly realises that this is the mother of George - George Nyembe, one of Razor Zulu's primary accomplices, and the person responsible for her own brutal attack. George had punched her, kicked her and stabbed her twice in the neck with a pair of kitchen scissors, and here Bronwyn sat giving some sense of comfort to the traumatised mother who was clearly upset and ashamed at all that her son had done.

"I'm sorry, I'm sorry," she said repetitively to Bronwyn

"I don't know why he had to do those terrible things to your family. I do hope that he is punished for them. I am sorry."

Showing her own strength and compassion within, Bronwyn gently squeezed this distraught mother's shoulder and replied, "I hold no malice against you, and I am sorry for you that you are in this situation. I can only send you love and wish you well," she says as she stands up and moves off to join her family once again.

In the midst of this moment of compassion and maternal connection, the entire court is still waiting to start. By 11h00 everyone is informed that the reason for the delay is that they are waiting for one of the defence lawyers to arrive. He is late. By 12h30 everyone is informed that they should rather just go and have some lunch and return to court by 14h00. The defence lawyer had still not arrived.

Needless to say this did nothing for the nerves and tension that had encompassed everyone all day. They all filed out as one, to try and find a quite place to sit and grab a bite to eat before returning and hopefully starting with the day's scheduled events. Thankfully this was still to be.

On arriving back at the courts at 14h00, they were informed that the lawyer finally had arrived and that court would be starting. Jamie was called first to testify. The rest of the family was required to wait outside. The courtroom was relatively full, with mainly friends and family of the accused, as well as a few representatives from the media and my parents, two lone Paterson supporters. The family were not allowed to be in court during each other's testimonies in order to avoid any influence between each other's statements. Jamie had been unable to identify anyone during the line-up processes, due to a combination of following instructions, to not looking at them as well as the bad lighting in the identification room. As a result, she's not able to be cross examined by the defence team. However, as part of the prosecution process she's required to give her statement and explain all that occurred. DNA evidence collected from the rape confirms that Razor Zulu was the perpetrator.

While Jamie, a small petite young girl, is standing on her own in the witness stand and having to recall in detail all that was done to her family and specifically to her that night, she's forced to look at Razor at one point. As she looks at him, the arrogant bastard has the audacity to wink at her. It catches her off-guard, but being the incredibly strong person she is, she is able to right herself quickly, quickly enough that nobody picks up on anything immediately. She continues to give her statement in a brave and controlled manner, until she is eventually excused from the stand, and court is adjourned until the following week.

The rest of the family would have to wait another seven days to give their own verbal recall of their nightmare at the hands of the Razor Gang.

Before adjourning court, the judge reiterates how irate and incensed he's at the tawdriness of the defence lawyer and his late arrival. He recommends to the victims that they report him with immediate effect to the legal society and that he, as judge, would be willing to sign confirmation and a formal complaint in this regard.

∾

Weeks after giving her testimony Jamie heads to the bush, the place where she finds refuge and solace. There, she finds herself talking to a friend about all that occurred that night and all they have experienced since. The friend shares with Jamie her own experiences when she too was attacked with an outcome not too dissimilar to Jamie's. While these two survivors are sharing in each other's strength, Jamie feels a tear rolling down her cheek and she realises she's crying, "But," she clarifies to me years later, "they're tears of relief not sorrow."

Wiping away her tears, Jamie realises that this is the first time she has actually shed a tear of any sort since the night it all happened. She has held onto all her internal strength from the moment Razor locked that bathroom door and climbed out the bathroom window and has continued to do so until that very moment. Crying for her friend and crying in relief, that for her it was now all over, these tears were the first and the last that Jamie would ever shed in this regard. She chose to focus on positivity and strength instead.

∾

The week goes by swiftly and the Patersons are back at court. It's Bronwyn's turn to testify. Before she starts, she's required to be sworn in. During the swearing-in process something shocking happens that scares them to their core.

Having fled their original family home and now safely ensconced in a new home, there was continually an underlying fear that the perpetrators would find out where they live and find some way to retaliate now that they were finally in court and in the process of testifying against them.

As Bronwyn is being sworn in, she's asked to state her name in full. Bronwyn answers and gives her name in full.

"Can you please state your physical address for the court."

Bronwyn goes cold. "No." she says. "I don't want to." There is no way she wants the four men who have shattered their lives to know where they now stay.

The Clerk of the Court informs her that she's required by law to give her address.

What about protection of the innocent once again? Surely such vital information could be obtained through more sensitive and private processes. Possibly the option of having the witnesses sign a document of sorts beforehand, stating confirmation of physical address?

But here Bronwyn sat with no option than to say out loud, in front of the four men she would have most wanted to keep the information from, as well as a courtroom full of their friends and family. Anyone, of whom could have opted for revenge if they so wished.

Bronwyn was forced to state the exact physical address, down to the last letter, where the family had now moved to and opted to set up a new life for themselves, a place where they had hoped they could feel a little safer once again. But in one sentence, that illusion of safety was swiftly removed from them once more.

Even more harrowing and with less logic than the requirement of a physical address, they were also required to state out loud what vehicles they drove and what the registrations were of the vehicles. A detail that to this day I am still not sure of its necessity. Obviously the now easy identification of them out on the roads made them even more vulnerable.

Incidents such as this, together with the experiences that occurred with the lineups, specifically my experiences in Hoedspruit, leaves me with absolutely no wonder as to why there are so many citizens in South Africa that opt not to stand witness against their perpetrators. They are just too afraid for their own safety as so many of our systems put them further at risk and create further fear, not protection.

It was not a good start for Bronwyn either, and shook her up before she even started. But with the continued strength that she's able to show, she manages to continue with the verbal recall of all that transpired that night. The day continues with Bronwyn giving her testimony and submitting to questions from the prosecutor. But progress was only due to continue for so long.

Just as they thought things were underway and starting to move, suddenly one of the accused decides that he wants a new lawyer. Court is halted to discuss this and there is no option but for the judge to postpone the case once again and allow enough time for the suspect to secure a new lawyer. The case is scheduled to resume a month later.

As time does eventually march on, a month later, the Patersons, together with my parents were back at court. Bronwyn is to continue on the stand, however, this time it's her turn to be cross-examined by the defence lawyers. Bearing in mind that of the accused on trial, she had recognised three of them during the lineups, this means there are three different lawyers she will have to face in cross-examination, each of whom will prick and prod, question and re-question and bully the witness trying to trip them up or create reasonable doubt in all that has been presented. So, she has to go through the harrowing experience, the first time, a second, and again for a third.

During her cross-examination the issue comes up regarding the height of George Nyembe, in relation to Bronwyn. As part of the process, the defence lawyer makes George walk up to Bronwyn and stand directly in front of her with his face millimetres from hers. This may have been enough to destroy a lesser person, but Bronwyn hides all her fear inside and stands resolute. My mother recalls being so impressed with Bronwyn and her strength. She's not sure that she would have been able to handle it all in quite the same manner.

After Bronwyn's cross-examination is over, she's allowed to remain in court to support her husband, Alan for his turn to take the stand.

As with Bronwyn, Alan too is requested to unwelcomely state his address and vehicle details out loud to the full courtroom. He too refuses and he too is informed that he has no choice as it is required.

Angus had refused to testify as he was far too young and frightened to do so. As the prosecutor believed there to be enough within the statements of Jamie, Bronwyn and Alan, they were happy to support this and to go along with this decision. Thus, Angus was spared this frightening experience himself.

Finally, all questioning and cross-examinations are complete and the family is released, however, no date is set or given to the Patersons for a verdict or, hopefully sentencing thereafter. They are left in the dark and have to wait it out and continue with their lives.

An entire year later, Bronwyn gets a phone call from a friend.

"Are you listening to Radio 702?" she asks.

"No, why do you ask?" says Bronwyn.

"They're discussing your case and the sentencing being given to the suspects," the friend replies.

"Sentencing?" Bronwyn exclaims. "We have not even been informed of a verdict, let alone sentencing."

Bronwyn phones around to get information and finds out that of the suspects on trial, only two have been found guilty; Razor Zulu, for the rape of Jamie and George Nyembe for the attack on her. Both have also been found guilty for house robbery. Razor is sentenced to 30 years and George to 20 years. The rest of the gang were acquitted due to lack of evidence and some apparent bungling of evidence on the crime scene itself, which deemed it inadmissible in court. I guess at this stage we had all learned that we could expect no less.

For us as a family, at least these two primary suspects are now finally convicted of something and will spend the next portion of their lives away from polite society and will no longer be able to create a reign of terror in the Johannesburg area as they have been so willing to do over the last decade or so. Although we still had our own long journey ahead of us, the pressure was somewhat reduced. Obtaining a conviction for

Mike's murder will never bring him back, so getting a conviction for that incident specifically was not the primary goal. Our main aim was to make sure that they were stopped in their tracks and could not bring the same hurt and heartache to other families as they had so callously been able to do for so long, and at least with the Paterson conviction and sentencing that could now be achieved.

⁓

During the days at court supporting the Patersons, mom had the fortune to meet up with a public prosecutor, Nerisha Naidoo that would also be of assistance to us in the months to come. Mom asked her for assistance in getting information on what was happening with Mike's case as we were still being given little to nothing from the standard channels at this stage.

Nerisha offered to look into it for mom and see what she could ascertain but made it clear that she was doing so as a private individual and in her own time. She eventually called mom back to let her know that as it was a murder case, it had now been moved from the Magistrate Court to High Court. Again, although a welcome move, it was a move nonetheless that we had not been informed of in any way. She supplied mom with the name of the new prosecutor who would be dealing with the case at a High Court level. Mom immediately started trying to contact this new prosecutor. It takes three months of phone calls before she's able to finally get through and have a candid conversation with this new prosecutor who will hopefully be responsible for the conclusion of Mike's case.

"There is a problem," he says to mom - a word that we were fast becoming familiar with. "There is a lack of evidence," he says. "I have taken it off the court role. We don't have enough to go to court on this," he continues. "I have instructed the investigating team to readdress all their evidence before I will put this back on the role again."

Unbelievably, Mike's case is off the role again. How is there not enough evidence? Ollie, the first private investigator had tracked down and found Mike's laptop, which was linked back to the gang. They had Mike's gun, which they had found in the possession of George Nyembe (although used by his cousin Rueben Nenzehlele at the time), they had gotten his vehicle back that same night, found abandoned in the area close to where they all lived at the time.

In addition, I know that a number of useable fingerprints were found on Mike's vehicle. George Nyembe had also sung like a canary and confessed to everything, so why was that not being used either?

Mom calls on the new investigating officer who is now in charge of the case to find out what they're going to do to correct these aspects (there had been a number of different investigating officers every time the case was moved or re-allocated over the years). She first challenges him about the laptop. "What laptop?"

"Mike's laptop," she replies. "It was found in 2008, four years ago, and was handed in to the police as evidence against the gang. It must be mentioned in the docket?"

The investigating officer gets a frown on his face. "I know of no laptop," he says.

He pages through the docket. "There is no record of the laptop in the docket either," he responds.

Mom is horrified. Immediately after this meeting with the investigating officer she contacts Ollie, and following his links, tries to track down the laptop. She has no success. To this day, we have no idea where the laptop or the reports and records of its recovery are. It was last known to be handed over to the police and from there, it has disappeared.

She then asks the investigating officer about fingerprints. "They weren't able to get any fingerprints off the car," she's told. This makes no sense as I was standing there when the LCRC officer exclaimed excitement at getting a number of clear and usable prints. What has happened to these prints?

She questions the presence of Mike's Gun as well as what the status of George's testimony is. "There are two problems with George's testimony," he says.

"The first is that when George made the original confession, the investigating officer at the time should have taken it to a magistrate court to be stamped and thereby making it official and usable in court. However, it seems that he took the confession back to his office, wrote his own report on it and put them both into the docket. It won't stand up in court."

Mom is horrified, how can a vital piece of evidence such as a confession be rendered useless because of administrative incompetence and the lack of an official stamp?

"The other problem is that we cannot use George's testimony for Mike's murder as he was not involved," she's told.

"What do you mean, he was not involved?" Mom asks. "He stabbed Mike 14 times."

"Stabbed?", he asks. "He was not stabbed, he was shot twice," he retorts pulling out the autopsy report and showing it to mom.

Mom is outraged.

"How can you sit there and tell me my son was not stabbed?" she asks, seething in anger. "I personally counted 14 different stab wounds on his body when they eventually pulled him out of the pool," she tells him.

He slowly reads through the autopsy again, just to make sure he did not miss anything. There is definitely no mention of stab wounds in the autopsy report. The investigating officer apologises to her profusely and says he will look into it.

He calls her back a week or so later, to tell her that she needn't worry anymore, they have changed the autopsy report. It now includes mention of 14 stab wounds.

It begs the question ... how on earth does that happen? Is an Autopsy not an official report and document? How can it just be changed, years after the fact?

During my research, I was able to obtain a full copy of Mike's docket. One of the first things that I looked for was a copy of the autopsy report. Needless to say, I was most surprised that there was no such document within his full docket and can only assume it may have been as a result of this issue. During my next trip to Johannesburg, I went back to the police station to look through the docket once again, just in case I had possibly missed it the first time around in making copies of the entire docket. There was still no autopsy report in the docket. The very helpful police officer that was assisting me with access to the docket also exclaimed extreme surprise that such a crucial document would not automatically be in the case docket and she went out of her way to go and get a copy for me from the mortuary the following week. Luckily there was still a copy on the mortuary's system, and she was able to email it to me. Interestingly enough, I can confirm that this copy does now reflect, at the very bottom of the page, the presence of both stab wounds and gunshot wounds. It, however, does not quantify the number of stab wounds, but at least outlines the presence of such, together with the already documented gunshot wounds.

With the inclusion of stab wounds on this document, it was then possible to thereafter proceed with charges against George as now officially, Mike was stabbed. But it left us mind-boggled at just how an official document, years after the autopsy and Mike's subsequent cremation, can suddenly be changed to reflect something as important and crucial as 14 stab wounds. Let alone the fact that this was left off the original autopsy report from the start. What on earth are we really dealing with here? Just what level of incompetence is really at play and just how "official" is an official document if it can so easily be changed?

Lives On Hold

"Justice delayed is Justice denied."

William E Gladstone

With the investigating officers now having to put renewed effort into the case so that the prosecutor will even consider putting Mike's case back on the role, we turn back to Ollie, the initial private investigator that assisted us with finding the first bits of evidence that pointed in the direction of the Razor Gang. Ollie works hand-in-hand with a lawyer, Karl Auret. We immediately take both on board once again to help secure enough evidence to get the case back onto the role and possibly towards a trial. Computershare and The Mike Thomson Change-a-Life Trust, are ever generous as usual and cover all the additional costs to enable their involvement. I can only shudder to think of how many South African citizens do not have the good fortune to have access to such financial support that will enable this additional furtherance and instead are left to the mercies of our clearly non-functioning systems. How many families have been so badly let down and have not been able to see justice obtained due to these failing aspects we were becoming so familiar with?

Karl and his team become an incredible asset to us and are of assistance that is beyond description. But, it's another three years before we are able to get the case onto the role again. It has now been seven years since the Razor Gang had been arrested and eight years since Mike's murder.

With the case back on the role, we are informed that only two of the suspects will be indicted – George Nyembe as he was found to be in possession of Mike's gun and has confessed to being in the pool with him and Mzilowo Tofele, known as Mzi, as Lorna had selected him out of the line-up. Apparently, they did not have enough evidence to charge Razor with. In the very initial stories at the start of their arrest, it was mentioned that Razor was responsible for the final gun shot to Mike. However, since the death of Thabang (Maxwell Kheza) during the Fourways armed robbery, the gang had changed all stories to subsequently say that Thabang was responsible for shooting Mike, as obviously the dead cannot argue nor defend themselves. Rather a convenient turn of events for them all.

Thinking back on the night of Mike's attack and everything that Mom, Dad and Allan witnessed with all the many people moving in and out the house, back and forth and potentially walking out evidence at a frightening rate, we can only sit in wonder, at just how much additional potential evidence there might there have been if the scene had been handled correctly.

Mike fought violently with his attackers. He knocked out Thabang, and nearly drowned George. There must have been evidence from both of them left outside by the pool. The gang then spent two hours in the house emptying every cupboard and drawer they could find. Excavating through absolutely everything! It's impossible for them to have not left other evidence behind.

Somehow, we are told there is a jersey that they have found that they're wanting to get DNA evidence on and if they can, they may be able to link one of them to the scene. Every time mom calls the investigating officer to ask if there is any result on this, he informs her that there is a massive delay and waiting list for DNA processing and it could be months before we get a result.

Mom calls Vanessa Lynch from the DNA Project and asks if she's able to fast-track a DNA process. She says that she can and takes down all the details. A week later, the police are handed the DNA results. The investigating officer is shocked and extremely impressed that we are able to arrange for it to be done so quickly. It begs the question, if it can be done so quickly, what is taking so long via the standard police channels?

Sadly however, the results are not able to assist or further the case for us, so we are back to working with the small amount of evidence currently available. Karl and his team continue to support with additional investigations and assist the investigating officers in putting together their case and all available evidence. Finally, there is evidence to charge four of them and the National Prosecuting Authority is going ahead with indictments against:

Accused 1 – Bongani Masumpa
Accused 2 – George Vincent Nyembe
Accused 3 – Raymond Bheki Zulu
Accused 4 – Mzilowo Elvis Tofile

For the following offences:
Housebreaking with intent to rob and robbery with aggravating circumstances and murder
Alternative Offences
Contravention of Riotous Assemblies Act and the Firearms Control Act – unlawful possession of a Firearm and Ammunition

It's early 2015 and we are informed the case will be going ahead in June that year. Megs is scheduled to go on a school tour, but Lorna tells her she will not be able to go as they have been told they will need to be in Johannesburg for the trial. Megs misses booking for the tour, only to be told, a few weeks before they were scheduled to fly up, that the case was being postponed and would now be in September. Megs misses her school tour for nothing.

The family now prepare themselves for a September trial.

Nick is playing hockey and is selected to represent his province at the annual Country Districts Tournament; however, the tournament is scheduled to take place in September. Nick has to pull out of the team.

Needless to say, a few weeks before they were scheduled to fly up to Johannesburg, they receive yet another communication to say that the case has been postponed yet again and would now be taking place in November 2014. Poor Nick has missed out on playing provincial hockey for that year, all for nothing. Yet again, the children are putting their lives on hold for this dreaded case and are then being let down by yet another postponement at the last minute.

No proper explanation is given for the delays. We do not even receive this information via the police or the responsible channels. Karl and his team find out all relevant information through their constant pestering on our behalf and pass it onto us. In recent years, as I have mentioned, I have tried to find records to substantiate each of these delays and just what the reasons were, but, as mentioned previously, I have been unable to find or to access any official court records on Mike's entire case or on the Razor Gang.

But should I really have expected anything less?

The Wrong Courthouse And A Rush Across Town

"The greatest glory in living lies not in never falling, but in rising every time we fall."

Nelson Mandela

Eventually, in early 2015, eight years after Mike's murder, we receive the call. The case is going to court. It will still only be an initial hearing so Lorna and the children are not needed just yet, but the four accused will be present. Mom and dad are adamant that they want to attend. They want to make sure they're aware of everything that happens from here onwards in order to pick up on any further problems or irregularities that may occur, and hopefully be able to counteract or mitigate them before it's too late. They're informed the case would be heard at the Randburg Magistrate Court, in the northern suburbs of Johannesburg.

Early on the morning of 4 June 2015 they head off to court. Luckily, they had decided to leave early as they were unsure of traffic firstly, and secondly had thought it would be prudent to get there early, and rather sit down relaxed with a cup of coffee and await the proceeding activities.

With an even greater stroke of luck, Karl had arrived even earlier at court in order to assess and confirm a number of details on what would be happening that day. On arriving there, he was informed that the case had now been moved across to the Palm Ridge Magistrate Court, which is near Thokoza, in the south-west of Johannesburg and entirely on the opposite side of town. Karl calls mom and dad quickly and tells them to change their route and tries to give a hasty explanation on how to get there. Mom and Dad, rush across town fighting immense traffic as they go.

Of course, by now my parents are neither surprised nor shocked that such a simple step as informing the family and supporting lawyer as to the location of the court case or any subsequent changes as there may have been, is omitted. This falls perfectly in line with all the incompetence and unprofessionalism that they had experienced every step of the way over the last seven to eight years.

Subsequently, they had not needed to rush in any event, as, as can be expected, court was late. They sat outside for what seemed like an age before everyone was called inside. Once inside it became apparent why there had been a delay. Two of the accused, George Nyembe and Bongani Masumpa, had decided to admit guilt and sign full confessions. They would also be turning state witness against the remaining two. Suddenly there was a little light at the end of this tunnel.

Karl explained to my parents that the case would now need to be split in two. The first would be to deal with the guilty pleas from George and Bongani and the second to continue the trial of State vs Raymond "Razor" Bheki Zulu and State vs Mzilowo "Mzi" Elvis Tofele.

As representatives of the family, my parents would need to come back to court the following day, during which the guilty pleas of George and Bongani would be presented to them and should they agree to the terms therein, sign acceptance thereof on behalf of the family.

This was duly done and on 5 June 2015. The official guilty plea of George Vincent Nyembe, admitting to

Charge 1 - Housebreaking with an attempt to Rob; and Robbery with aggravating circumstances;

Charge 2 – Murder.

As part of the guilty plea, the following proposed sentences were outlined:

Count 1: 15 years imprisonment.

Count 2: 20 years imprisonment.

The sentence in count 1 is ordered to run concurrently with the sentence imposed in count 2. Effective sentence is therefore 20 years. That the 20 years be ordered to run concurrently with the sentence the accused is currently serving, which is 28 years.

That it be ordered that the accused be declared unfit to possess a firearm.

At the same time, the official guilty plea of Bongani Masumpa admitting to Housebreaking with an attempt to Rob; and Robbery with aggravating circumstances was officially signed.

Similarly, in his guilty plea, the following sentence is outlined:

Count 1: 10 years imprisonment. That the 10 years be ordered to run concurrently with the sentence the accused is currently serving, which is 28 years.

That it be ordered that the accused he declared unfit to possess a firearm.

Two down. Two to go.

Missing Paperwork

"You can have results or excuses, not both."

Author unknown

Finally, after nine years of delays, postponements and revised dates, in February 2016 we are told that the last two remaining gang members, Raymond "Razor" Zulu and Mzilowo "Mzi" Elvis Tofile will be going to trial. Raymond is to be charged with house robbery and murder and Mzi would be charged with house robbery.

Mzi was apparently the getaway driver and supposedly never in the house. But, somehow Lorna had pointed him out in a line-up and so the police were able to bring charges of house robbery against him too. However, apart from the line-up identification, they had little else on him.

Megs, Nick and Annie-Rose had grown up considerably and are now far from the frightened children they once were. However, a new fear grips them now. It has been so long since that fateful night and they have spent so many days, weeks, months and years trying to forget all the scary parts of that entire event, just in order to survive emotionally and to be able to move forward, and now they would be expected to remember it all.

Not just that, but they would be tested, prodded and questioned on all the tiny little details involved, the nuances, the minutiae and the specifics. What if they could not remember it all? Nick had lived as many years of his life since the event and without his father, as he had lived before the event, together with his father – he was nine years old at the time and it had been nine years since. This day had taken so long to arrive for all of us! Their fear now was what if Razor and Mzi got off because they can't remember correctly or, heaven forbid, confuse facts; what then? Once again, the undue pressure on them was immense.

In order to prepare for the court case, Lorna, Megs and Nick flew up to Johannesburg the day before court was scheduled to start.

I arrived in Johannesburg an hour or so after Lorna and the children, and arrived at Allan and Sarah's home, just in time for a meeting with Karl.

Karl was now sitting with Lorna, Nick and Megs running them through the process, what would happen in the courtroom, the expected bullying and type of questions to expect from the defence's legal team and what generally would be required of them in turn.

He also went through what would legally be okay to say and to answer if they were unable to remember anything specific. He assured them and let them know it was quite okay not to remember everything. In this instance it would be totally acceptable. The failure here was not theirs at all, instead it was the courts and the state's for taking so long to bring this case before a judge and to successfully get it to where it was hopefully going.

However, with full knowledge of the Patersons' experience in court, and just what abuse they had been exposed to at the hands of the defence, as well as the defendants themselves, we were all justifiably nervous and terrified as to what the expectations and potential horrors of this next phase they would have to go through, would in fact entail.

That evening we all spent it together in a scene reminiscent of those first few nights all huddled together in Allan's Lounge. We busied ourselves with dinner and watching DVDs. We tried to distract our minds from torturous thought processes and presumptions of what tomorrow would hold and to keep Lorna and the children distracted and focused on anything other than courtroom visions and assumptions that might be creeping in.

Court was scheduled to start at 10h00 the following morning on 10 February 2016. The case had been elevated to a High Court, court case but would be facilitated within the Palm Ridge Magistrate Court near Thokoza.

The state prosecutor had requested Lorna, Megs and Nick to be there as early as 08h00 so he too could prepare them for what was to come, and to individually go through their original statements so they could re-align themselves with everything they had put down in those first few frightening days following the attack.

A very tired, red-eyed and nervous family as well as Helen, who had originally driven me up to Johannesburg through the night from Hoedspruit, all those years ago, and Karl, arrived at the courthouse the following morning.

We were all on edge and very nervous. Finally, not being able to hold it in any longer, one of the children exclaimed, "I don't want to have to look at them again. I'm too scared. Will I have to look at them? Please tell me I don't have to look at them at all."

The fear of seeing any of these thugs that had terrified them so much that night and had occupied their nightmares ever since, was just too much to deal with.

I immediately tried to allay their fears and talked them through the physical process of what was to be expected. "You will be outside the court for most of the proceedings," I tell them. "You will only be required to come in when it's your turn to testify and the court orderly will come outside to call you. When you walk into the courtroom, you need only look ahead, focus on the judge or the prosecutor who will be standing in front of you and just keep looking at him or her." I continue, "The prisoners will be brought into the holding cells below the courts and will be brought up separate steps into the courtroom. They will be sitting in a box to your right, but you do not have to turn your head and look at them, unless for any reason you are asked to do so. Just keep looking forward and your eyes focused on the judge and the prosecutor," I add, nodding towards the prosecutor who was by now standing in the passage with us. I raise my eyes questioningly at him for confirmation on all I have said.

"Yes," he confirms. "In fact, if it will help, you can take them down to the courtroom now and show them the layout and how it will work."

I look to the children for their input and they both nod in agreement. The prosecutor calls a court orderly who takes us down to the allocated courtroom and we take Megs and Nick inside to familiarise them with all they will have to do and see. This simple bit of extra knowledge and preparation seems to put them at ease somewhat and we all head back out the courtroom to find some coffee and wait for the dreaded 10h00 to arrive.

With nervous tension very high, we are not able to wait outside any longer and we head back to the courtroom at about 9h30 to sit on the long benches lining each side of the hallway linking one courtroom to another. Conversation is halted and nervous. We are finding silly things to get the children laughing at and laughing about; anything to keep their minds off what is looming closer and closer as 10h00 continues to roll around. I turn to the children and ask each of them to start drawing me and pose as "professionally" as I can – I am trying all I can to distract them and keep their minds off what is to come. They had both been doodling in notebooks at the time and I wanted to create something more focused and concrete for them to keep busy with.

The courts and hallways start filling up as victims, families, friends, interested observers, media and lawyers start arriving to face their own dates with the judicial system.

I am looking up the long length of the hallway watching all the throngs moving back and forth and wondering what each of their stories may be and what misfortune may have brought them to this point in their lives and this appointment with Lady Justice, when I suddenly see something out of place.

Shuffling slowly down the middle of the corridor are two men tightly surrounded by four officers from the Department of Correctional Services.

Taking a closer look, the slowness and shuffle in their movements becomes clear, I see the two men in the middle are fitted with leg irons and handcuffs. They must be prisoners I realise and continue to watch them as I am wondering why prisoners would be brought in through the main entrance and down the public hallways and not through the secure holding cells and prisoner's courtyard as one would expect. They pass the first courtroom; they pass the second and the third. I now realise they're heading our way and before I know it, they're guided to sit on the bench alongside us.

Lorna and the children turn white and are immediately silent.

I approach the investigating officer who is busy talking to my parents. "Who are they?" I ask, nodding my head in their direction but deep down knowing the answer.

"That is George Nyembe and Bongani Masumpa," he replies confidently and almost nonchalantly.

"What the feck are they doing out here?" I burst out.

"It's all ok," he tells me, "remember they're on your side now. They have turned state witness and are testifying against Razor."

"I don't frigging care what they're doing now," I respond, "that man" pointing to George, "stabbed my brother 14 times and left him at the bottom of the swimming pool." I exclaim. "And that one," I say, now pointing to Bongani, "Was responsible for tying them all up."

I turn my attention to Lorna and the children to help them cope with this shocker that has just been thrown before us and made to sit alongside us on a bench as friendly equals. Lorna cannot sit there any longer, she gets up and moves to the large glass window at the end of the passage. I re-engage the children. I sit back on the bench opposite them and pull a comical pose for them to continue drawing, and now, more than ever, to keep their attention elsewhere. It seems to take forever. The children get tired of drawing.

Nick is staring at the rats that have been the object of his nightmares for the last nine years. I watch him and can only imagine what must be going through his mind. The last time he was face-to-face with these thugs, he was a frightened little boy of nine. They had terrorised him, broken him and stolen his father. Now, he's a strapping 17-year-old, bigger and stronger than any of them by far.

What he must be thinking and just what he would do right now if given the chance, I can only imagine. I walk over to him and give him hug. I quietly ask him "What would you like to do right now?"

He turns to me with near tears welling up in his eyes and quietly shakes his head and turns back to stare at the rats in front of him once more.

It's only 10 minutes until 10h00. Surely, we could all last another 10 minutes, I thought. At least it wasn't. "The Nasty One" sitting out here with us, the one that had created such fear in them and had dragged Nick around the house on more than one occasion with a gun to his head, bleating profanities and threatening to kill his family if he did not give him what he wanted.

No sooner had I had that silly thought, when I then heard the sound, I had got to recognise only minutes before; the clanking and awkward shuffle of someone in leg-irons.

I saw the same scene as previously, this time with only one man on his own, escorted between two officers from the Department of Correctional Services. They too were definitely heading our way.

I turned to the investigating officer. "Please do not tell me that this is Razor Zulu they're bringing down the hallway?" I ask him.

He turns to have a look and casually nods his head.

Razor Zulu, a vilified name that we had come to dread, to hate and to despise, and here he was shuffling down the passage towards me, towards my parents, towards Lorna and the children.

"What about the holding cells, what about them only being brought straight up into the courtroom when court starts, what the hell is going on here?" I ask.

The investigating officer, Captain Baloyi who has been very helpful to us over the last couple of years, is at a loss for words. He shrugs his shoulders and tell me that he will go and find out. He disappears into the courtroom.

Razor and the officers sit down, about three metres away from us. He turns to look at us and sneers. He makes subtle intimidating and threatening gestures to us, his face a mirror of aggression and arrogance.

I turn to watch the children, as they turn away from him, the fear and confusion visible in their eyes. They had been promised and assured, (I had promised and assured them) that they would not have to look at these rats if they chose not to. But here they were, not only looking at them face-to-face, but having to sit next to them in close enough proximity for jovial conversation if it were on the menu.

Razor continued to sneer and taunt them, thriving on the power he gained from once again instilling fear into them.

I see the interaction and feel the need to do something - to do anything to stop this. The desire to walk over to him and perform some act of aggression myself is so intense but the reasoning part of my brain knows it is not possible, nor advisable, so instead, I do the only option available to me. I stand up and move across to him. I sit myself down on the bench directly opposite, I lean forward with my elbows on my knees and I meet his stare, aggression for aggression, arrogance for arrogance.

I want him to think that he has no effect on me and does not scare me. Although my insides are quivering like jelly, my outside demeanour is as hard as rock. Mostly, I just want to draw his attention away from Lorna and the children. Every time he turns to look at them, I exclaim harshly, "Hey!" and he looks back at me again.

I become so involved at staring down this aggressive and arrogant thug, I barely notice the time.

Somewhere to the side of me I hear my mom asking what is going on. It's now 10h30 and we are all still sitting outside the courtroom with these deviants. I turn to look and am relieved that Lorna and the children have all moved off to the end of the corridor. I can move away from Razor now because his intimidating stares can't reach them there.

Together the prosecutor and the investigating officer come out to talk to us. From the look on their faces we immediately know that something is wrong. The sleepless nights and emotional build up to get to this point has been immense and all we needed was for it to be over. We just knew it would not be, not today, anyway. "Postponement" was written on the two faces in front of us.

I turn to where the deviants are sitting and seethe in anger as they sit there calmly laughing and chatting away. All that was missing were the teapots and cupcakes.

"The judge is busy with another case," we are told, "and needs to finish with that before he can start with ours. He's not available to attend to your case just yet. We are going to need to postpone," the prosecutor said.

The three shackled thugs plus the fourth accused – Tofile – who is out on bail, thus appearing under his own recognisance, are led into the courtroom and we are left outside feeling deflated and confused.

I am intrigued as to why they have been led inside. Together with Helen, I head into the courtroom to see what is going on.

To my surprise I walk in just as everyone is being requested to stand on ceremony for the judge who is about to enter the courtroom. Everyone is upstanding, the judge duly enters, and we then all then take to our seats once more when he's seated in his.

My mind is spinning, and I am trying to work out what is going on. If the judge is busy with another case and apparently unavailable, how come he's sitting here in front of us, clearly present in this courtroom? Why were the four of them brought in but nothing was requested of us? It doesn't make sense.

The prosecutor is talking to the judge and I have to strain to hear them. I think I may have heard what he just said but I am not sure and I think, "Surely that cannot be?" I see the judge's reaction and I realise I most certainly did hear what I thought I heard.

The judge is furious, and his tone raises to such an extent I no longer need strain to hear what is being said. I can hear it loud and clear. The reason for the impending postponement had nothing to do with the judge, nor a jam-packed court role, but everything to do with the inefficiency and ineptitude we had come to know so well over the last nine years. The case was being postponed because the court orderly had lost the court procedures file and it was not present in court that morning and thus the hearing could not continue! They were busy looking for it now!

Looking at his previous notes, the judge blurts out angrily "How can this happen? I thought I made it quite clear at the last hearing that there is not to be another postponement in this matter. This case has gone on for long enough now and we need to see this closed. Why did you not arrange a copy file if you cannot find the original? This is totally unacceptable!" He is livid.

There does not seem to be any suitable answer nor solution given and the judge has no option but to postpone, declaring as he did so, that this will be the last postponement accepted and come hell or high water, the case will start at the next hearing and best everyone make sure that all necessary paperwork is present and ready.

Nine years and a world of tense emotions and re-organised lives to get us to this point, and someone could not make sure the proper paperwork was present! We have no words.

Bundling Lorna and the children into the car, and feeling just as frustrated and deflated themselves, my parents took them away from the dispirited courthouse as quickly as they possibly could.

Having Razor Zulu so close to me and having looked at him directly in the eye after nine years of imagined visions of who and what was behind this name that had become a part of stilted family conversation, I suddenly decided that I wanted to get a photo of him on my phone as he exited the courtroom. I wanted to burn his face to memory and know everything about this deviant and thug.

As the family fled the courthouse, Helen and I continued to sit outside and wait for him to exit. Bongani and George are taken away, Tofile walks out, the lawyers leave, the investigating officer leaves, the prosecutor leaves and yet Razor has not exited. Helen and I popped our heads into the courtroom to investigate. Except for a lone female interpreter, the courtroom was empty. Helen asks her what had happened to the criminal from this courtroom. She points to the stairs leading to the holding cells and says, "He's down there. For his own protection."

Apparently, I have been deemed a potential threat to his well-being and they're not sure why I am still waiting outside the courtroom. How ironic, the holding cells are now being used to protect him from me and not to protect us from him.

Suddenly this rat supposedly needs protection from me. I shake my head in wonder at the thought, and giggle quietly within. I have no option but to leave without my photo. I walk confidently down the hallway with large airborne strides, down the same hallway that they will hobble him along later, leg irons and all … when I have left, and all is presumably safe for them to bring him out and shuffle him back to his prison cell and hopefully one day, if we can get this system to work, a life of incarceration!

"Courts daydream" – Nick's memory of that day

The clouds littered the sky. People littered the streets. The car rolled slowly down the road. The bulk of an ugly building amassing before us. The car stops. The brooding justice department sulking over the skyline. I noticed very little of the grim surroundings as I walked by the small courtyard before the doors. The interior didn't inspire a sudden spike of observation. It was a typical government building, plain and empty. Those who worked there gave the building a run for its money. I was glad they stopped us to check for weapons and tasty treats, but a bit of life may help the general atmosphere. The blank stares and frowns on every face, did nothing to improve my already gloomy mood. There weren't many people trying to squeeze through the lonely metal detector but still I waited. I waited on the inside for my family to join me. I waited for someone to notice me. To tell me what to do. But I was alone.

I could feel the tension building in everyone. Nine years of grief bubbled to the surface. I knew I was close to breaking. One wrong move and what followed would not be pretty. So, I avoided it. Monosyllable answers. Blank stares, downcast eyes. I blended in with those around me.

Waiting for my turn to speak with the prosecutor, to go over my statement and get a brief idea on the courts proceedings, left me a lot of time to think about what happened nine years ago. What I remember and how I feel. But I was also exposed to the pity dripping out my family's eyes. I hid by pouring my emotions onto paper. I wrote to release the flood building inside.

Nine years earlier, I was a small boy who couldn't sleep. Kept awake by the bark of the dogs. The movement of my dad as he locked up the house. But one thing drew me out of bed. Four unknown black men shoving my mother and older sister into my room. Ignorance is bliss they say. That statement could not have better described many of the situations and emotions I found myself in after that night. They were here to help. He's sleeping outside. The guns. The threats. Mom's scared and frantic actions. The dark mass at the bottom of the pool that made her scream. The strange pictures. The play *therapy. Ignorant thoughts from an ignorant child.*

Maybe if I was older I would have understood everything sooner. Seen how thinking they were here to help, was irrational.

My turn came and went too quickly. The prosecutor shook my hand, sat me down and he read through my statement. The core of what I had said nine years ago was the same as what I remember now but many of the small details had changed: things appeared and disappeared. I was glad proceedings were under way but it meant the trial would start soon. Soon they would call me in to testify. Soon I would sit across from them and see their faces. Faces that I had forced from memory a long time ago. It was a shorter wait than I expected. We were sitting in the hallway, as the witnesses are supposed to do so. Waiting for our turn. Boredom runs wild in a place bereft of joy. So, I drew. I drew my aunt's face. And I noticed a change, the tightening of the jaw muscles, a burning fire sparking in her eyes. The change in atmosphere was almost tangible as two of the men who did it were just down the hall from us.

I have always said I wasn't scared the very first time I saw them, and I wasn't scared when the third one who held a gun to my head walked through a door no more than ten centimetres to my left. The one thing that surprised me the most, about seeing them, was that I felt no anger. I had just been face-to-face with the man who murdered my father and I was not angry – I felt no resentment.

I may not have stepped into the courtroom. I may not have received justice for the murder of my father. I may have found some form of forgiveness for them, but I may not have, I don't know why I felt the way I did. But if there is one thing I learnt.

I would not wish this on anyone.

Nicholas. T. Thomson

And Again ...

"When a nation's posterity is determined by a group of nefarious incompetent dolts there is only one possible outcome – a sophisticated chaos."

Ibiwoye Oluwatosin

The next date we received was the 25 April 2016 and once again, we set our sights on re-doing all that we had experienced in February, this time without Megs and Nick.

Megs had completed Grade 12 the year before and had planned a gap year overseas before heading off to university to study. She had organised herself a job in the USA as an au pair and had already delayed her departure date to attend the February trial. There was no way Lorna was going to let her put her entire life on hold while inefficiency keeps delaying progress. Their lives had already been stolen and turned upside down by these men, and now those who were supposed to be bringing us justice were causing the same. From the very first moment that postponement was mentioned in February, Lorna made it clear that the state would need to re-organise their case in order to go ahead without the children's testimony. This entire process had already taken so much from them and eaten into so much of their lives over the years, that she was not letting it impact their lives any further.

Nick was in Grade 12 that year and had already missed a few days of school with the trial (or lack thereof) in February. It would now be too detrimental to him to continue missing any more school. Especially if we had no confidence that the trial may actually go ahead. Thus, it was agreed that only Lorna would be attending.

Based on these conditions, the trial was all set for April. Or so we thought!

It was explained to us that according to their knowledge, the case should have priority status and thus would be heard first on the day. This together with the resolute demands from the judge that no other delay or reason for delay would be accepted, gave us a mild sense of confidence that it would actually go ahead.

On the morning of 25 April, the family, Helen and Karl once again arrive at the courthouse and make our way to the prescribed courtroom. We take our seats on the benches in the hallway, just as we had done two months prior and we start the same old wait for court to start. Just as had happened before, I hear that clanking sound coming down the hallway, and turn my head to look. George, Bongani and Razor, bound and shackled, are surrounded by their pillars in brown and are making their way towards us and towards the courtroom.

They were once again deposited on the benches adjacent to us. The rest of the scene played out just as it had before. Lorna went to the window at the end of the passage, I took my place on the bench opposite and once again we started the staring challenge.

It all felt too familiar.

This time, however, it was not long before they filed them all into the courtroom and opted for them to remain there while we waited for the judge. Thinking that possibly something was about to happen this time around, Helen, my sister and I followed them in while my parents remained outside with Lorna. We sat at the very back of the courtroom.

Razor noted our entrance, turned around in his seat and attempted to continue with an aggressive and intimidating stare. I continued to give it back. Once again, I barely noticed time, until I perceived conversation occurring with the prosecutor and lawyer up front and once again, I heard mention of that word: postponement!

Not again! How could this be?

Once more a solemn party made its way to Lorna and my parents in the hallway. This time ironically, the previous excuse seems to have materialised, the judge has been allocated to two different cases for these dates, and ours has been side-lined.

To say we were angry would be a severe understatement. We had been assured that our case had priority status and so should two cases be allocated the same slot on the role, such as in this instance, ours would have been given priority and would have been heard first.

In order for our over-loaded courts to deal with the large number of cases passing through, judges are often assigned two cases in the same block and time period. Should a case be postponed for a viable reason, the judge is not left twiddling his or her thumbs and wasting time, but instead can then continue with the second case. Should two cases come up to start at the same date and time, either the oldest case would be heard first, or should either of the cases have been given priority status, that one would be heard first. Therefore, the fact that our case supposedly had priority status, and was nine years in the waiting, it should not be postponed in lieu of another case and should instead be heard first.

Even the defence team is furious. Everyone wants this case to be over with. We are also informed that the case has now been allocated to a new judge and she's not aware yet of its full history, nor the promises and demands of the previous judge.

The prosecutor and Karl manage to arrange an urgent meeting for all parties with the new judge. Everyone wants answers on why this is happening yet again.

Karl departs the judge's offices and shares the bad news. There is no way that the case is going to go ahead today, nor any day in the upcoming weeks. It needs to be reallocated on the new role.

Court roles are structured and assigned per quarter (three months) and they have suggested using this to our benefit. The new judge, now fully apprised of the situation and the desperate need to get this case over and done with, has put through a request for the case to be re-assigned back to her in the new quarter, but more specifically, to be assigned to the very first day of the new quarter. This will also ensure that no continuation or extending of a previous long running case can interfere either.

The judge requests an orderly to further look into why this case is not currently carrying priority status when it should be and definitely was previously. She also demands that priority status is re-issued with immediate effect.

The justification brought to us shortly thereafter seemed vague but had a modicum of explanation to it.

The case most certainly carried priority status at the onset, when the actual trial phase was started; about two years prior. When George and Bongani opted to plead guilty and turn state's witness and Razor and Mzi maintained their innocence and opted to go ahead with a trial, the case was split in two. The first sector to deal with the guilty pleas and the second to continue with the trial. Apparently, as had by now become totally predictable, the subsequent blunder was due to an administrative error. When the case was split, the priority status and label was thereafter attached to the portion dealing with the guilty pleas and not to the case continuation as it should have been. Therefore, once the pleas were signed and sentences given, the priority status was cancelled as that portion of the case was successfully concluded.

The continuation of the case and the trial of Razor Zulu was then followed through onto the following court role without priority status! Yet again, administrative ineptitude was proving to substantiate the continued and repetitive delays we were experiencing.

Were we ever going to get through this?

Just as we had heard before, we were assured that by the next date the case would definitely go ahead. The judge had ensured that everything was in place to confirm its activation. We had by now lost all energy and all momentum and were simply dragging our feet and ourselves through towards the finishing line.

The next quarter was due to start on 25 July and our case was scheduled for day one of this new quarter, with priority status! We just had to wait for another three months. We had no other option and anyway, what is another 3 months on the already almost nine-year wait. We could only hope that this would be the last.

The Final Court Case

"Apologies are not meant to change the past; they are meant to change the future."

Kevin Hancock

The court date finally arrives. We all head across to Palm Ridge Magistrate Court once again. There is no heightened anxiousness, nor nervous tension this time, as we've done this all before. It almost feels routine now. Emotionally, we are totally drained, and no one has the energy to even comprehend what we will do or how we will cope if any further postponement is proposed, but after nine years of delays, we have come to expect nothing less – it seems an ever elusive illusion that this will actually conclude.

Once again, we take our seats on the benches outside the courtroom. Just as before, we hear the sound of the shuffle and clank of George, Bongani and Razor as they hobble their way down the main corridor. It's unbelievable to me that six months down the line that they still aren't using prisoner's entrance and courtyard, the holdings cells and the steps leading directly up to each courtroom.

As I watch the three of them head towards us, I notice that there is no jovial communications or interactions between them this time. Razor sits down first on a bench opposite us and to the right, the others seem to make a pointed effort to head to another bench further down to our left.

I prepare myself to head over and sit in front of him again at the first sign of any aggression or intimidation. My insides no longer quiver like jelly at seeing him, there are no explosions of adrenalin, this is now just something I am used to and something I have done before.

He looks up at us, I am steeling myself for that usual sneer, but it doesn't come, instead he hangs his head, looks at his hands and starts picking at his nails. The air is palpably different. He says something to one of the warders sitting next to him and they all stand up and move into the courtroom.

Once again, the clock by-passes that 10h00 deadline and we are all still sitting outside. We start preparing for the inevitable. If things have not started yet, it can only mean another delay, another postponement. We have almost convinced ourselves as much, when the Capt Baloyi comes to talk to us.

"There has been a change," he says

"No," we shout in unison, interrupting him before he can say anything more.

"No," he corrects us back, "it is good news," he says

What on earth can be good about another change we are all wondering.

"Razor wants to plead guilty!"

After nine years of arrogance, nine years of aggression and nine years of claimed innocence, after dragging this from court case to court case, and courtroom to courtroom, the man wants to now plead guilty!

With a mixture of shock, disbelief and relief, we realise in that one short sentence that it's all over.

"There is just one issue we need to discuss," Captain Baloyi says, "The state is concerned that it doesn't have enough evidence to successfully prosecute Mzi. It recommends that we drop charges against him."

We all look at each other in question, still trying to get our heads around this massive change of events. Lorna is the first to say something, "Yes, yes, we will agree to that," she says. And with that, the end was finally in sight.

The resultant emotions are confusing. There is no elation, no excitement, no victorious fist pumping in the air, instead we are all quiet, drained and confused. We can only wonder at what has brought about this change. It doesn't feel victorious; in fact, it's just the opposite. Why did the rat have to wait nine years and put us all through this extended hell, to give up, give in and admit wrongdoing in the end? We had all this pent-up emotion and didn't quite know where to place it. It was like someone had popped our really big water balloon.

However, regardless of how backwards and upside down the moment seemed, we would take it. Hell, we would take this rather than the alternative, any day.

It's done, it is over, Lorna hasn't had to get bullied on the stand, or go through all the Patersons experienced, or had to face them or their lawyers in a show-down as had been dreaded for so many years. We only had to wrap things up tomorrow and then all was done and behind us – FINALLY!

It was a very different family carrying very different emotions that arrived back at Palm Ridge Magistrate Court the following morning. This time, instead of heading straight to the courtroom, we headed to one of the available offices nearby. With the family, Karl and the prosecutor present in the room, the plea bargain drawn up by Razor and his lawyers was presented to us. We had presumed his reasoning for pleading guilty would be to try and get a lesser sentence in return, and we were prepared to fight against this. However, in the document before us, Razor and his lawyers had requested and included maximum sentencing for both the murder and the house robbery charges.

Once again, we were dumbfounded. Where had this come from and what was his reasoning behind it?

Mom and Lorna signed the document on behalf of the family and with the last flick of the pen, the case was closed. Raymond "Razor" Bheki Zulu, aka Mandla Skosane, aka Moses Zwane, aka "The Nasty One", was to receive another sentence equivalent to life.

We all headed down to the courtroom for the final meeting between Lady Justice and ourselves. Razor was already in the courtroom and as with his demeanour the previous day, turned to look at us sheepishly and then buried his face in his hands.

We sat one row behind him this time, almost as if our choice for close proximity might give us some answers on what had changed within him. The judge came in and we all stood. Once seated, the plea bargain was presented to the judge. The judge sat looking at it in silence for a moment, paging through the notes in front of her and looking up again. She tells the court that she would like to call a recess for 30 minutes to an hour as she would like to go through all the facts of the case to confirm that the proposed sentence is justified.

With the finishing line looming so close, we can almost touch it, we all stand up and opt to wait outside. I linger a little behind the family, watching this man who I have spent ages sharing aggressive and hardened stares with and here he sits now as weak as a lamb. I notice him trying to get the attention of Captain Baloyi who walks across to him. They exchange a few words and I see Baloyi's eyes widen in surprise. He looks towards me with a look of shock and amusement on his face. "He is asking to talk to your mother and to Lorna," he says to me in an animated stage whisper "he wants to apologise!"

I walk outside the courtroom, shaking my head in wonder and head straight to Lorna and my parents. "You won't believe this," I tell them, "Razor is asking to see you, he wants to apologise."

"Why?" Lorna asks, "What does he want?"

Karl, who was standing with my mother is trying to discern the confused look on Lorna's face. "You don't have to talk to him of you don't want to," he tells her, "it's entirely your choice."

Lorna nods her head but says she will go, and she and Mom head into the courtroom once more with the rest of us trailing behind to witness this mind-blowing development.

Lorna and Mom stand in front of him. He's still sitting on the accused bench with his head in his handcuffed hands. He looks up at them and bleats, "I'm sorry." Shaking his head, he carries on, "Sorry, sorry, sorry." Talking first to mom and then to Lorna, he says, "I'm sorry that I killed your son and I'm sorry that I killed your husband. Please forgive me."

Initially Lorna is not sure what to say to him and stands speechless. Mom finds her voice first, "I'm sorry, I can't! It will be a long time before I will ever be able to forgive you" she says, "you killed my son. But …" she adds, "I acknowledge and thank you for your apology. It takes courage to do that and for that I thank you, but I'm sorry, I most certainly cannot forgive you and am not sure I ever will," she concludes as the tears well up in her eyes.

Finding her voice, Lorna looks him in the eyes and with tears in hers she whispers, "You have made my children grow up without a father." Razor drops his head so hard that he hits it audibly on the railing in front of him and he starts to sob.

The judge returns to the courtroom and declares she's happy with the sentence proposed: 20 years for murder and 15 years for house robbery. The nine years he has already spent in jail does not count and it all starts from now and from this day forward.

It's now truly and officially over.

Mom and Lorna quietly walk out the courtroom and everyone else follows. Dad is still sitting on a bench behind Razor and he suddenly looks so lost and distraught he cannot move. He stands but is unable to put one foot in front of another, he's just staring at this man in front of him that murdered his son, for nothing more than greed, he's lost in his own emotions. I stand with him, just to make sure he's okay and to help him out the courtroom.

The warders come to take Razor away. As he starts to shuffle out, he sees Dad and me still standing at the back of the courtroom. He looks at us both, with hands together and bending his knees in contrition, he apologises to us again and again.

My father and I simply looked on as they took him down the steps and down to the supposed safety of the holding cells. We head out the courtroom for the last time to join the rest of the family outside. Everyone was involved in animated conversation as regards the turn of events from Razor. No one had seen it coming. The warders, the prosecutors, the Investigating officer, they are all standing with the family expressing their own surprise and amazement at it all. They all explain how Razor has continued to maintain a state of aggression and arrogance with them from day one, and thus, they would never have expected this in a million years. No one seems to be able to offer any reason or explanation for this turn around.

We notice Bongani and George still sitting on the bench nearby to where we are all standing. We have nothing to say to George. He stabbed Mike 14 times and left him at the bottom of the pool. Lorna heads over to Bongani. "Are you the one that tied us up?" she asks him.

"Yes," he sheepishly replies.

"I just want to say thank you for being so gentle with my children when you did so, you could have made it worse." He nods his head and hangs it in shame.

She turns to Mzi Tofile who is sitting next to him and has just had all charged dropped against him. "You have been given a second chance," she says, "I hope that you will make the most of it and stay away from people like them," pointing to George as well as the direction Razor was last seen.

"Yes," he promises, "no more crime."

Whether he means it or not, we'll never know, but with that, the Thomson family walk out of the Palm Ridge Magistrates Court for the very last time.

It is over! It will never bring Mike back, but after nine years, there is some form of justice for his brutal and unnecessary murder. It does not bring peace, joy, relief nor accomplishment. It only brings closure. We will always miss Mike and wonder what could have been. There will always be a gap as a father, a husband, a brother and a son, but we cannot hold onto the past, it is time for us to move forward and to focus on all the positive ways we can honour him instead.

∽

A month later we receive a final and official letter on South African Police Services letterhead, outlining the closure of the case, and true to nature, inefficiency and ineptitude reign supreme once more. The letter states:

Kindly be informed that the case docket Parkview CAS 647/09/2007 was received back from the Palm Ridge High Court and the following outcome was received:

Accused no. 1 and 2 was found guilty on House Robbery and was sentenced to 20 years imprisonment.

Accused no. 4 was found guilty on House Robbery and was sentenced to 15 years imprisonment.

The case against accused no. 3 was withdrawn.

The office regards this matter as finalised and closes the file.

There's not a word about Mike's murder! You have got to be kidding! We have been through nine years of hell, we have fought for justice for Mike and at the end of the day, that the official document can be so insulting as to disregard this and all that has occurred and officially claim to us, that these rats have been charged with house robbery only.

Yes, inefficiency and ineptitude reign supreme! No wonder the criminal and justice system is in such shambles and we seem unable to come out on top of it all.

PART IV:

Finding The Humanity Within The Nightmare And The Aftermath Of It All

"I see only one hope for our country, and that is when white men and black men, desiring neither power nor money, but desiring only the good for their country, come together to work for it.
I have one great fear in my heart, that one day when they are turned to loving, they will find we are turned to hating."

Alan Paton, Cry the Beloved Country

Taking A Gamble At Sun City

"You gain strength, courage and confidence by every experience in which you really stop to look fear in the Face."

Eleanor Roosevelt

In early 2016, after the February delay of the court case due to the lack of court proceeding documents, I had started playing with the idea of putting this whole ridiculous process into a story.

Looking back on all that has happened, I believe that our story encompasses and represents those experiences of a large portion of the population. There are many South Africans who have shared in the same frustrations and shocking revelations that we have. Not only have we faced South Africa's crime firsthand, but we have also experienced the countless issues that have followed thereafter.

In the words of Karl our trusted lawyer who helped us so vociferously to see justice done, "We have been well and truly screwed by the system and have had the dubious "honour" to meet its problems head on again and again."

Most South Africans are not aware of what happens behind the scenes (or does not happen, as may so often be the case) and if I were to share our story, then possibly someone with the right training, the perfect opportunity and the right frame-of-mind will come up with the solutions needed to counteract this or, by a remote stroke of chance, government may be convinced to finally come to the party. This sad state of affairs cannot continue if we want to move this country forward from the crippled state it's currently in and if we want to stem the copious tears this beloved country is bringing to its citizens.

We can only fix something when we can identify what is in fact wrong in the first place. I have obviously had plenty time to think this through myself over the last few years as we have been forced to experience each of these issues, and I will expound on some of my thoughts as we continue in the book, but for now, I needed to focus on bringing all the issues and experiences together into a single diatribe, with a single thread and story, weaving between. This would mean also verifying all the information we had been given along the way and down the years, so that when I put pen to paper here, each has been justified, confirmed and corroborated. Where I have been unable to get documentation to vindicate information or where role players have not been willing to confirm, I have changed names or stated as such, otherwise, everything else espoused in this story, has been confirmed and clarified, and invariably I have files of information to support it.

Apart from the solid facts of all that had happened, I also decided that the book would not be complete without getting to know the deviants and rats themselves. To get to know their story, to try and understand who they are, why they have made the choices they have made and just what they have been through in their lives, that brought them to this point in ours. I have always believed that you cannot truly judge another until you have walked in their shoes, or at least tried to understand the path they have been on, and although I have never looked kindly upon this group as a direct result of all they have done and chosen to do, I am also willing to understand that they too will have been victims of our society and beloved country, and of their environment along the way, and there has to be some level of understanding and compromise in this regard, and I would dig deep and find it in myself to give them that opportunity and to hear what they had to say.

I also thought it would be worthwhile to try and find out from them what had made them plead guilty in the end, specifically Razor Zulu who fought so aggressively until that very last trial.

And so I set my sights on establishing meetings with these men in prison so that I could start getting to the bottom of what initiated this story and all we have been through over the last decade of time.

Little did I know at the outset, just how challenging this would prove to be. And, that this would not only continue to show me that inefficiency continues in the world of the Department of Correctional Services as well, but would also open me up to a criminal of a different sort – the kind of criminal you don't see coming and don't recognise for the rat and the deviant that he is, but rather the one you think is a good hearted Samaritan – until it's too late! But life is for learning and life is for living and I would have to find my way and learn as I go along.

∽

Razor, George and Bongani had all been scheduled to serve out their time at the Johannesburg Central Prison near Southgate Mall. This facility is euphemistically called Sun City because of how bad it really is inside.

A little over a month after Razor was sentenced, I reached out to the Head of the Johannesburg Central Prison as well as the Area Commissioner and his secretary via email. After a week, I'd heard nothing from any of them. I kept on resending the emails. August and September go by and still I hear nothing. I keep trying … nothing! I look up the Department of Correctional Services website and access a range of contact numbers and I start phoning. My frustration increases when I cannot get a single call answered. I try one number after another. I try them again and again, but not a single ring is answered. Do the phone lines or the phones themselves just not work or does everyone choose to simply ignore them?

Two months of repetitive attempts at communication and using different resources yet not one of them is successful. I am feeling very frustrated as by now, I have no idea how I am going to get this organised, and I am not quite sure what to do next.

Then once again, fate intervenes; a little twisted this time around, but intervenes none-the-less.

I am woken up in the early hours of the morning in October 2016 with an emergency call to support a victim of kidnapping. The man that was kidnapped in a neighbouring province two days prior had been dropped off, badly bruised and beaten, in the middle of the orchards in Hoedspruit. He had managed to make his way to a nearby farmhouse to summon help.

As this was a cross-provincial kidnapping incident, Hoedspruit was graced with the presence of some old school policemen from various specialist units around the country. They had been working around the clock for the last 48 hours to ensure his safe return. One of the policemen, Danie, was from Johannesburg.

A few days later, still frustrated with more unanswered emails and more unanswered phone calls, I sat thinking about how else I could gain access to Sun City and ultimately the three men within. Although I have lots of contacts with various police and detectives, most of them are from

Limpopo and Mpumalanga and they too would not have much to do with Johannesburg Central Prison or anyone else within. I started thinking about the policemen I had just met.

On the off chance that he could help, I contact Danie whom I had met at the farmhouse in the early hours of that morning. His response is immediate and positive. I only need tell him whom I want to talk to and he can pull them out from Sun City, take them to a local police station and I can talk to them there. "Why do you want to talk to them?" he asks.

I tell him about my brother and about the Razor Gang and all they have done and my idea for the book.

"Ok," he replies a little more thoughtfully, "If this is for a book, then we will need to go about it differently." Evidently, convicted criminals are wards of the state and their rights have to be protected. "But," he adds, "I have potential contacts to help us go about this the right way. It just might take longer," he says.

He calls me later with some news. One of his senior colleagues tells him there is a relatively new legal process I can tap into and arrange conversations with these men, it's called Victim-Offenders Dialogue (VOD).

Even though he's remarkably busy himself, Danie continues to chase up options for me. I am exceptionally grateful. Danie gives me the name and phone number of Collen Gilfan[1] who apparently works on profiling of prisoners and assists with rehabilitation programmes in the prisons. He can apparently assist us with VOD. I phone Collen and immediately feel that I'm going to get somewhere at last. Collen immediately related to all I am saying, adds in a few thoughts of his own and truly sounds enthusiastic and willing to help. I feel like I have taken a big step forward.

We talk a few times over the ensuing weeks, but don't really seem to be getting anywhere. He explains to me that he normally works in the

---

1   Not his real name

Pretoria prisons and thus doesn't really have contacts at the Johannesburg Central Prison, but he is using his contacts to make new contacts and will see what he can do to help me. Everyone seems to be facing the same challenge in getting a phone call answered in Johannesburg.

In the meantime, however, he suggests that I look at possibly going to visit the men in prison during regular visiting hours as a standard visitor. He says that I should tell them that I want to enter into VOD with them and request that they then start the process from inside through the prison social workers. It's of benefit to them on their prison record if they have done VOD, so there is a chance that they will cooperate.

This sounds like an exceptionally daunting option, but if it's going to get me what I need in the end, then it's worth considering. I steel myself for the task ahead.

Visiting hours at the prisons are on weekends and public holidays only, so I plan a trip to Johannesburg on the first available weekend I can get away. I have absolutely no idea what to expect.

Before arriving at the prison, Collen kindly offers to meet me at a coffee shop at a nearby mall so he can help talk me through what to expect. I'm amazed and so grateful that he's going out of his way to assist.

I arrive at Sun City and park my car in the large visitor's reception parking area. I need to sit quietly in the car for a few moments while I take a deep breath and gather myself together and not think too much about what I am going to do or whom I am going to see. I haven't really thought about what I am going to say when I see them. I guess I'll just have to wing that when I get there. I have, however, prepared letters for each of them to give to their social workers to initiate steps to start the VOD process from the inside. Collen has told me that I can take nothing inside, neither a bag, nor a phone. I can, however, take a pen and paper. Thus, armed with a notebook and ink I head to reception.

At the reception area, there is a large hall filled with hundreds of waiting hopefuls. I have to fill in a slip of paper first with all the details of whom I want to see. I fill in three slips; one each for Razor, George and Bongani. Handing the slips in, I then go and sit down with all the other hopefuls wanting to see their loved ones, while warders on computers punch in the details from the slips of paper into their screens and ascertain where each prisoner is located within the prison complex.

After waiting for what seemed like an eternity, I get called to the front and make my way to the warder who has just called my name. "Ma'am" he says, "We have a little problem."

"Problem" - there is that word again – one I have gotten to know so well!

"This man here" he says, waving the slip of paper that I have written Raymond Bheki Zulu onto, "he is no longer here. He has been moved to Leeuwkop Prison," he tells me.

I let out a loud sigh of frustration. It has taken a lot of internal dialogue and mental convincing to get to this point, and now he is not here.

"But, this one" he says waving the slip of paper that I have written George's name on, "he is here. You can see him," he says confidently.

"And what about the third, Bongani?" I ask

"Ma'am, that one is a problem," he replies, "we don't know where he is. I can't find him on the system at all"

Well that most certainly is a problem, I deliberate, but a problem I would have to deal with later. For now, I could at least see George. One out of three is not great, but at least it is something and not a total waste of a day.

Looking clearly like a fish out of water, he is looking at me questioningly, "Why do you want to see him?" he asks me.

I mention, what I am to learn quickly are magic words, "VOD. I want to speak to them about VOD," I say and his attitude changes in a flash. "Ask for Mrs Magakwe when you get there" he says, "She will help you.

But firstly, you need to go through the security check there" he points behind him in a helpful manner, "there is a bus waiting just outside that door. You need to get onto the bus and tell the driver you are going to Medium C. That is where you will find George. Mrs Magakwe will be at the entrance door to the prison. Just ask for her, she will help you."

The bus makes its way through the prison complex, stopping every now and then. "Medium A," shouts the bus driver and a handful of visitors climb off the bus. "Medium B," he says at the next stop and another handful alights. "Medium C," he says. I climb off the bus and head into a second security area, this time dealing specifically with Medium C visitors. I get taken into a cubicle and searched. Passing this security check, they ask who I want to visit. I hand them all three slips and am given the same response, "One here, one at Leeuwkop and one unknown."

I am directed to sit on a bench, this time outside in the sun, and wait my turn. My name is called, and I'm told to go down this cement road running around the side of the building towards a large, thick, heavyset, solid metal door, the size of two busses. I walk down to the door and knock on it just as I have been instructed to do. One of the large doors opens slightly to allow me in and I find myself heading into a large courtyard with the prison building on the far side.

There is a lone warder sitting on a chair in the middle of the courtyard. He is watching me. I have to walk past him to head to the door into the prison block; presumably where I need to go. I start walking. As I walk past him, I quietly greet him, and I look ahead to continue towards the door on the other side of the courtyard.

"Hey," he says to me, "I know you. You must be here to see Razor"

I stop in fright, my nerves hit an all-time high!

"How do you know me?" I ask him gingerly, my mind racing around what the options could be.

"From the court," he explains. "I used to take Razor every time. I remember you and your family."

I can breathe again. That is a reasonable answer and one I can live with.

"That's right," I say back to him. "Although I believe Razor is now at Leeuwkop so I can only see George today."

"What," he says with a frown on his face, "no, no he can't be. I do all the transfers and I haven't taken him there," he explains. "Who told you that?" he asks me.

I show him the name I have written down of the man at the reception area who gave me the initial information.

"Oh," he says as if accepting that this man should know. "Maybe someone else took him, but I don't think so." Suddenly remembering, he adds, "Just on Wednesday I had to take him to court again for another case, that he also pleaded guilty to by the way, and I brought him back here. That was only three days ago." He then shrugs his shoulders and adds, "But maybe …" as if that can cover all possibilities.

I ask him where I can find Mrs Magakwe and he point to two women sitting at the door ahead of me. "That's her," he declares without really indicating which one she may be. I walk towards the two women.

Putting on my sweetest demeanour I ask, "Hello ladies, which of you is Mrs Magakwe?"

"Who wants to know?" is barked back at me in an unfriendly manner.

I introduce myself, tell them the name of the man at the main reception who told me to ask for her, I explain why I'm there and what I want, and then I mention the magic words, VOD. Her attitude changes in a flash and suddenly she couldn't be more helpful and what a wonderful help she was.

Working on what I had just been told in the courtyard, I explain to her that I am here to see George but was hoping to see Razor as well. "The man outside reckons he's here but the system shows he's at Leeuwkop," I explain. "Can you please check for me?"

She comes back a few minutes later to say that Razor is definitely at Leeuwkop but George is here and he's waiting to see me.

My heart stops briefly, and I catch my breath.

George stabbed my brother 14 times and left him at the bottom of the pool. He stabbed and beat Bronwyn Paterson to a pulp, leaving her for dead and he raped and beat Jenny Redmond, and here I was about to sit down one-on-one and have a conversation with him. "Are you friggin' crazy Debby," I thought to myself, but there was no turning back now!

Mrs Magakwe takes me to a large visiting room with two or three rows of benches facing each other and hundreds of men donned in prison orange, facing girlfriends, mothers, brothers, sisters, friends and colleagues; all talking at the same time and over the top of each other. Each communicating couple had to sit with their face's mere inches from the other, just to be able to hear each other over the noise. The only space available for George and me was on the same bench on the nearest side of the room to the door - as close as two strangers could get. I had no choice but to sit right next to him. This time, there were no leg irons, and no handcuffs, just him and me and thankfully, Mrs Magakwe.

I'm trying to tell him why I am there and what I want, but its noisy and with all the other prisoners and visitors talking at the same time, we can barely hear each other. I can now see the need for communicating face-to-face inches apart. I am finding a natural tendency to need to lean forward towards him to hear what he's trying to tell me and for him to hear what I have to say. I am not comfortable at all. Mrs Magakwe sees this and taps me on the shoulder. I am able to lip read her words "This is not going to work. Come let's go to my office," she mouths at me and thankfully, we all stand up and move through to her office. Communication is suddenly a lot easier and I thank her.

I turn to George who is now sitting on the opposite side of a desk to me. I tell him why I am there and what I want. I give him the letter for the social worker and tell him to give it to her on Monday and to start the VOD process from within. I ask him a few questions and he replies, but I don't encourage much communication. I want to keep that all for when we can talk properly with the aid of a social worker, as I plan to really challenge him on who he is, why he has done all that he has done and what has driven him to do so. This is just a start.

While we are talking, I can't help but look at him in wonder. He looks like a fresh-faced youngster with soft rounded features. He's a nice-looking man. I can't believe that this can be the same man that has been so violent on so many different occasions and by all other descriptions was a hard-faced nasty criminal. I would never have predicted it at first glance.

I ask him if he and Razor are still friends. He shakes his head emphatically and replies, "No." I don't ask for details but make a note of it as something to explore when we eventually have our proper meeting.

I have one last question for him before he leaves, "Do you know when Razor was transferred to Leeuwkop and why?"

His brow scrunches up in a questioning frown "What?" he says, shaking his head, "No. He is here, I saw him this morning," he confirms.

I look up at Mrs Magakwe and ask her "Did you hear that? He says that Razor is here."

With a frown on her face she says, "Let me check again," and leaves the room, leaving me alone with George. I suddenly feel very vulnerable. There is nothing but a desk and a plethora of office equipment and potential weapons between us and he's not bound nor restrained in any way. I try keep him busy with questions about his mother and his family. Mrs Magakwe comes in shaking her head in amazement, "The system definitely has him at Leeuwkop, but you are right, he's here, he's coming now."

I see George squirm in his seat. "Do you want to leave?" I ask him "Yes," he replies quickly. "Okay," I say, "you can go."

He stands up and says, "I'm sorry we killed your brother, my intention wasn't to kill it was only house-breaking."

"But George," I respond, "If you go somewhere with a weapon in hand, you must be prepared to use it." I say, "Killing is already an option in your mind."

"Yes, but I only had a screwdriver for housebreaking, not for murder," he responds.

I just nod my head and point him to the door. I am not going to get into it for now, nor why he would so unnecessarily have stabbed Bronwyn when she offered him no threat whatsoever. I'll deal with those issues and that discussion when we meet again. For now, I am about to sit across a desk and actually have a conversation with the vilified name – Raymond "Razor" Zulu – head and mastermind behind The Razor Gang!

I needed a quick breath before I continue.

I turn to Mrs Magakwe while we wait for Razor to arrive.

"This one", I say looking at her, "you don't leave me alone with this one."

"No" she says, "I'll be here with you all the time."

Just as I had done with George, I look at him in amazement. The man before me is a small scrawny thing. Not the kind of person one would presume could instil so much fear in people, nor have affected so much damage in people's lives over time. It is amazing what the effect of drugs and alcohol, and the presence of a gun can do.

He susses me out almost nervously and takes a seat in the office chair on the opposite side of the desk to where I am sitting. Mrs Magakwe moves to stand behind the desk to my right.

I ask him if he knows who I am, "No," he responds. I tell him who I am, why I am there and what I am wanting. I tell him that we don't need to talk about it today, but I am going to come back in the New Year so we can meet properly and talk then.

"I want to know about you," I say, "who you are, where you grew up, about your childhood, about what hurt you that has made you need to hurt others so much," I continue", "what made you turn to crime and why you chose to be so violent."

By the time I have said all this, I seem to have opened up a floodgate within him. Despite having said that we don't need to talk about this now, he just starts talking and does not stop.

He told me where he was born, spoke of his mother, his father, his brothers, how he left school at 10 and home at 14. He hit the streets hard. He started speaking of his entry into crime and eventually to violent crime. Once again, the dead Thabang got all the blame. According to Razor, he was the violent one, he always carried the guns, he organised the jobs and he did all the shooting.

"We can only wonder why they were never called the Thabang Gang instead of the Razor Gang," I muse facetiously to myself.

I let him talk and talk. I did not try to stop him. I just kept writing down as much as I could while he continued to talk. Every now and then I would nod in response or ask for a small clarification, but other than that I just let him continue. I noticed Mrs Magakwe was writing everything down too and was as involved in all he had to say as I was.

I knew that a large portion of what he was saying was probably a wild extraction of the truth or a twisted version to help him continue to not yet take responsibility for his actions, yet I wrote it down all the same. I will ask him the repeat questions when we meet again and would see how his answers then might relate to these now.

As the dialogue with a seeming lack of self-admonition continued, I felt the sudden need to ask him one question in particular. After a lengthy output, he sat quietly for a minute and I took the gap.

"Razor" I said, grabbing his attention, "Tell me, why did you rape Jamie?"

There is suddenly a change in his demeanour. He briefly puts his head in his hands then looks up at me. I can't quite place it, but there is a tangible difference in the man and I suddenly catch a glimpse of the hardened vicious criminal and then it's gone, the scrawny one is back.

"Eish," he says to me, "I was drunk, drunk, drunk, drunk," he over dramatises.

Holding his hands in the shape of a gun in front of his face he continues, "I even gave my gun to my friends afterwards," and moving it up to the side of his head he continues. "And, I told them just to shoot me now, because I had hurt this poor girl. She would be sad for the rest of her life," he says to me feigning shock and horror at his own actions.

I so badly wanted to ask him "What about the others that you raped afterwards. Did you say the same every single time?" But I hold my tongue.

I don't want to challenge him just yet. I need him to feel confident and comfortable enough talking to me so that he will work on the social workers on his side, and not feel too threatened by me. He continues to find a way to blame the late Thabang for the rest of his deeds.

As the conversation continues, I become aware of a subtle but distinctive action on his part. While sitting on the office chair on the other side of the desk, one of those manoeuvrable sorts with castor wheels, he enters into a repetitive process of leaning back and forth in the chair. Leaning back into the chair whenever he was going into thought or recalling something new and then leaning forward with his elbows on his knees, each time he verbalised and responded. The constant rocking back and forth subtly hides another game at play. Every time he leant forward; he rolled the chair a few centimetres towards me.

It was not long before I had noticed that the chair had moved around the corner of the table and he was now situated near the table edge 90 degrees to the right of where I was sitting. As the conversation continued, he in turn continued to slowly move towards me one wheel-roll at a time.

I took this to be another play at power control on his side and a possible attempt to see if he could rattle me, intimidate me or scare me in any way possible as he slowly rolled me into a corner. I most certainly was not going to let him succeed. I subtly caught Mrs Magakwe's eyes while he was turned away and indicated to his current position so she could hopefully also be aware of what was at play.

Once again, I quietly looked around me and took note of what my options were as regards potential self-defence weapons from the office stationery available should it be required, and other than that, I did my best to not let him know that he was getting to me or intimidating me in anyway whatsoever. As with previous occasions, my insides were quivering like jelly and my outside demeanour as calm and collected as I could muster.

In my mind I drew an invisible line alongside the desk and had decided that should he cross that line and things become a little too close for comfort, I would ask him to move his chair backward. If that did not work, I would stand up and end the meeting. I did have visions running through my brain of just how wrong the situation could go and watched the invisible line closely as he drew nearer.

Just as he was almost upon it, there was a commotion and a lot of talking just outside the office. A warder walked in and told Razor it was time to go, visiting hours were over, and they ceremoniously led him out of the room. With a huge sigh of relief, I could stand up and move away from my corner behind the desk, relieved at not having to test just what the man was attempting.

I asked Mrs Magakwe if she had noticed what he was doing, and she confirmed that she was about to tell him to move back herself. I thanked her profusely and asked if I could buy her a cold drink at the visitor's tuck shop to thank her for all her help. She gave me a hug and said, "No my dear, that is not necessary, this is my job, I am here to help you."

Even in amongst the failures of the day, it is so encouraging to be reminded that within our defunct system, we do have some incredible gems at work, and a very small handful of individuals who not only are committed to what they are doing but who do their utmost best with the limited resources and crumbling systems around them and truly seem to care about all they do.

By the time I head out of Medium C and out of the security gates, to wait for the bus to return, the majority of the visitors have left. I wait by myself for an age for the bus, ruminating on the entire day's experience. I have also arranged to meet with our hero cop Bruce Mac Intosh for the first time that afternoon, so I needed to get on my way. With the bus still not arriving, I turn to the security guard at the gate and ask if I have to wait for the bus or am I allowed to walk back to the main visitor's reception area myself.

"You can walk if you want," he tells me, "but, it's far."

I smile humorously and say, "Not a problem, I'm going to walk."

It feels good to walk, to take in a bit of fresh air and to get a good look at the entire prison complex as I pass through. I ruminate on it all, on the concept of prisons over time and our need to remove certain individuals from society as they become a threat to said society; about how does one develop a society where this is not necessary and where we can bring up individuals who believe that the needs of the society should be given as much priority as the needs of the self.

I ruminate on what are we really doing to the souls behind each of the extensive lengths of electric fences, razor wire and brick walls that I am walking past. Are we helping improve them or are we helping to further destroy them? Is this really a productive and beneficial system or are we creating a never-ending cycle for generations to follow? I think about the South African systems, and our situation specifically. After all that we experienced over the last nine years, it should come as no surprise that

I experienced system and administrative malfunctions at Sun City too.

To think that prison records show a prisoner as violent and deviant as Razor to be in one prison, while he's in fact in another, is frightening. How do they keep control of all the prisoners, if this is what is going on behind the scenes? If he had to escape, would they really know? If this is the situation here, just how often is this happening in the prison system, nationally?

Then as for Bongani, how can they not find him on the system at all, and where could he be? I take cognisance of the fact that the criminals all seem to use different names so often when they are arrested and possibly he has been checked in under a different name, however, as I have in my possession, the legal guilty plea agreement signed by him, using the name Bongani Masumpa, and he was now incarcerated on the back of the signing of that document, surely he would have been booked in with some connection thereto?

I would need to find someone to look into this for me and to track him down and see if he is still in prison or what the story can be behind the seeming lack of records under that name.

By the time I have thought through this all, I start making my way to my car, to head off to meet this Hero Cop I have heard so much about from my mother and from the Patersons and that I have already started sharing with you. I want to chat to him and find out more about his side of the story and sadly why he felt the system had let him down so much he had no choice but to leave the force and stop with the fantastic and lifesaving work he was committed to.

Looking Beyond The Bars

"But to punish and not to restore, that is the greatest of all offences."

Alan Paton, Cry the Beloved Country

Nelson Mandela said that no one truly knows a nation until one has been inside its jails. Well, if that quote holds water, then we are well and truly in trouble!

Ask anyone who has been inside, and they will tell you that prison is not easy. Not only is prison not easy, but at this stage, it can be considered yet another failure of our society.

Searching for an article or report that contains beneficial effects and successes of our correctional services is, well, close to impossible. I have scoured the Internet and read report after report looking for any such feedback, however, apart from finding a 2017 documentary called "Inside Prisons" that looks into positive reforms and change that have been implemented in the Krugersdorp Prison, and the positive effects it has had on the prisoners within, there is very little else to be found.

In 2011, an inmate takes to blogging about his experience as he's arrested and goes through the judicial and correctional services. It is an eye-opening read for anyone who is interested in what prison life is really like and if only all our criminals would take to such civilised processes as reading, it may assist in halting them in their tracks. In one of his blogs in June 2011, he lists a number of primary prisons around South Africa and the reputations that they have amongst the prisoners themselves. His comments on Krugersdorp Prison in 2011 reads:

"Exactly like Sun City except for the location... not for the squeamish and soft-hearted. Avoid if possible, folks!"

As I have mentioned before, "Sun City" is the euphemism given to Johannesburg Central Prison as it's so bad and such an awful experience it's in fact nothing like the real Sun City (which is a gambling and pleasure resort). It is also where Razor and George are currently incarcerated and it is also the prison where I ventured to visit.

This inmate bloggers account is largely about Sun City and he expresses aspects such as the following: (this is not the full blog, but each paragraph is a different section I have taken out of his blog. To see his full blog, I have included the URL in the reference section of this book, titled, Thinking back, a prisoner's diary).

"Most Johannesburg suspects are detained in the P-4 wing of Sun City until your trial in court. If you are squeamish and soft, I guarantee you will NOT survive this experience ... Literally!"

All the rights that according to our beloved Constitution you are entitled to...forget it. You get food once a day, you don't get any exercise, there is hardly any medical service and the conditions are sub-human ... period. Anything you want is only possible via Smokkel [smuggling]. Imagine not seeing sunlight for two years. Your skin actually becomes translucent. It's scary to see.

Legal visits are virtually impossible as around 8000 detainees have to share three consulting rooms, it's just a complete nightmare. On an average you will fight roughly every second week, but like I said it's as if you become totally used to this kind of life. It even seems normal after a while

The routine in terms to get to court is appalling, especially if you have a trial ranging from one week to three months. You are woken up between 03h00 and 04h00 in the morning and taken down to the court cells. All the detainees of all the various courts in Johannesburg are taken down to the reception area. It's noisy, dirty and extremely crowded. Food is a scarcity, and everybody is divided according to the court they attend into cages. Yes, cages. So, everyone attending High Court will end up in a cage together, Protea court in one cage, Yeoville in another and so forth with Brixton, Wynberg, Randburg, Roodepoort, Jhb-Central, Krugersdorp, etc all having their own cage.

Depending which court you attend, you arrive back at Sun City between 17h30 and 19h00. Now one by one everybody is processed back into the prison and placed into the cages once again. Here you wait until the last Gomban [transport vehicle] returns and group by group you are taken back to your sections at around 21h30, sometimes even as late as 23h00. Then the routine starts the next day again between 03h00 and 04h00.

NOTE: I didn't mention food as you don't get any during the day, unless your loved one's bribe a "Gatta" at court to buy you some food. To think I followed this routine for nearly three months every day while still trying to argue with my so-called lawyer and having to deal with the condemning media. I didn't stand a chance! I failed myself, my family, my friends and now I'm stuck in this shit hole due to my own failures ... or is it?

Currently, it's hard to deny that our prisons are soulless places of hopelessness, frustration and desolation. If we are to have any hope of lessening the number of criminals in South Africa, this needs to change.

In the 2017 documentary called "Inside Prisons", (currently available on YouTube), Krugersdorp Prison reports on a number of successful reform processes they have initiated, and the successes these processes are bringing.

Part of this process included progressive visions by new management to get the community involved in refurbishing the prison. These new improvements included, a computer, a fully equipped gym, a "fun room" (with snooker tables, ping pong and other activity offerings) and paint to brighten up the prison. Creative and inspiring murals have been painted on the various walls and includes a water feature in the outside courtyard.

Nico Lotter, the Deputy Director of the Krugersdorp Prison extols on some of the decisions taken and the benefits achieved. He explains that initially there was a lot of violence in the prison between inmates as well as between inmates and warders. There was a high level of inactivity within the inmates with them literally doing nothing day in and day out. He further reports that from the moment they started initiating the changes there was less aggression and less assaults between the inmates which he continues to attribute to the fact that there is less frustration and boredom experienced.

He also comments on the fact that he immediately started noticing a massive increase in the self-esteem of the inmates, which enabled them to develop a sense of pride in themselves and in what they were doing. Self-esteem is a very necessary building block to enable self-growth and personal change of any sort.

Lotter also continues to report that the prison has also now developed sports clubs within its walls, practical workshops such as glassworks, and woodwork skills and all the while that he's talking, the camera is showing different scenes from inside the prison; all of them full of colour, with creatively painted walls and operational facilities within. Apart from the bars on the windows and solid iron doors, there is little else to give away its identification as a prison according to the visuals we are used to seeing.

In the same documentary Lotter makes a statement that immediately strikes a chord with me. He says, "*We cannot rehabilitate a prisoner, he has to rehabilitate himself. Our responsibility is to supply the facilities, training, learning of skills to motivate him and to try to change his attitude and his self-esteem. If you can change that, and he accepts that, then you can say that that prisoner will rehabilitate.*"

He states that prior to this reform, the prison released an inmate who was far worse of an individual than before he came in, now however, they're releasing more and more inmates who are rehabilitated and, for all the reasons listed above and the opportunities and changes now offered to them, have a far greater chance at becoming responsible and productive members of society.

He further extols on his thoughts as regards many people's views on prisons. He states:

"*The community usually wants us to punish him twice. They think that usually if you lock up a prisoner, you should also punish him inside. I think it's the wrong perception, because the fact that his freedom is taken away, is punishment enough. At 16h30 we start lock up and then he's still a prisoner again.*"

As many famous inmates have previously reported, the loss of one's freedom is a challenge hard to bear and can be impossible to cope with.

In comparison, this same documentary looks at the conditions in Polsmoor Prison where overcrowding and lack of staffing is a massive issue.

Within the first two minutes of the documentary, Mike Green, section head at Polsmoor, opens up a cell and turns to the camera to report ...

"*Accommodation for this cell is 18 [number of beds provided], and the* "unlock" [number of inmates inside at the time of unlock] is 46.

He then continues to explain that due to staff shortages, inmates are locked up in the cells for 23 out of 24 hours. They get let out and are allowed outside for one hour only. He then adds to this further by stating that occasionally, once again due to staff shortages, as well as occasionally due to other factors such as weather, this does not happen every day and they in fact may end up being locked up in the cell for the full 24 hour period in a day.

How on earth can we ever expect any positive growth or rehabilitation in these circumstances? This means that 46 inmates are cooped up in a small room designed to house only 18. Not only are the cells overcrowded, but the inmates are under-stimulated, frustrated and angry; a recipe for disaster.

Green also explains that they have two social workers and one psychologist for 3500 inmates. This is the sector of our society that is most greatly in need of social worker intervention and psychological assistance and all we can spare and afford them is a total of three between both fields? Once again, how on earth can we ever expect any positive growth or rehabilitation in these circumstances? We are only creating breeding pools for the troubles that afflicted us in the first place. It makes absolutely no sense whatsoever.

One of the prisoners is filmed shouting from within his cell:

"For us prisoners who get sent to prison to rehabilitate, but here, you can't be rehabilitated. Here, you come to learn about crime. It's just a warehouse where criminals come together. There are murderers, housebreakers, rapists, thieves. I – who am here for six months for theft – am put together with these and that is how I learn more about crime."

Another humane aspect implemented by Krugersdorp Prison in the last two years, is the installation of around 16 phones throughout the prison complex. The primary motivation for this was that they wanted to be aware immediately if anything was wrong in the prison. This has had very positive results as now the prisoner has an opportunity to phone lawyers, human rights activists, unions and even Lotter himself. This enables the prisoners to establish a sense of self-worth and self-respect when they know that there is someone out there looking after them. And, should anything be wrong, there are open processes and channels in place that will allow them to convey such issues and concerns when required.

I know that many of you are shaking your heads right now and saying, "What on earth are you thinking. We should rather just lock them all up and throw away the keys." But let's look at the situation with an open mind. The reality is, is that most of our prisoners get out at some stage of their lives and are back on our streets, very few actually stay in prison for ever, and I personally would far rather have an ex-inmate from Krugersdorp living near me, that has developed some sense of responsible citizenship and belief in himself, than an ex-inmate from Polsmoor that not only is now far more angry and frustrated than when he came into prison, but has also now learned a ton of new skills to use, in which to take out his increased anger and frustration on my community around me and possibly, heaven forbid, another of my family.

Just to get a clear understanding of what the potential threat is that awaits us and is breeding in our prisons as they currently stand (apart from Krugersdorp Prison, of course), the following statistics give us an indication of the high numbers of criminals within our prisons and that we are slowly denigrating further and further into lesser human beings.

In 2014/2015, there were 42077 Remand detainees (awaiting trial), 115064 Convicted Criminals and an average total of 157141 prisoners overall in our prisons countrywide.

In 2015/2016, there is a slight increase to 42380 Remand detainees (awaiting trial), 116951 Convicted Criminals and an average total of 159331 prisoners overall.

By March 2016, the total average had further increased to 161984 prisoners housed in our various prisons that are built to accommodate a total of 119134 bed spaces only. This is an over-population of 42850 prisoners overall.

At some time over the next five to 20 years, the large majority of these 161984 prisoners will be released back onto the South African streets, and unless we do something serious and very quickly about rehabilitating and assisting these individuals to become worthy and responsible individuals, we can only guarantee that crime will continue to get worse.

It cannot be argued, where Krugersdorp Prison at least has the chance of producing a rehabilitated and responsible member of society, Polsmoor Prison is guaranteed to do just the opposite and is nothing more than a criminal breeding ground and a school to increase one's criminal skills.

If Krugersdorp Prison is our future, then we at least have a chance to save our country and to stem the tide. If Polsmoor Prison is our future, then we are well and truly lost as a nation and there is no hope for our future as a country or as a society and the words of Nelson Mandela need to incite deep concern into our every being. *"No one truly knows a nation until one has been inside its jails."*

A Different Kind Of Rat

"It is not permissible to add to one's possessions if these things can only be done at the cost of other men. Such development has only one true name, and that is exploitation"

Alan Paton, Cry the Beloved Country

It's 2016, December rolls around and I decide that I need to at least have made some progress in setting up VOD processes before the year ends, so that I can start 2017 with some sort of action plan in place.

Not wanting to rely solely on Razor and George working through their social workers, I continue to try every channel I can, to knock on the doors from outside. Collen Gilfan promises to keep on with his contacts too.

"Operation Vala" is coming soon, he informs me. This is where the prisons are shut down from mid-December to mid-January and no visitors are allowed in or out, no exceptions, I am told. So now I am pressured for time and to get things moving.

In the beginning of December Collen contacts me, he has had a meeting with the social workers he deals with in Pretoria as regards contacting the social workers in Johannesburg on my behalf. They have apparently put him in touch with a third-party organisation called Magna Projects, that is involved in profiling projects within the prisons. There is supposedly an opportunity that I can sign up with them as one of their project implementers. Through this process I should be able to get access to the prisoners.

We continue to communicate via Whatsapp, me asking for more info and he offering what turns out to be vague and non-committal answers.

I push for more information, but never seem to get it. Answers are seemingly complex and filled with jargon and complicated processes; all seemingly exceptionally helpful yet still not really giving me any direct answers.

Finally, Collen sends me forms I need to fill in on Department of Correctional (DCS) Services letterheads. My first thought is, "How typical for what I have come to experience with DCS – the forms are very unprofessional and badly laid out and the logo is a little blurred." It's also stated at the bottom that the forms needs to be completed and forwarded to the National Conventional Arms Control Secretariat and I am now wondering how that all fits in. But I am in uncharted territory here, and certainly don't know enough to question vociferously and thus, just continue to go ahead with what has been presented to me.

I am so extremely grateful to Collen for all that he's doing, and this truly does seem like an option that can work. I go ahead with it all blindly and willingly.

I do, however, do a Google search on Magna Projects to see if I can find any mention of them or reference to them on the Internet. I obviously would like to know more about who I am going to team up with. I'm surprised that I can't find anything on them. However, at this stage there is no need for me to be concerned as Collen is just being so helpful. I cannot believe my luck at having found one of these true Samaritan gems who just enjoys helping people. And, as always, I am ever grateful for his help.

Collen calls me the following day to tell me that he has taken all my documentation to the Magna Projects offices and dropped them off for me. He said that they wouldn't accept the documents without payment for the vetting/administration fee. "But, don't worry. I just paid it for you, and we can sort it out in the new year."

"Wow, thank you," I say. Once again I am so grateful for all his help. "Please just send me through all the information as I'd rather pay you back as soon as possible, if I can," I respond.

Naïvely, I was expecting an administration fee of anything from R100 to possibly R800 at the most. Thus, I was stunned when I received the receipt and transaction report made out to me by Magna Projects for R16900.

"Holy poop," I thought and called him immediately. "This is huge, Collen. Wow! A lot more than I had expected and in fact, if I had known it was this much, I would not have gone ahead with it," I told him. "Being largely a volunteer worker, I most certainly don't have this kind of money now but I will pay you back as soon as I can," I add.

"Please don't worry about it. Just pay whenever you can," he assures me.

Once again, I am filled with such overwhelming gratitude that a stranger is willing to go to such an extent to help me, it brings me to tears. All I can think of is that there is still some humanity in this world and that there are still some unselfish intentions in our country, and I am just ever so grateful.

Two days later, I prepare to leave for Johannesburg to do more research for the book and thereafter I will head to the South Coast to join the family for Christmas as we usually do. I have arranged to have lunch with a friend of mine, Ingrid, before I depart for Johannesburg. Collen calls while I'm having lunch with her. "There is a little problem," he says.

"There is that word again," I think to myself.

He had just popped into Magna Projects office to check what is happening with my application and they'd told him that they were unable to accept his payment proxy on my behalf. He said, "The payment is an indication of commitment from your side and they would need you to pay at least 10-20% back to me before the end of today in order for them to complete the process before Christmas."

"I'm going to be running around all day today, but if you can send me all the details in an email, I will look at it when I get home tonight and will do it before I leave for Johannesburg tomorrow," I respond.

I put the phone down and turn to Ingrid as she asks me what that was all about. I start telling her and freeze mid-sentence as I hear what I am saying myself, and my brain starts spinning at one hundred miles an hour.

Suddenly, after all this overwhelming gratitude, this is now raising 100 red flags and ticking every box for a potential scam. Now that there is an urgent request for payment, I am starting to see things differently. I start running through all the indicators of a scam that I am aware to look out for and recognise and mentally tick them off in my mind.

1. Find a target who is elderly or has an emotional need and who is emotionally vulnerable – TICK
2. Develop an emotional connection and relationship bond – TICK
3. Win their trust and confidence in you – TICK
4. Give the impression that money is no object and of no concern – TICK
5. Create an unusual situation that creates a need for money to be paid to them, usually for something towards the victim's own benefit. – TICK
6. Set up a situation that has tight time limits and time pressures so

that the person has to pay quickly and does not have time to think about it or query details. – TICK

This new thought process and revelation is so overwhelming I sit staring at Ingrid in shock. "What is it?" she asks me, "What is wrong?"

I am still trying to comprehend that this could all be a con, considering the subject matter; it just does not make sense. Ingrid has always been a very level-headed thinker and I start telling her the full story, mainly to judge her reaction and thoughts, while simultaneously going over it again in my own mind and comprehend for myself what the situation may be.

Immediately, and without the emotional vulnerability that I am carrying, she is convinced it is a scam – why or what for, we are not sure, as the money outlined so far barely seems worth it – unless of course there was more to come hereafter.

There is still a part of me not wanting to accept this, "It can't be, he was introduced to me through a policeman," I say.

She replied with one simple thought, "I don't know what you mean by that?" and I suddenly realise that I don't either.

Even though I now suspect the worse, I decide my best option is to call Magna Projects before coming to any rash conclusions. It plays continuously in the back of my mind that if I am wrong, it's incredibly rude and insulting of me to think this of Collen when he has done nothing but go out of his way to help me.

I get home and immediately pull up the invoice for R16900. I want to call them and hear what they have to say. I sit and stare in disbelief. I had been so shocked at the amount on the invoice; I hadn't taken note of anything else. There was no phone number present, only a physical address in Pretoria. Another red flag and another potential scam box ticked. This was not looking good. I went onto Google Earth to see what I could glean from the address and to the best of what I could see, I am looking at a residential area – could this really be the base of Magna Projects? Another little red flag for me. Sadly, things were looking less and less likely to be genuine as I am finding very little to support it in any way.

I then decide on a compromise. His recent email that I received that afternoon, is requesting me to pay 10-20% of a total over R16900, therefore, I would pay the small amount of only R1600 for now. Tomorrow, I was heading up to Johannesburg and thus would divert my route to take a drive past the address on the invoice and see what I can ascertain from there. If it all turns out to be a scam, then firstly, it was not a huge amount of money I would be losing and secondly, as there had in fact been a monetary transaction, I would have a basis to instigate legal proceedings against him. If it all turns out to be a genuine story, at least I would have paid something towards what I owe him.

The following morning, I arrived at the address in Pretoria. Not only was it a residential address, but those within, knew nothing about Magna Projects. However, they knew exactly who Collen was and were very unhappy at being roped into his scam.

Leaving the Pretoria address feeling deflated, angry, confused and desperate at the thought that there are criminals around every corner, I drive into Johannesburg churning over all that's going through my mind. I came to the conclusion that he's a con-artist and the worst kind of rat. Razor and the rest of his gang don't pretend to be what they're not, they live as low-life rats, and they come to you as low-life rats. From the minute you see them, you know that you are in trouble and you know what is to come, but this kind of rat – he's a rat of the lowest sort.

He hides in the disguise of a good Samaritan. He preys on the emotionally vulnerable and he pretends to be what he's not. He creeps up on you unawares and he gains your trust and confidence first. Just when you think all is safe and well, he whisks it all out from under you when you least expect it. I have no respect for men like Razor Zulu, I have even less for men like Collen Gilfan.

Collen has obviously found out that I have been checking up on him and he tries to call me while I am driving after leaving the non-existent Magna Project offices. I ignore all his calls. I have nothing to say to him at present. He's not worth the energy or input. He has also never been so persistent to get hold of me - possibly a little guilt and self-protection at play?

I send him a text message stating that if the R1600 is not returned to my account by that evening, I would be starting legal proceedings the following day.

Surprisingly, the money is back in my account before the end of the day. From that moment on I decide to have nothing to do with him again. Keeping my head held high, I choose to walk away and rather focus on achieving something on my own. I will focus on communications with the social workers in the prison that Mrs Magakwe has put me in touch with. I could do this on my own and did not need the likes of Collen and his crooked ways.

Reaching my brother's home that day, still in shock at all that had occurred, I could not help but ruminate - My beloved country is awash with criminals of every kind and I cannot help but cry.

Even A Hero Suffers Defeat Against The System

"I do this not because I am courageous and honest, but because it is the only way to end the conflict of my deepest soul."

Alan Paton, Cry the Beloved Country

Following our initial meeting after leaving Sun City, I meet with Bruce Mac Intosh, our hero cop again in December. I want to get to know this "Man Born for Blue" better and find out why he left the service he had committed his entire life to.

I meet him and his wife, Larha for coffee at the Mugg and Bean in Paulshof, next door to where my parents had been living the night they received the life-altering phone call.

I ask Bruce to share a little more about himself, his career and of course, the process he went through to identify and capture the Razor Gang.

He tells me stories that put him in the midst of nine different shootouts in just two years. In three of these, he was entirely on his own. In one of these, he was shot and wounded.

He starts off regaling about some of the most notorious gangs in Johannesburg, the Sandton Knife Gang, the Rolex Gang and others; and with a glint in his eye, he tells me about his interactions with them and his involvement in their subsequent arrests.

Just prior to turning his attention to Raymond "Razor" Zulu and the rest of the Razor Gang, Bruce's primary focus and attention had been on the Sandton Knife Gang – so called as they typically would break into a home unarmed but would immediately arm themselves with knives from the victim's kitchen and attack the family thereafter.

During their reign of terror in the Sandton area they were reported to have invaded 18 homes, each in some of the most secure complexes in Gauteng. They were responsible for stabbing four people including an 18-year-old karate champion and an older man who almost died.

The gang was primarily made up of five brothers from Alexandra Township.

For months the gang bypassed high walls, electric fences, alarm systems, cameras and the watchful eyes of 24-hour guards. They spent about an hour inside each of their victims' homes, always wore dark beanies and gloves and smoked Courtleigh cigarettes. They tied up homeowners while holding sharp knives to their throats, loaded up their spoils in their victims' cars and fled.

Bruce and his colleagues were behind their eventual arrests. Working with the aid of informers, together with their superior detective skills, they homed in on the suspects. They revisited each scene, studied detailed evidence, one of the primaries being the cigarette butts left behind on each scene, and re-interviewed victims and witnesses.

In a single month, with three different raids, they managed to arrest four out of the five brothers. It was not long after that they arrested the rest of the gang. Police recovered about six carloads of stolen goods including jewellery, clothes and electrical equipment.

Remarkably (in South African terms), the Sandton knife gang was convicted three years after its arrest. Yet during the three years between arrest and conviction, the case was also subject to numerous delays and errors; a few of which included the escape of some of the members of the gang. In another incident a further two members of the gang escaped with Razor Zulu from the holding cells at the Alexandra Magistrate Court.

Additional errors reported, include collapsed charges due to victims emigrating, as was to happen with the Redmonds (I am led to believe that this happens far more often than we would like) as well as missing court records, as we had experienced too. Witness statements included the unsettling testimony of a man who was stabbed 17 times by the gang as well as the burglary in 2005 of the-then Deputy President of South Africa, Phumzile Mlambo-Ngcuka. The leader of the gang was reported to have opted for her home because he was bored with the usual break-ins and wanted something a little more exciting and daring.

The next gang that Bruce starts talking about is known as the Rolex Gang – so named as a result of their modus operandi of identifying shoppers at high-end shops in the Sandton area and then following them back to their homes where they rob them of their luxury goods.

Recalling this story, I can see immediately, spikes Bruce's adrenalin and the glint in his eye sparkles just a little brighter.

It's 2014, and the Rolex Gang has just pulled off another robbery in Sandton. As usual Bruce does his due diligence and visits the scene to find as much information as he possibly can from the evidence left behind. They had prior information of the vehicle that the gang normally used for their operations - a Chevrolet Lumina. Finishing up at the crime scene, Bruce heads home, looking forward to seeing Larha and the usual cup of tea that would be waiting for him.

Stopping at the traffic lights at the intersection between Witkoppen and Rivonia Roads, Bruce cannot believe his eyes. He has stopped directly behind the very car he knows to be on the lookout for; the well documented Chevrolet Lumina. He can see the vehicle is fully loaded with individuals he knows so well: the Rolex Gang.

Bruce immediately calls his supervisor, Captain Killian, and tells him that he's sitting in the traffic behind the gang. He's going to follow them until backup arrives and they can then pull them over. At that moment one of the suspects turns around and spots Bruce sitting in his Golf 7 GTI. The gang knows Bruce well. Recognising him, they immediately open fire and shoot at him straight through their back window. Bruce still on the phone with his supervisor, shouts down the line that he's taking fire and is going to take them down now. Captain Killian is telling him to wait for backup, but Bruce has no other option. They continue shooting at him and drive up over the closest island, into the oncoming traffic to get through the traffic light and then speed away up Rivonia Road. Bruce is not going to let them get away and he chases after them. The chase ensues up Rivonia Road, all the way through Rivonia and into Morningside. As usual Rivonia Road has nose to tail traffic, but this does not stop them. At 12th Avenue they swerve into the opposite lane and rush headfirst into oncoming traffic. Bruce follows them and they continue to fly up Rivonia Road only pulling back into the correct side of the road at 7th Avenue. Gunfire is constant as the cars are speeding up the road.

As they get to Morningside and they're flying past the Sandton Police Station, the Lumina hits a taxi and rips one of its front wheels off. The vehicle manages to continue a short distance on three wheels before hitting another vehicle and coming to a standstill. Bruce jumps out of his car and rushes up to the Lumina. With the constant fire from both sides, Bruce's magazine is empty. He turns his body slightly to reload his weapon. At this moment the gang open fire on him. He ducks and dives, but a bullet hits him in the back. This doesn't stop him though, and he turns around with his re-loaded weapon and he opens fire once again.

Bruce ends up taking them all down. Two are wounded, one losing his left testicle in the process, a third ends up cowering behind the car and the fourth, the driver, never makes it out of the vehicle. It turns out that in all the chaos, one of his own men shot him in the head which is potentially the cause of the initial impact with the taxi.

Bruce is injured and needs medical attention but not before he manages to securely arrest those still alive. Our hero cop brings down yet another group of major criminals in Sandton, and this time, all on his own.

This particular event affects Larha and their son Logan badly and Bruce starts realising the impact that his job has on his family. Larha never complains nor demands that he stop, but he can see the extent of stress that she's now experiencing and just how much this is all impacting on her and her wellbeing.

After the Rolex Gang shootout, Bruce is involved in nine shootouts over a two-year period. The last one Bruce recalls is a gang that they have started profiling using the modus operandi of municipal workers. They arrive in a bakkie with an orange light on the roof and a ladder on the back, they all wear orange high-visibility jackets. They pretend to be working on a section of road, while assessing neighbouring properties. As soon as they see an opportunity, they use a ladder to get into houses and rob them. Some of the group remains outside on look out, still keeping up the ruse of diligent workforce members.

Bruce is driving up Summit Road in Bryanston when he spots them. There is something about them that flips a switch in his limbic brain. He just knows these are not genuine workers and this is his gang in operation. He swings the car around and comes back down the road just as they're exiting a house. They see him and open fire. He fires back. A shootout ensues. One suspect is wounded, and Bruce manages to arrest two out of the four. Once again, Bruce is entirely on his own.

Leading up to this event, Bruce had been having a difficult time at the station. Regardless of all his successes and all his achievements, he was still operating under the rank of Warrant Officer. Some of his colleagues, many who were riding on his coattails, were being promoted above him due to political reasons.

The final straw came when Bruce had been requested to take over and run one of the specialist units at the branch, a position that normally came with an increase in rank. He was told that although they wanted him to do the work and take on the responsibility, he couldn't be promoted because he didn't fill the correct political criteria.

Having lost his soul and energy and now having just narrowly missed another bullet flying past his head, Bruce suddenly found himself asking the question "What for?" Looking at the affect this was having on the ever-loving and ever-supportive Larha as well as their young son Logan and having had just about enough corruption and political abuse as he could handle, he suddenly could no longer justify his decision to remain in the police force any longer. Coming home that night and sitting down with Larha and their usual cup of tea, Bruce poured his heart out to her once again and together they made a decision. Having dedicated his entire life to "the blue" and having literally put his life on the line again and again to "serve and protect", he could handle the negative side of it all no longer. Bruce was done, the system had let him down, despite his lifetime commitment to all it stood for. Bruce would be a policeman no longer.

And so it was in April 2015, Warrant Officer Bruce Mac Intosh was to wake up one morning and for the first time in his adult life, it would be without a badge and without a rank. He was now simply Mr Bruce Mac Intosh, husband to Larha and father to Logan, businessman and security consultant, extraordinaire. This was his new life and although it hurt to leave the old, he would face the new with the same commitment, aptitude and dedication.

At the time of Bruce's resignation there were many that were deeply upset and affected by his resignation. The following excerpt is a post that was shared on his Facebook page by a Wendy Vorster-Redmond – a member of the Sandton CPF.

Bruce's departure is so seriously regretted at Sandton CPF. Bruce has been a stalwart in the fight against crime in our precinct over many, many years. The thugs know that they had little chance when moving into our space. As much as we are sorry to see Bruce go, we wish him everything of the very best for his future career. You've served your time mate - and done so with distinction. Nonetheless I am annoyed that Bruce leaves as a W/O without having being given the promotions he so richly deserved. Bruce is one of hundreds who have reached the proverbial "glass ceiling" in SAPS - how many more good officers - of all races - must we lose to the political nonsense that prevails and that precludes good people from ever reaching the top in their careers? Go well Bruce!!

April 3, 2015 at 14h38

Losing people of Bruce's calibre is a devastating loss to the country and our ability to fight crime. Taking all of our statistics into account, it is most certainly a loss that we can ill-afford. We should be holding onto people like Bruce, promoting people like Bruce and leading the way with people like Bruce. There certainly are other heroes in the police force that espouse Bruce's principles and ethics in the fighting of crime, both from the new order and from the old. I personally am to meet and work with a number of them in the years to come, however, the sad reality is that they're most definitely in the minority and there are not enough of them left in the services of our police force and they remain with the unenviable task of fighting against the tide and working with colleagues they are never truly sure of, nor can fully trust. It is a job I most certainly do not envy them of, but I do most certainly and without doubt, applaud and respect them for.

Causes And Origins

"I envision someday a great, peaceful South Africa in which the world will take pride, a nation in which each of many different groups will be making its own creative contribution."

Alan Paton, Cry the Beloved Country

One of the important aspects for me, and something I have spent many hours digesting, reading, researching and thinking of, is the "how and why" of it all.

Why is it that in a country that is surrounded by beautiful and peaceful environs, we should be surrounded by so much violence, in a country that not only functions on, but regales about "African Time" and a relaxed attitude to doing things "whenever" or "just now" – a term that for the rest of the world means with immediate effect but in South Africa we know it means … "in our own time!" With cultures that have bred terms such as UBUNTU and BOERE HOSPITALITY and when needing to stand together and show incredible unity and community support, like standing behind our rugby team, we have done so beyond expectation.

Should we not then be the most relaxed, the most hospitable and the most unified culture in the world? What is it that overrides all of these aspects and instead has created and developed this culture not just of crime, but VIOLENT crime and this acceptance that it is okay to violently hurt one another?

In order to really understand the problem and what started this journey in the first place, I started researching crime and violence in South Africa. In doing so, I am exposed to the superior minds of Rudoph Zinn, Thobane Mahlogonolo, Hennie Lochner, Annelieze Burgess, the Institute for Security Studies and The Centre for the Study of Violence and Reconciliation. Each of these offered extensive options in this regard and I was able to glean a far deeper understanding of why we are where we are, and what was the reason and cause behind the factors that initiated this journey that I, and my family, as well as many other South Africans, have found ourselves on.

It's here that I can expound on the many complexities and reasons behind this and there certainly are very understandable reasons why, however, in the interests of brevity I will instead talk only about the five primary reasons that I believe are the causes behind it and possibly, at least, could form initial starting blocks towards the correction of and mitigation of crime. These include:

- Breakdown of the family structure
- The normalisation of crime and violence in community upbringings
- The failure of systems
- The challenges faced by the South African Police Services
- Current levels of Emotion Intelligence, also known as EQ

∽

Quite simply, the breakdown of family structure as well as the normalisation of crime and violence is where one of South Africa's biggest challenges lies.

The first aspect to acknowledge and recognise, and something that has happened repetitively for many different reasons, is the breakdown of family structure. We know that many families were broken up across the country, with mothers and fathers having to move to the cities for work and children being left behind on the family homesteads in the rural villages. As a result, these children in the poorer sections of South African society have grown up either in a single parent family – most commonly with the male parent being absent through working on the mines, or in the cities and staying in urban townships or hostels, or in some situations with both-parent-absent households.

Social studies the world over have shown again and again, regardless of culture or colour, that children growing up without strong parental guidance, have deep emotional difficulties and more specifically, those growing up without male parenting are far more likely to turn to violence and alcoholism.

South Africa has been, and still is, ubiquitous with broken families and youngsters growing up in such situations. Even further to that, where many households saw the absence of both primary care-givers, and thus the children were left at home to be brought up by grand-parents or in some situations with older siblings who neither had the strength, ability nor authority to establish boundaries, develop emotional dependability and create a stable and loving environment for the children to grow up in.

Thus, we cannot but be surprised that we have had entire generations growing up in such conditions and that so many may have turned to violence in response to life's many challenges.

The next issue that is a major contributor towards the violent crime in South Africa is the normalisation of both crime and violence within many of our communities.

Speak to many of our leaders who grew up in townships and one of the first things they will tell you, is how there often was a total normalisation and acceptance of crime in the township areas and there were many opportunities where youngsters were in fact educated in the skills of crime and encouraged to do so – specifically if it was directed towards the wealthier, more affluent sectors of our society. In such instances, criminals were seen as heroes amongst their communities and they were lauded with a Robin Hood type status. This only inspired younger generations to follow in their footsteps and for the culture to continue to grow.

In addition to this, in the darker days of our history, our previous police force was focused more on the upholding of segregation laws in the townships and rural communities, than on combatting or preventing the growth of crime within. As such, by the time we entered the new dawn in South Africa, there was a strong crime culture already in existence.

Sadly, as we have continued to move through the new era of South African history, this factor has never been properly addressed and as a result, it has now grown so extensively that all South Africans, regardless of colour, culture or wealth, are now targets of this destructive attitude. Crime is everywhere, and in fact, the poorer communities are now seen as easier targets as they do not have the means or resources to protect themselves in any way. It only takes a small handful of criminals to destroy their own communities from within.

Sadly, it's also remnants of our darker past that has also endowed us with the extension of this problem – the high level of violence that accompanies crime in South Africa. As a starting point, I would like to request that we take the concept of racialism and hatred off the table, as where there may have been a few incidences that this may be clearly evident, the reality is that the cause is in fact a lot more complex than that.

Many of the youth 30 to 40 year ago, specifically in the urban townships, were regularly exposed to high levels of violence, whether it be from nightly raids by the police or conscripted soldiers, or violence as a result of social frustrations within the community itself. This has contributed to a desensitisation process towards violence and an acceptance of violence as a natural aspect in daily lives.

During violent episodes such as those previously conducted by police and/or the soldier raids, the youngsters also witnessed their parents being subjected to brutal and humiliating harassment, and as such, studies have proven that many lost respect for their parents during this process, and the parents in turn, lost the ability to discipline or control their children. This left large gangs of youngsters, that parents had no control over, rebelling against any form of authority they may have been exposed to, and as part of a natural process, the exploration of boundaries with violence was one of the tools used.

This in turn, has continued to not only exist, but to grow.

In more recent years, communities, frustrated with the levels of crime and the seemingly inability of the police to respond, have often taken justice into their own hands; often violently. Inevitably, if the police are not able to step in and mitigate the justice implemented, the criminal under attack is normally beaten to death or a state close to death. The justice meted out is brutal.

Having seen numerous videos of such "kangaroo courts" being implemented in the communities within our greater region, there is one aspect that continues to horrify me each and every time. Apart from the exceptional level of violence that is being implemented, I am always horrified to see the number of children either participating in, or simply standing by and watching, all that is going on.

What lessons are we teaching these children? Not only are they being desensitised to violence, they're also learning that violence is an acceptable means of dealing with one's problems.

In townships such as Diepsloot, there are groups of women who openly admit to running investigations on potential rapists and they will then go out and attack them. They start off by beating them repetitively as their intention is that when the rapist dies, he must die hurt. Once he is bloodied and beaten, they will then use petrol and tyres to burn them alive.

The irony about this situation is that these women state that their motivation behind what they do is to protect their children and to enable them to grow up in a safe and secure environment, when realistically, by exposing them to such actions, they are in fact in turn, potentially creating violent citizens of tomorrow, whose first reaction when faced with a problem will be to turn to violence themselves as a corrective measure.

Taking mob justice one step further, there is even a dance that has been created called "after tears". It's used to celebrate the successful killing of a rapist or criminal in the townships. Not only are children learning that violence is an acceptable means to deal with problems, they're also learning that killing someone, if the reason can be justified, is an event to be celebrated with music and dance. The messages we are sending these children and our South African citizens of tomorrow is frightening.

This issue in turn is then linked to the failure of our systems in either controlling crime, mitigating crime or bringing justice once it has been committed. It's through the failure of our systems that communities feel they have no other choice but to take matters into their own hands.

I have already highlighted a number of system failures, through sheer incompetence and maladministration in our story so far. However, as I have continued with my voluntary work and doing all I can to assist SAPS in the mitigation of crime in the Greater Lowveld, I have come across additional system issues that severely hinder our ability to fight crime or more directly, may contribute towards the causes of crime.

One of the biggest challenges we face, both for SAPS and for community response units, and the private sector involved in safety and security, is that South Africa is home to "a nation of unaccountables".

It is without fail that every single person that is ever arrested, will ALWAYS tell you that they do not have an ID book, nor know their ID number and are less than forthcoming with other info such as their date of birth... or even their true and proper name. Generally a slightly different version is supplied every time or at least a different spelling variation each and every time. Siphiso Chilwane may become Sipho Chiloane a month later. Razor had given the names Mandla Skosane and Moses Zwane during previous arrests. He also sometimes listed himself as Razor Zulu and at other times as Raymond Zulu. The concerning aspect is that criminals are initially recorded onto what is termed the Criminal Administrative System (CAS), based on the name supplied and linked to the specific incident concerned. This system, I believe, has great room for improvement.

During my research I wanted to get a list of all the crimes that Razor was linked to. A trusted friend in the police force assisted me by going into CAS. At present, the only way to link potential suspects is through their names or CAS numbers they have been charged with.

As CAS records are then completed on the back of the names supplied by the suspects themselves, one person may have six different records that are difficult, if not impossible to link to each other. If any ardent detective is able to find and create these links, it is not achieved without hours and hours of work trolling the system looking for potential links and connections. Time that could be far better spent with a more efficient system.

Sitting in the office for almost four hours, I was still unable to get a list of all Razor's crimes. Even more horrifying is that the few that I was able to find are grossly inaccurate. Mike's case number is allocated to Razor, however, it still only reflects a charge for house-breaking – nothing at all about murder, as well as no CAS number for the Paterson attack and nothing at all about the rape of Jamie. According to the state, my brother was never murdered, and Jamie never raped. If I were a new detective looking into who Razor is and what crimes he has been involved in, I would have no way of knowing that he has been found guilty on both murder and rape, let alone the many other cases that are just not showing up on his record.

Knowing that Razor was initially linked to 22 different cases and being aware of at least four that he has been successfully charged for, I should have easily been able to find this linked to his name. However, apart from Mike's case, which as I have stated is listed incorrectly, I could not find a single other known case linked to his profile.

I could extol on story after story of experiences I have had with the CAS system and trying to find basic information that should easily be available but is not or is improperly recorded. It is of major concern that, as with the prison systems I had experienced previously, this system that is supposed to control and coordinate the effective recording and linking of South Africa's most dangerous individuals can be so highly ineffective and inaccurate.

If we are truly to get on top of crime, it is my personal opinion that the current CAS system needs some serious reviewing and a concerted overhaul and improvement. And step number one, would be to link it to an automatic and immediate fingerprint scanner, that regardless of the name supplied, that particular individuals' previous records will be brought up immediately and can then be added to as is required in each situation.

∼

The failure of systems such as CAS are also closely linked to the next issue, which is as regards the challenges faced by the South African Police Services (SAPS).

The challenges faced by SAPS officials are extensive. Sadly, it seems that the large majority of police may be corrupt or tend towards corrupt behaviours. This being said, there are similarly a large number of highly committed, honest and hard-working policemen who want nothing more than to sort out the crime situation in South Africa. They live to catch criminals.

There are many from the same mould as our hero Bruce Mac Intosh. I myself work with a small number of them within the Limpopo and Mpumlanga regions. These men and women already have a hard-enough time within the realms of their basic job description. Combine this with having to conduct it all within ineffective systems and then to be doing so for a community and country that automatically presumes the worst of them, and criticises all they do and are, simply due to the uniform they wear, must be soul-destroying on all levels. I personally get very defensive when I hear comments of general negativity towards all SAPS members and I am very quick to extol facts on some of the hardest working men and women I have met.

Apart from working amongst corruption and alongside corrupt colleagues, SAPS are hugely under resourced and even more so, hugely understaffed, and overtaxed with work hours and expectations piled upon them.

We are faced with this fact often in our daily operations as Farmwatch.

There are many an occasion when requesting assistance, we are told that there are no officers nor vehicles available. Subsequently, there are many an occasion where a single officer is left sitting in the Community Service Centre – also known as the Charge Office on their own. In the last year in Hoedspruit alone, we have lost 17 police officers through death, resignation or transfer. Not one of these members has been replaced. Hoedspruit station is severely understaffed, and we know for a fact that this is not a unique situation nor the only station in the country facing this challenge.

It is on the backbone of this situation, that community organisations such as Farmwatch or Community Policing Forums that work with and support SAPS are invaluable. It is impossible for the small handful of staff to man a station, respond to incidents, attend court, complete admin and paperwork and chase up on criminals, leads or suspects and fight one of the highest crime rates in the world. It is physically impossible.

These challenges faced by our police today, severely affects their ability to effectively control crime and is without doubt creating a landscape that allows for criminals to successfully hone and develop their skills. Research the world over has shown that the younger a person enters into a criminal career and the longer they are therefore able to enact on this career, the more violent they become as they progress – yet another contributor towards violence in our country. Therefore, by allowing crime to continue as is currently the case in South Africa, we are inadvertently allowing for more and more violence to develop and for criminals to become more and more skilled at what they do

Tied in together with the lack of manpower at the stations and police effectiveness, is the lack of resources. I'm not only referring to operational resources required for daily implementation, but I'm also referring to various forms of technology that could assist our police force to catch up with the rest of the world in the 21st century.

There are many occasions where our police do not have stock of DNA swabs to run on their arrested suspects as per the new DNA law; in the greater Lowveld area, there is only one breathalyser to be shared amongst nine police stations; and on a larger scale, there are often no vehicles available to assist police officers in effecting an arrest.

Walking into a police station it is very evident that available technology is way out of date if existent at all. There is so much phenomenal technology that could assist either the officers on the beat, or the detectives trying to chase up links, leads and suspects, yet sadly there has been no move in South Africa to bring our stations up to this level. Further to resources, this can be applied to structures and facilities as well. As already described, the majority of police stations in South Africa do not have proper facilities to run identity parades and thus result in some of the horrors I have discussed earlier in this book. I could write a chapter alone on identity parades and what victims have had to go through supposedly to assist in the successful identification and conviction of their attackers, which as a result, have sadly all failed.

Technology and infrastructure of our police stations need some serious attention. Committed SAPS members work twice as hard trying to implement strategies manually and without the structures, facilities and beneficial technology that could make not only their jobs easier, but certainly a lot more efficient.

We as a community organisation do whatever we can to assist our SAPS and supply them with resources where possible and where required and assist them with the use of technology that enables them to increase their levels of impact and effectiveness wherever possible. The effects of this input are already very visible to see and are continuing to grow each day, not just in the resultant arrest records, but also clearly visible in the renewed enthusiasm and commitment of the SAPS members we work with.

One sector of our SAPS that is possibly the most advanced and to a certain extent is supplied with and does make use of advanced technological resources is the Local Criminal Record Centre (LCRC) units. This is the term used for our forensics department who come out to a crime scene to collect DNA, fingerprints, and other forms of evidence, as well as photograph and record all details of the scene. However, here too we have a challenge.

The challenge here is how these units are established. LCRC offices are based at a cluster level. This means that one LCRC office may serve five to ten police stations within a cluster. Our LCRC office for example is based in Phalaborwa, but also serves communities as far as Giyani. Phalaborwa alone is 80km way from us and Giyani is almost 200kms away. This one office may have to visit a scene in one town and then have to rush to another on the opposite side of the region. As a result, we often find that we may need to sit on a crime scene for up to five hours trying to protect the scene and protect the evidence. Apart from being exceptionally difficult to do, specifically in a public setting or a place of business, it also means that often evidence at crime scenes is destroyed before it can be properly collected and processed. Or even worse, evidence is not collected at all.

We all know that evidence is crucial in the successful identification and conviction of a suspect, the collection of evidence should be given primary status and should be collected and recorded as soon as possible to avoid destruction or contamination thereof.

We may have laws in place now to allow for the collection of and processing of evidence such as DNA and other vital clues, but the implementation process on the ground, is severely hindering its ultimate effectiveness.

∽

The last cause I want to bring in, once again goes back to social issues and not just who we are as a nation, but who we are as a species. No matter which way we like to spin things, there is but one reality ... Human beings are an emotional species.

Emotions are what makes us tick, emotions are what makes us thrive and strive, emotions are behind everything that we do and everything that we are, and the ability to recognise and deal with emotions is what makes one person more successful than another.

This ability to deal with our emotions is known as Emotional Intelligence or EQ (Emotional Quotient) and has been stated to be far more of an indicating factor towards success in life, than IQ (Intelligence Quotient).

Emotional Intelligence was first written about by psychologist and science journalist, Daniel Goleman in 1995, in his book, *Emotional Intelligence - Why It Can Matter More Than IQ*. It was in this book that he first introduced the world to the concept that an ability to understand and manage emotions greatly increases our chances of success.

Individuals with developed EQ show characteristics such as being able to think about their feelings; have the ability to control their thoughts; they are able to receive and benefit from criticism; they are authentic to themselves; they keep their commitments; they help others; they have the ability to discern between what they need and what they want; and finally, the big one here, they are able to show empathy.

In contrast, an individual with low EQ levels are easily stressed; they have limited emotional vocabulary; they have difficulty asserting themselves; they make assumptions quickly and defend them excessively; they hold grudges; they often feel misunderstood; they are not aware of what their "triggers" are and how to deal with them; they blame others for how they feel and they are easily offended.

With a bit of a better understanding of what Emotional Intelligence is and is not, it can be a little easier understood as to how the lack of EQ may lead to maladjustment and inability to achieve desired goals and there are a number of research studies where the relationship between low levels of EQ and crime has been investigated and direct correlations have been found. Studies done on criminals in jails all show to have very low EQ levels.

Research interviews revealed that the internal process of self-reflection instigates an increased state of self-awareness. Self-awareness is the foundation for developing responsible decision-making skills and the motivation to desist crime.

Looking at EQ within South Africa as a culture, one of the first things we may notice is that many of South Africa's cultures are paternalistic. By this we refer to societies where men are considered to be in charge and in control; and are required to be tough and brave and are not encouraged to show any feminine characteristics such as emotions or feelings. Thus, in both black and white cultures "men need to be men" and are not allowed to cry because "real men don't cry".

This expectation that a man has to be strong and not be allowed to show emotion, has resulted in millions of our men not being taught to explore, nor experience their emotions, which in turn results in a diminished EQ. This characteristic is in fact prevalent in many cultures around the world, specifically where women are considered weaker or inferior species, and thus it's not unique to South Africa. However, it's most certainly highly prevalent in this country and, through its ability to diminish EQ, it can be a strong contributor towards the crime.

Without a culture or a home base where this is taught and encouraged in both men and women, it can have devastating results socially. The wonderful thing about EQ is that where IQ is a genetic trait, EQ is in fact a learned trait; and even more encouraging, it can be learnt and developed at any age. It is never too late to become Emotionally Intelligent and thus more socially and emotionally successful.

Increasing the general EQ of the nation, can in itself lead to a more stable and secure society, something we are greatly in need of in South Africa.

Filling In The Gaps

"It is not 'forgive and forget' as if nothing wrong had ever happened, but 'forgive and go forward,' building on the mistakes of the past and the energy generated by reconciliation to create a new future."

Alan Paton, Cry the Beloved Country

Looking back on the small amount of information I could find on Razor and George and how they grew up, I can see many of these theories and issues that I came across in my research can be reflected within their experiences too.

Both of them grew up without a father figure. In Razor's case his father was "there" but quite clearly wanted nothing to do with his children. He had, in fact, violently rejected them from his life. In addition, the only male figure Razor had in his early life, his uncle in the Eastern Cape, had also rejected them violently.

In George's case, his father lived and worked in another part of the country, and as their extreme poverty restricted the ability to travel at all, he grew up never knowing his father at all.

Both of these situations, according to international studies, have the ability to lead towards the propensity for violence.

Similarly, both were subject to extreme poverty, with many nights spent on the streets or going to bed hungry or with just one piece of bread in their bellies. This would have initiated a basic need for survival and where there may have been no other option but to turn towards crime as a solution to ward off starvation.

Similarly, a lack of community and family structure and stability are evident. Alexandra Township was (is still) a maelstrom of people, cultures and chaos. There is no tribal authority to lay down the law, people of different traditions and tribes come from all over the country and are squashed into overflowing streets and shacks. There is no sense of belonging, sense of purpose, nor a sense of identity. Thus, Alexandra Township comprises a crowded group of individuals with no single purpose and direction but purely focusing individually on the need to survive and carve out a living. This was the chaos that Razor found himself living in after they had fled from Natal. George was born directly into this chaos and knew no different from the start. It was inevitable, that with no alternative guidance, nor teachings, they would turn to the streets and the gangs within, to find some sense of belonging and sense of purpose in order to "find themselves" as all young people are prone to do as they start to hit the double digits of age.

Having turned to the streets at a very young age, and specifically for Razor having witnessed his uncle's reaction to his mother's decision to move to Natal and then having to witness his father's reaction on their arrival in Natal, they were both exposed to violence as a general course of action from a young age. They subsequently would have been desensitised to its effects and occurrence as well as having been taught that it was an "acceptable" means of dealing with one's problems.

Similarly, having turned to the streets at a very young age, and having started their criminal "careers" as very young boys – Razor was as young as 13 when he started, they have had plenty time and many, many years to expand on their experience. And, as studies have shown, the longer they are involved in crime and the earlier they start their criminal careers, the more likely they are to turn to violence. With each of them with as much as 15 to 20 years of crime under their belts at the time of coming into our lives it is no wonder that they had extended to the levels of violence that they had. They had had many years to get there.

Looking at this all, it is very evident to me how both Razor and George had developed as they had and made the life choices that they made. Conditions in their lives strongly contributed towards this downfall.

I am in no way trying to make excuses for Razor or George as ultimately, they still had a choice on what direction their lives would take and their subsequent journeys are a compilation of their own life choices. For it is a freedom that we all have, it is still up to us each individually to decide on the kind of person he or she wants to be, and on the impact, we want to leave on this world.

I have met some of the most remarkably inspirational people who have come out of the exact same situations, but who have a moral compass that can only be admired and a sense of self, that can lead to nothing but success. One of the only differences I can find between them and someone like Razor or George, is that they had wise counsel, guidance and teachings from a parent or mentor that they had constant contact with. Teachings that not only enabled them to build their moral compass but also allowed them to develop a level of emotional intelligence that in turn gave them the self-belief and self-confidence to rise above everything around them.

My purpose, as I've said before, is not to make excuses for Razor and George. I'm trying to understand the path that led to the shattered lives of the Thomsons, the Patersons and the Redmonds. And, of course, for all South Africans that have been affected by crime. One can only truly heal and move past something if one is able to fully understand and comprehend all that has happened as well as why it may have happened. Understanding is an important starting block towards healing.

The Magic Words; VOD. Just What Does It Entail?

> *"Meneer, said the captain, if man takes unto himself God's right to punish, then he must also take upon himself God's promise to restore."*
>
> **Alan Paton, Cry the Beloved Country**

With the intention of wanting to get to know and understand the Razor Gang, I had started on a campaign to try and get to meet them, to sit down and talk to them, and to hear from them what had resulted in them entering our lives. It was again time for me to focus on arranging VOD (Victim-Offender Dialogue).

VOD, the three letters that I had learned during my first visit to Sun City, seemed to carry a magic all of their own and could change a person's acceptance of your purposes and presence at the prison, immediately.

When looking into our justice system, on paper, it all looks wonderful. Progressive theories and objectives are outlined; restorative as opposed to retributive processes are to be implemented and attention towards healing of the victim is prioritised. However, as we have already outlined while looking inside our prisons, the reality is totally different.

It is however a small comfort, for whatever that may be worth at this stage, that in theory, potential foundation work is in place.

In documentation on the VOD process, the Department of Correctional Services states that, "It fully understands its place and role in the new corrections" – and includes a more focused paradigm in which partnerships with families, communities and the state and all other stakeholder are of vital importance. Additionally it is convinced that rehabilitation and the prevention of repeat offending are best achieved through correction and development as opposed to punishment and treatment and lastly, their approach to rehabilitation is based on the confidence that every human being is capable of change and transformation if offered the opportunity and the necessary resources.

The process of VOD is not necessarily focused on forgiveness and reconciliation (that's up to the victim), nor is it a requirement for parole. VOD is not a settlement process and neither a counselling nor psychotherapy situation. Its purpose is to provide an opportunity for both victims and offenders to discuss the offence, to express their feelings, for victims to get answers to their questions and for victims and offenders to develop mutually acceptable restitutions plans that address the harm caused by crime.

VOD can be initiated by either the victim or the offender and similarly can be refused by either party. It's an entirely voluntary process from both sides.

As this process has only been around for about six years at the time of writing, it is still a fairly new process and is not known by many. Obviously, a primary factor and requirement in the initiation of this process is for the identification of a perpetrator and the successful arrest and conviction thereafter.

Unfortunately, statistically only 6% of our murders are successfully prosecuted (read between the lines, you have a 94% chance of getting away with murder in South Africa), thus most victims will never have the opportunity to face their attackers in a VOD process. However, for anyone who is, "fortunate" (I use that term lightly for obvious reasons) enough to have had their perpetrator both successfully identified, arrested and prosecuted, and if one feels they have the strength to sit opposite such perpetrators without quite literally "losing their cool", then this is a process that I would recommend.

There is without doubt a certain amount of resolution to be obtained by sitting around the table with one's attackers, or the attackers of one's family as in my case. Talking through all that occurred, getting unanswered questions answered and having the opportunity to let them know what kind of an impact their attack has had on yourself or the primary victims and extended family of such an attack can be of tremendous assistance.

Even if you are not successful in increasing (or creating as it may be) any levels of empathy in the offenders towards your position, the simple fact that you have had the opportunity to at least try to do so, can be very healing and helpful in itself.

Heading Back To Sun City

"There is only one way in which one can endure man's inhumanity to man and that is to try, in one's own life, to exemplify man's humanity to man."

Alan Paton, Cry the Beloved Country

In February 2018, 15 months after my initial visit to Sun City to initiate meetings with Razor and with George, I start my phone calls in earnest again. I call Mrs Mabala, the kind and accommodating social worker responsible for them, and that Mrs Magakwe had put me in touch with. I request the possibilities of VOD once again. Mrs Mabala knows exactly who I am the minute I mention my name and she immediately recalls who it is I am trying to see. Bearing in mind it has been at least eight to ten months since I last called, this gives me the idea that either she has a phenomenal memory or, there are not many people requesting VOD, making me something unique and possibly worth remembering.

Having agreed to a date with Mrs Mabala, she then refers me to an auxillary social worker by the name of Tumiso Malapeng. It is his job to make final arrangements and assessments for the impending

VOD session. I have a meeting booked with him at the Department of Correctional Services offices in downtown Johannesburg – an area of our country where I feel most like a "fish-out-of-water". I would rather face a wild animal – any wild animal, head on and face to face, before having to face the traffic, congestion, one-way streets, the constant feel of impending danger, and the reminders of destitution that are all so common in this part of town. The only thing I hold onto is that this is not too far from where Mike was working, for Computershare, at the time of his murder and thus would have been taking a similar drive into town himself – a drive that had so many things been different that night, and in our country, he would possibly still be making to this day.

I arrive at the offices and phone Tumiso. He meets me outside the offices so that he can direct me to the underground parking. From the minute I meet him I'm immediately relaxed with him. He is a very personable individual.

We park the car and head up into the bowels of the building. There is very little else that can be used to describe the building itself other than being a typical government-style building, looking very worn and old, with 70s style linoleum flooring, off-white walls and certainly no intention to inspire anyone within, whether full time employer or visitor alike.

The elevator does not work properly on his floor, so we have to take it one floor above and then take the stairs down a floor to get to where his office is located.

He unlocks the door and we walk in. There are two desks in his office and five different chairs, and piles and piles of folders, dockets and paperwork neatly piled in some semblance of order, everywhere that piling, not filing, can be done.

Other than that, there is very little else. No basic office equipment nor stationery requirements are visible, as one would expect in an office of this nature. There is no computer, nor filing cabinet to help keep all the paperwork in order. There is, however, a telephone on the desk but I note amusingly that the telephone cable is wrapped tightly around the phone, with the connection plug dangling down the side of the desk on the side that I am sitting. There's definitely going to be no calls made from that telephone.

Tumiso sees me looking at the phone. He shakes his head and says, "We don't have working phone lines in all the offices. I had to go to one of the offices in the floor above just to call you."

He then points to a neat pile of folders standing about as high as three full reams of paper, in the right-hand corner of his desk. "These are all cases where the offenders are requesting VOD sessions with their victims. It's my job to try and track down the victims, make contact with them and see if they would be willing to sit down with the offenders for a VOD session. It's a very difficult thing to do when I don't have basic resources such as a computer or telephone," he tells me.

He shows me a far smaller pile against the wall adjacent to his desk of potentially completed cases. I can only imagine how much quicker, easier and successful his job would be if he were to be supplied with the correct resources. Once again, my mind boggles at the very idea that in today's age, our government can have any sort of an office for any reason without at least a working telephone and a basic computer. Surely these are standard necessities for any kind of job to be done. I am fairly confident that the majority of our Ministers are not even aware of the lack of resources in offices that may be considered as insignificant as an auxiliary social worker within the Department of Correctional Services.

Tumiso and I immediately fall into a comfortable conversation, despite the real reason behind what it is I am there to do.

As part of the VOD process, it's Tumiso's responsibility to meet with victims beforehand. First, to assess their state of mind and preparedness for meeting the offenders face on, and second, if required, to initiate a level of counselling and preparation for the impending session.

He starts off asking me a few questions to assess where I am emotionally. I immediately respond with questions of my own with the intention of assessing his perspective on a lot of the issues that I have already discussed in this book. There is immediately a lot of agreement as well as alternative viewpoints put forward in exploration of some of the theories and thoughts.

I also ask him what his thoughts are about criminals like Razor and George, and whether they too can be considered victims of our defunct society, our collapsing systems, and of their upbringing in general.

He agrees with me as in just about every case with criminals, there is a similar story behind them. However, he states, that this does not take responsibility away from them as at the end of the day, it's still their own choices that have brought them to this point.

He explains to me what he means by this "I grew up in poverty as well and I grew up with very similar circumstances to them" he says, "however," he continues, "in all my levels of desperation, I have never felt the need nor desire to turn to crime. If anything, it just pushed me harder to succeed and to make something of my life" he concludes.

I ask him a few more questions with the intention of finding out what in his life may have given him the inner strength and ability to do so. He starts talking about his mother and he says something to me that immediately lets everything else fall into place.

"Regardless of our situation," he says, "my mother used to tell us one thing only," he continues, "she has always expressed the need to love." If I came home upset with anyone or had witnessed anything violent or traumatic, her standard response to me was, "You just have to love them my son. It's not your job to be angry with them or to hate them. If they're truly bad people, give them enough of their own rope and they will hang themselves. It's not up to you to do it for them. In the meantime, all you need to do is just love them for who they are and who they can be. Love them all, try and understand them all, and if you can, rather try and help them than respond in anger towards them."

Wow, what an amazing mother and what wise words to teach a child.

The result of her loving guidance can be seen in the man today. Looking back on the small amount of information that I have found out about Razor and George, I have no doubt that each of their mothers loved them in their own way. However, what potentially was missing, was the ability to talk about emotions and to explore what they may have been feeling and learning the ability that they could in fact choose what to feel in a situation - you can choose to react in violence or you can choose to respond with love and understanding. Introducing one to their own emotions is nothing less than wise counsel and guidance that could have helped to guide them and direct them through the quagmire of hopelessness and desperation in the overcrowded, poverty ridden townships and rural areas.

Through introducing one to their own emotions and control of one's own emotions, you are inadvertently building crucial social foundations such as EQ.

Either, from not receiving the same guidance themselves, or possibly with all they had had to experience and survive in their lives and trying to raise children in squalid situations, neither George, nor Razor's mothers would have had their own resources, emotionally or physically, to offer the nurturing guidance that would be required to get someone successfully through such a difficult childhood. These mothers may have been so overwhelmed with the struggle to supply physical needs to their children that the emotional needs were overlooked.

Subsequently, if George and Razor were to raise their own children, they too would potentially not have the resources, as they were never given nor taught such things themselves, and thus they too in turn would not be able to pass this onto their children, and so the cycle continues.

༄

I wake up early the following morning and suddenly realise I am filled with more dread at the thought of the peak-hour city traffic I will have to face to get to Sun City, than I am at the thought of facing Razor and George. I giggle as I realise just what a rural recluse I have become.

I meet Tumiso at the Southgate Mall and together we drive into the prison complex so that I can get inside with relatively little effort and problems. We head directly towards Medium C prison and I am immediately able to recognise where I am from my initial visit 18 months earlier. We park the car and head towards the inner security gate that I had walked through all those months previously. At the gate we have to fill in a register and while doing that I hear a voice behind me. "Debby?"

"Yes," I reply.

"It's Mrs Mabala," she replies

"Aaaah, great to finally meet you face-to-face," I say to her giving her a hug.

Mrs Mabala is the original social worker that I have been talking to all these months in trying to arrange this. I point to Tumiso and I say, "Thank you for putting me in touch with him. This is a good man you have here."

"I'm glad to hear that," she replies.

Once we are all signed in and through the large security gate, we head down towards a building on the side of the large courtyard I had walked across on my previous visit all those months ago. Heading through thick security doors one-at-a-time, we head into the building. We go through a maze of steps, corridors and different floors before we eventually reach a boardroom. It's not a very large room but is comfortably equipped with a large table in the middle and at least 16 chairs around it. There is coffee and tea on the side.

As we walk into the room, I see George sitting on the far side of the table. My stomach jolts. Linda, the social worker in charge, and walking me in with Mrs Mabala sees him too. She quickly instructs the two warders with him to move him out of the room until all is ready. She turns and apologises to me and asks if I am okay.

She immediately sets to organising the room exactly how she wants it. She tells me to come and sit down at one of the seats in the middle section of the table. "I am going to make them both sit there," she says, pointing directly to the two chairs opposite me. "I want you to be able to look at them and watch them when they talk. Are you okay with that?" she asks. I nod my head and sit down.

As I am sitting there and waiting, the enormity of what I am about to do suddenly hits me and I have to work really hard to keep my heart out of my throat and to keep my head together for this. I am not allowed to write or record anything and so I keep telling myself I need to remember every little detail that occurs and is said, and for that I need to keep my head as sane and clear as possible.

I pull myself together just as George and Razor are both led into the room and made to sit in the two seats opposite me. They're surrounded by five warders. On my side of the table, I am flanked by an array of social workers, auxiliary social workers and prisoner advocates. There are 14 people in the room.

Linda asks everyone to introduce themselves and what their role is in today's session. Linda starts proceedings by saying she's going to ask George and Razor to start and to give them the opportunity to first tell me exactly what happened that night, from start to end, in their own words.

George starts. He's clearly very nervous, but he runs through everything he can recall and exactly how it all went down. There is nothing new nor startling that he tells me, apart from the mention that in targeting the house next door, they had originally been given information from the domestic worker that there was lots of money in the house. Once they had robbed them, they were supposed to share the money with her and with her son.

He also mentioned that Tofile (Mzi) was actually far more involved than we had initially been told. It seems that Mzi is a taxi driver and is the person that many of the domestic workers approach with information on a potential target and he will then contact Razor and Thabang and they then put a team together for the job. Between Razor and George there are nine different names that they rattle off of which I know them all, bar two. Mzi, it seems, is responsible for getting all the information in to assist with planning and then he uses his taxi to drop them off at a target's house. He does not hang around at all, as the plan is usually for them to steal the victim's vehicle to leave the scene.

George starts off his story by telling me that as soon as Mike approached them hiding in the bushes in the courtyard, as he was emptying out the leaf-litter basket, they immediately told him to cooperate, "But, he would not cooperate," George says. I feel my blood starting to boil as it seems that George is trying to put blame on Mike. I sit calmly allowing him to continue, my face a mask and hiding what I am really feeling inside. Truthfully, I would love to reach across this table right now and slap him as hard as I can for that one sentence alone. But of course, I don't. He tells me that Mike then threw him in the pool and started drowning him. He was close to passing out. During this time, he stabbed Mike again and again. He shouted for help in the midst of the scuffle and during one of the short interludes he managed to get his head above water, and he saw his friend Thabang come outside and shoot Mike first in the shoulder and then in the head.

There are a few facts there that I immediately recognise as untrue, however, I let it ride for now. Razor interrupts and asks if he can go to the bathroom. Two warders take him outside. I quickly turn to George and I say to him, "George, while Razor is not here, please tell me who really shot Mike? When you were first arrested and you confessed, you said that Razor shot Mike, but since Thabang was killed, suddenly now the blame is put on him. If you are too scared to tell me in front of Razor, then please tell me now, who was it?" I plead.

At that moment Razor walks back into the room and the opportunity is lost. "Thabang shot him," George says and looks down at his hands while he's talking.

Once George has completed his story, it is Razor's turn. Just as in our first meeting, Razor's behaviour is very dramatic. There is a lot of hand movement, covering his face with his hands, throwing his head on the table into his folded arms whenever I asked him a pertinent question and, there are even tears. I take all this in, trying to look carefully at every nuance, to assess whether it is at all genuine or simply the flashings of a psychopath. It's difficult to say.

While I am sitting there listening to both of their stories, I find the same thought going through my mind again and again. Out of all the millions of different faces that Mike would have seen and come across throughout the thirty-nine years of his life, these two faces before me, were the last two faces, that he would ever have laid his eyes upon. These two faces were the primary focus of the very last thing he ever saw on this planet. This is a portion of his last moments on earth, and these two faces were the cause of his last moments on earth. I find my emotions totally overwhelming me at one point and have to work really hard to swallow my heart that is currently sitting in my throat. I manage to do so and can continue to listen with a mask of control on my face.

Razor starts off his story a little differently; he first goes into a detailed explanation of picking the different individuals from the gang up at different places, some from Alexandra Township, others from Diepsloot. He also mentions that there were seven of them altogether at one stage. He then decided that there were too many, so he sent those without weapons, home. This left four and Mzi, who was to drop them off.

Razor also explains how they had targeted the house next door but were not able to get inside directly, and so jumped the wall into Mike's garden. He also explained how they were hiding in the bushes when Mike walked outside, for what he thought was to empty out an ashtray.

It had obviously all happened so quickly for him as well that he had not really been able to take note of what was really going on. He, however, said that he rushed up to Mike first and told him to cooperate. Contrary to George, Razor mentions a number of times that Mike did cooperate. However, when they told him to lie on the floor, he refused, and this is when the fight started. According to Razor, Thabang was the first to approach Mike with the gun in hand, along with George, and in the meantime, Razor was the first to rush inside.

He suddenly mentions that Thabang had also cocked his gun at Mike, presumably in an attempt to scare him and to show that they meant business, but the gun jammed and Thabang was left trying to sort out his weapon for a while. According to Razor, this is when Mike then pushed George into the pool. Once Thabang had sorted his weapon out he shot Mike, first in the shoulder and then in the head.

Razor continues to explain how he then heard someone shouting "Razor, Razor, Razor." He came running out of the house to find George climbing out of the pool and Mike left at the bottom. Thabang was seemingly very scared and unhappy that he had had to shoot Mike … apparently! Thabang wanted them all to leave the scene immediately. However, Razor said that they could not call Mzi back because if anyone saw him in the area again, they may get suspicious so instead they need to take what they can and use Mike's car to get away. This was his story as he relayed it.

Immediately I realised, that even though it was requested at the start, and even though they had been through days of preparations leading up to this, They were still too afraid to speak the truth and were still using Thabang as the scapegoat.

Having spent hours and hours scouring over every detail in Mike's case file, studying the crime scene photos, going through the autopsy and ballistic reports and reading statement after statement from first responders, to suspects, witnesses and of Lorna and the children themselves, there are a few pieces of key evidence that I recognise immediately that do not match up with either story.

As we never had a court case nor trial in the end, there is no way that Razor nor George would even be aware of its existence within Mike's docket, so presumably feel fairly safe with the stories they have concocted.

The first is that a single unspent 9mm cartridge was found next to the pool. I must add that it was found by Allan. The horde of first responders missed it whilst wondering aimlessly through the house. He pointed the cartridge out to the police immediately. This would make sense and would fit in with the story about Thabang's gun jamming when he tried to cock the gun in order to threaten Mike. However, further forensic evidence clearly states that both the bullets that were found in Mike during the autopsy, behind his lung and in his skull, were the unusual calibre of a 7.65mm weapon. In reading through all of the arrest statements I also noticed that on Razor's second arrest, he had in his possession a 7.65mm weapon. Thus, it would make perfect sense to presume that it was in fact Razor who shot Mike.

Additionally, looking at the description of the trajectory of the bullet into the lung, it would make better sense that this bullet was shot from more or less an equal height, possibly with Mike bending ever so slightly down at the time to throw out the leaf litter basket as there is a slight downward trajectory from the right clavicle to just below the trapezius muscle at the back, but certainly not from an elevated position such as one would be, if standing on the edge of the pool shooting down on someone below.

Similarly, the forensic photographs also clearly show the bullet wound being on his right side just below the armpit, which would have been impossible to get to if he was already in the pool with his arms downwards while attempted to drown George – his arms must have been in a raised position either in an attacking or a defensive mode motion.

Additionally, it's described and can also be seen on the forensic photographs, that there was powder tattooing at the bullet-hole entry, and this too would only be possible for a close range shot which would not have been possible for someone standing up on the edge of the pool.

The headshot, however, clearly shows this elevated trajectory with the path being described as "downwards and backwards" towards the back of the skull.

Based on this, and having to then read between the lines of what George and Razor were telling me, I can only assume that what really happened was the following:

They were all hiding in the bushes as described when Mike came out to backwash the pool. Knowing Mike, who was always level-headed, and not a naturally aggressive person, if he automatically went into fight mode, there would have to have been something that brought this on.

I suspect he may have bent down slightly or was leaning forward towards the bushes to empty out the leaf-litter basket when Razor first came rushing out with his 7.65mm weapon in his hand. Mike may have raised his hands immediately when asking, "Hey what do you want?" or they may have been slightly raised while he was throwing out the leaf-litter basket. This would have exposed the section of his body just under his right armpit. This first shot into the side of his chest most definitely would have done the trick and put Mike into an automatic fight mode response. I suspect that Razor then rushed past Mike and into the house to prevent Lorna from calling for help or reacting in any way if she had just heard the gunshot outside. Bongani presumably was rushing into the house with Razor.

Thabang and George remained outside, and in trying to now stop Mike who had gone into attack mode and was possibly hitting one or both of them already, Thabang would have then tried to cock his weapon in order to give Mike a fright and threaten him with another shot, or with the intention of even using it if need be.

Thabang's weapon then jammed and while he was trying to sort it out, an unspent 9mm cartridge was dropped to the floor and this also then gave Mike the chance to retaliate and sent Thabang flying. Presumably, this was then followed by a rush and attack from George, who Mike then threw into the pool and jumped in after him.

Coming around again, Thabang would have seen Mike drowning George and as he was unable to assist with his weapon, then possibly called out to Razor to come and help. Bongani at this stage, was already tying up the family inside, so Razor could then come outside with his weapon, see what was going on, and give off the final shot. As the bullet entry is from the front left of his skull down towards the back righthand side, Mike would have been facing him at the time and Razor's face looking down at him in the pool, may have been the last thing he ever saw.

This was one of the main thoughts running through my brain as I initially sat in front of these two and listened to all they had to say.

From all the evidence that was on the scene, together with what I have been able to piece together from the reports and statements in his docket, as well as from my knowledge of my brother and how we would typically have responded to such a situation and of course with reading between the lines of what both George and Razor were, and were not telling me, this I believe to be the most likely scenario of what actually happened.

If it were to have happened the way George described, then the trajectory for the shot in the lung would have been wrong, it would also be impossible for there to have been powder tattooing on his chest. If Thabang was shooting down on him in the pool, as they're still insisting happened, this would have been an impossibility.

Similarly, if it had happened the way that Razor explained, then how does he explain the two different calibre bullets – Razor's story is that the only gun that was fired that night was Thabang's however, the unspent cartridge next the pool was a 9mm and the shots fired off at Mike were a 7.65mm calibre.

I truly believe, where George was definitely responsible for the 14 stab wounds in all parts of Mike's chest, Razor was without doubt responsible for both of his gunshot wounds. And, where the second shot may be argued to have been in "self-defence" of George who was about to lose his own life under Mike's hands in the pool, the first was without doubt not, and was an immediate and instant shot in order to gain power and superiority in an unplanned situation.

Evidently, once Thabang had been killed during an armed robbery in Fourways, it was much easier to pin everything on him as he's obviously not around to defend himself. The dead clearly can't argue back.

This, however, seems to be the story that George and Razor are now going to stick to and somewhere deep inside I need to come to terms with that, and just hold onto what I have been able to piece together with the evidence supplied and just be happy within myself that that is more than likely the real story. Ultimately, we will never know.

Once they have had their say as to what had happened that night, Linda then turns to me and says, "Debby it's now your turn, what questions do you have for them, and what do you want to say to them?"

Suddenly my mind freezes. I have prepared for this moment for so long and suddenly, without my notes, I am at a loss as to where to start.

I start speaking and find my voice is weak and shaky, I stop, take a deep breath and try again. This time I am able to say, "Well where do I start, how do I even start getting to the bottom of all you have done?" I swallow hard and continue, "Start by telling me about yourselves. I want to know who you are, where you came from and what made you turn to crime in the first place."

They both seem very comfortable to answer this question and start talking without much prompting required.

They tell me very broken stories both of which I have tried to capture in the first two chapters of this book. I would obviously have liked to have spent much longer time with them, if not days, in trying to find out more and get more stories on their childhoods and find out about experiences that may have affected them and the choices they made, however, I know this is not going to be possible and I have to make the most with this limited opportunity I have been given.

One question leads to another. I ask them what made them plead guilty in the end. George looks away and out the window as he answers. "I know I did that thing and it was wrong," he says quietly, "I had to face it now."

I turn to look at Razor for his response. Once again, he starts off dramatically. He puts his head on his folded arms on the table and sits there for a while until Linda says to him, "Razor, please answer the question."

He looks up at me, tears streaming down his face. "That boy," he says. "When we did that thing, he was manyana," (Zulu word meaning small) he says grouping the tips of his fingers together and moving his hands downwards to indicate something small. "When I saw him next, he was big." Now indicating with a flat hand, palm facing down and moving his hand upwards towards something of height. "I realised then that I had made this boy grow up without his father," he said.

I realised he was talking about Nick and when he had seen him once again at the initial court case, the one with the missing paperwork. Little did we realise at the time, what an effect that very moment would have on Razor and his decision to plead guilty. And, that while he stared at us with his usual aggression and arrogance, deep within there was turmoil and confusion of his own emotions on the go.

Razor continues to explain to me, "I did a very bad thing and I deserve to be in jail." The tears are still welling up in his eyes and tumbling down his cheeks, yet somehow, there is so much drama in all he says and how he's saying it, that I am battling to feel the reality in it all. He just seems to be playing this game really well. I constantly ask myself if he's just telling me what he thinks I want to hear, or does he genuinely mean this. It all just seems too dramatic and too "correct". However, on the flip-side of the coin, I remind myself, that after nine years of aggression and arrogance, he did suddenly change and do a 180 degree turn that caught everyone off guard. Possibly there may be something genuine within it all. I will never truly know.

I mention the other cases that they have been involved in. I mention the Patersons, we talk a little about that, and Razor tells me the same story that he had told me eighteen months ago. This time he gives further background to it all. He tells me that he had always been very clear with his crew that no one was allowed to rape or murder. If this sort of thing happened, the police would be more adamant in investigating and tracking them down. If it was "just" an armed robbery, it would not be given the same focus and attention. (Even the criminals are aware of this focus of our police force and how far too many crimes are considered "ok" if no one is severely injured or killed.)

He had always made it very clear that if any of them raped anyone, he would shoot them there on the spot. Possibly now, after the incident with Mike and murder had now been committed, he was less compelled to stick to his own rules. Thus after the ordeal that he put Jamie through, and after climbing out through the bathroom window and meeting up with the others outside by the vehicles, he then put his gun on the vehicle bonnet and told them to just "shoot me now as I have done a terrible thing".

After telling this story he turns to Linda and says to her in Zulu. "It seems that she knows that family, please tell her to ask them to come here too, I want to say sorry and speak to that girl as well."

Raising her eyebrows, Linda turns to me and repeats his words to me in English. I just stare at him in response, trying my best to get a proper reading on what he's really feeling at the moment and if all of this is genuine.

"Why did you do it then?" I ask him.

Again, he gives me the same answer as 18 months ago, accompanied by the same dramatic hand movements and covering of his face, "I was drunk, drunk, drunk, drunk," he says.

Razor continues talking, he tells me of the bullets that they found in the Patersons' safe and that they then believed there to be a gun in the house too. He tells me that this incident was never pre-planned, they were just very drunk when they initiated it and just decided on the spur of the moment to go and rob. He does not make it clear what made them choose their house. He blames his lack of sobriety on all the decisions taken. He also talks of them finding the kitchen scissors and how they then used them to torture Bronwyn. However, he mistakenly relays that they used the scissors to cut her again and again. "No," I say to him, "You did not cut her, you stabbed her, in the neck."

"We did this," he says, using his fingers to imitate scissors cutting.

With a frown on my face, I turn to George, "That's not right? And anyway, it was you that attacked her, wasn't it?"

George looks at me and immediately agrees. "It was me," he says, "I stabbed her, here," indicating the part of the neck just above the shoulder, "I cut her ear," he continues, and once again looks down at his hands then out at the window; possibly in shame.

I then ask them about the fight that Bronwyn had heard one of them having with Razor in the passageway when she had presumed they were fighting over Jamie. George immediately responds and says, "That was me, I was fighting, but not about the girl," he continues.

"So what were you fighting about?" I ask.

"The plan was always to put everything together in one place when we steal, and we then share it out between everyone afterwards. I saw Razor putting some of the jewellery in his pocket for himself, so I was fighting with him about that," he said.

I then ask them about the Redmond attack. They are both quick to deny any involvement therein. This case was dropped and has never been brought to court mainly due to the primary witnesses, the Redmonds, having fled the country and refusing to cooperate any further.

However, being in possession of copies from that case docket which includes statements written and signed by each of the members of the Razor Gang, in which they confirm and list the participants in that event as Razor, Thabang, George, Sibusiso (Mashinine) and Armand (also known as Serge or Fergo), and this was followed with evidence linking them to the incident, I know it all to be true. I'm angry that they still choose to deny this so readily. As frustrated as I am with their denial, I guess I have to understand it somewhat, in that any admissions on their side will also more than likely carry the fear that this case can then go back to court and they may get more convictions and potentially more years added onto their already lengthy incarcerations.

We continue to talk about a few other details and questions that I have and that they have for me. Razor again apologises and tells me that he's sorry, for what he has done as he has heard that Mike's wife has turned to drinking as a result and is not in a good way.

I actually laugh at him and tell him he could not be more wrong. I tell him what a phenomenal person she is and what an excellent mother (and father) she has been to her children. I make it clear that he has hurt her beyond measure, but he most certainly has not broken her. That story belongs to another family that he and his gang have changed forever, but it's not my place to share those details here. He had been given the right message but about the wrong person.

I then ask him if he knows anything about the man that he killed, my brother, and what sort of a person he was. I tell them who Mike was and what sort of an impact he had on everyone around him, what he had achieved in his life, and what a loss his death was to the family and his community.

I let them know that at his funeral, there were over 700 people who attended, that after his murder, there were many families that lost hope with South Africa and moved away overseas. That to honour him as a man and to stand against all that both Razor and George had done and stood for, we had started a trust in Mike's name and to date had raised close to R40-million to fight crime and to make sure we could put people like both of them in jail, and hopefully rehabilitate them onto the right track. Once again George hangs his head and looks down at his hands, and Razor does another dramatic movement, covering his face with his hands and then burying his head in his folded arms on the table.

There is one last question I need to ask them. "What do you think in your life needed to have been different to have prevented you from choosing a life of crime?" I ask.

George immediately replies, "A job and a skill. I want to be able to do something, to be something," he explains. "I have already decided to try do this thing here in jail and when I get out, I want to be able to work with my hands, like building or with wood," he continues. "There is nothing here at Sun City but there are workshops at Leeuwkop where we can learn to be a carpenter." He then informs me that he has already put in a transfer request to go to Leeuwkop so that he can learn such skills and benefit from the courses offered.

"And you?" I say, turning to Razor.

"Also a job and a skill," he says.

"And are you looking at training while you are here?" I ask.

"I haven't looked yet, but I will do that now," he promises. And once again, he puts his head into his hands and buries his face.

He looks up at me again and says, "I am sorry, very sorry, please forgive me," he pleads. George nods his head in agreement alongside him.

My mouth goes dry and I look at them for a while before I answer.

"I am not sure if that is something that I can ever do. Taking someone's life for nothing more than greed is a very difficult thing to forgive," I say. "However, instead of you asking me for forgiveness, I would rather ask you for something."

They suddenly both look at me with question in their eyes.

"You know in life we are all connected," I start, "There' is an energy between us all and links us all to each other." I continue as they look at me with confusion on their faces.

"Sometimes in life, we get to take, but then we also need to give. Life is a constant process of give and take. You have both only taken; possessions, lives, innocence and happiness. It is time that you start giving."

"From this moment on I want you to wake up every day and decide how you can give to someone else and to make someone else's life a little better today. It does not have to be anything big and it does not have to be someone important. It can even be the person sleeping next to you in the cell, here in prison. You just need to find one thing every day to give back and improve someone else's life. You can also talk to all these people with us here today and find out how you can get involved in talking to children and preventing them from turning to crime. I am sure they have programmes that you can get involved in and to help with," I continue and look towards Linda for confirmation. She nods her head in agreement.

I look back at the two of them and say nothing more, I want to see what their response is to what I have requested. They slowly nod their heads at me, and I then continue. "You want me to forgive you so that you can feel better. That I cannot do. But instead I am asking you to do something else that will not only make you feel better but will also have a positive impact on someone else's life. That is more important and that is what you need to do for me."

"Yes, we can do that," they both say in unison. Of course, I'm not convinced and deep within I obviously don't hold out much hope.

And, just like that, the VOD is over. George and Razor are taken out of the room and back to their cells. I say goodbye to Mrs Mabala, Linda and the other social workers present, and walk out with Tumiso back to my car. I ask him how genuine he thinks Razor was with all those tears. He shakes his head and also states that he's not sure himself. If it was an act, it was a very good one. Tumiso, did, however, add that George was apparently terrified and really dreaded what I would have to say to him. Somehow, I just feel that all of his responses as well as his actions and commitments towards improving himself are far more genuine than Razor's at this stage, and possibly there is hope for him somewhere down the line. But as with most things in life … only time will tell.

I leave the session thinking on the futures and the emotional states of everyone involved in that incident that night. While trying to make sense of what exactly may be going on in the minds of Razor and George, I of course think about Lorna, Megs, Nick and Annie-Rose and all that they have had to deal with and how well they have dealt with the massive trauma and loss thrust upon them. Their bereavement and heartaches still so evident in all that they do and in all that they are, but their internal strength and continued love for the world is inspirational.

In order to help them heal and find their paths to peace again, they have all taken to writing and have proven exceptionally proficient at it too. Below is a poem that Annie-Rose, at the age of 16, wrote for a school project on her thoughts, her life and her memories. It's a beautiful piece that speaks of the wonderful memories of her past with her father, the loss of her father and their lives that they shared with him. It also speaks to the remarkable future they have made for themselves and how they have risen above the evil and the hurt and have become remarkable young adults today.

Music of the Past – Annie-Rose Thomson - Aug 2016

music of the past
music of the present
music of the future
they sing their melodies in my mind
they are alive and ever-changing
memories remembered
memories made and
memories expected
a personal river of time
flowing unhindered on its course
through my mind

it sings to me songs of the past
of the first act
of four familiar faces
who became five when I entered the show
it sings to me of my darling Buckingham
my palace
my paradise
it sings of animals who were loved and cherished
my underwater companions
my friends in the sky
my not so slow trundling land companion who was always looking for
adventure
my most beloved dogs whom I will never forget
and most of all the undomesticated friends
whose wild calls sung me to sleep at night and woke me with the sunrise
it sings to me of the rivers rest and a refuge from strayed elephants
my much-loved N'tsiri with its simple yet beautiful impala lilies

it sings to me of my wooden hut and the house in the sky
made out of the love of a man who gave everything for his family
it sings to me songs of longing
songs of sadness and loss
and then comes the final scene of the 1st act
when five become four
when once happy yellow walls are painted white
the curtains are drawn
the scene ends
act two begins.

this is a happier song
it is the song of my present
my sweet sanctuary
my safe haven
my wondrous house by the sea
my friends from my past could not follow me on my journey
but I have made new ones
my friend that is always watching over me sits in the sky,
my spotted friends who live in my garden and are always making a racket
and the mysterious ocean lullaby that sings me to sleep each night
replacing my much-loved N'tsiri songs
I miss my old life
my palace
my paradise
my songs of the past
but I love my present with all my heart
there is but one thing I would change
to make us four
five once more
but life goes on and time continues to flow unhindered
the past cannot change but the future is still undetermined
and with that act two ends
and the third and final act begins

this last song is one that is the most changing and undecided
just as it seems to be certain
it swivels and sweeps onto a new course
one of unlimited possibilities
one of notes unheard

songs unsung
it is wonderful and frightening
one note is thousands
thousands of notes are just one
in the end when the songs of the future
meet up with the songs of the past
and the songs of the present
they will create an ocean of melodies
they will tell the story of a life
my life
one filled with love and loss
happiness and pain
one with endless possibilities but only one choice
my future is still uncertain
that song is still unsung

music of the past
music of the present
music of the future
they sing their melodies in my mind
they are alive and ever-changing
memories remembered, made and expected
a personal river of time
flowing unhindered on its course
through my mind

Life Changing In The Lowveld

"I have always found that actively loving saves one from a morbid preoccupation with the shortcomings of society."

Alan Paton, Cry the Beloved Country

If one has to look at historical crime statistics in South Africa, one cannot but take note that, together with the Northern Cape, Limpopo has always had the lowest crime rate in the country; particularly as regards the more serious and aggravated crimes. This was just one of the many, many things I loved about the Lowveld.

I moved to the Lowveld a year or two after leaving school, for what was supposed to be a six-month holiday job in the middle of a three-year round-the-world travel experience.

Once immersed in the lifestyle it had to offer, I fell in love. I fell in love with the simplicity of life in the bush, I fell in love with the excitement of life in the bush, I fell in love with Hoedspruit, I fell in love with the mountains and I quite simply ... fell in love. Yes, there was a khaki clad man in the mix too. I could think of nothing better than making this my home. I had been travelling the world in order to find myself and decide what it was I really wanted to do, and it took a little trip home and to the Lowveld for me to do just that.

I started off in conservation, immediately registering to study for my diploma through correspondence with Technicon SA and I set myself to learning everything I could about my world around me. As a family, we had owned a share in a game reserve in Hoedspruit called N'tsiri, so I had been coming down here every holiday and long weekend since the age of about 11 or 12, however, not once did I allow myself to be immersed in the culture and lifestyle that a small rural bush town offers and instead, with all the pseudo-wisdom of the city-born, would look down at it and wonder with criticism, "What on earth does anyone do all the way out here?" I was soon to learn. And, it was not long before I was soon to love. I loved it all.

One of the things that I loved the most, was the sense of freedom. There was no traffic, no crowds and there was no crime. My first home in the bush, was a tent, which then progressed into a structure made of 3½ wooden walls and a canvas roof, with no door. We would use a table and chairs to barricade up the open section if we heard the leopards or lions prowling around the camp at night. It was wild and it was wonderful.

I would frequently pat myself on the back congratulating myself on the choices I made in life. We had no money; one certainly does not work in the bush for financial gain, but we had freedom, we had life and we had passion, and it was what I was truly after from the start.

However, as time has progressed, life in the Lowveld has changed too. Other 'city-born' eyes started noticing all the wonders as I had, as regards life in the Lowveld and rapidly, development started occurring.

However, in the earlier days, regardless of the increased development occurring, crime in the area still remained minimal and uncommon. We would notice gangs moving into the area during busy holiday season, who would come and pick pocket or shoplift but would move off rapidly once the tourists all left. That was about it as far as the existence of crime in our area extended.

And then things started to change. It started off a little gradually and then snowballed and snowballed until life out here is now no different to life in the cities. Sadly, this is the situation in most of our rural towns and villages across South Africa today. There is close to nowhere in this beloved land of ours that can be considered free from crime.

Due to its location and the various activities occurring around us, Hoedspruit and all its surrounding towns, villages and regions, are now subject to some of the country's most renowned and noteworthy crimes: rhino poaching, farm attacks, vehicle hijacking and cash-in-transit heists. Boy has life changed.

Although no official study or report has yet been produced on the matter, those "in the know" are fairly confident that the development of major crimes in the area, can be linked, directly and indirectly, to the initiating cause of rhino poaching through the common perpetrators of organised crime syndicates and their recent movement and focus into the area. One crime has now fed into another, and suddenly we are finding ourselves having to prepare for all levels of threat possible.

The onset of rhino poaching has personally affected us on levels far greater than ever expected and ever reported on.

Rhino poaching itself needs no introduction. There has been a plethora of information, documentaries, social media posts and articles written on the subject and all those involved, or at least the aspects that those interviewed are comfortable enough to talk about on camera and openly with public media. Many of us on the ground, however, know a far deeper and far more frightening reality to what is going on. Regardless of the level and the depth, we, as Hoedspruiters and Central Lowvelders obviously live directly in the middle of it and feel its impacts personally on a day-to-day basis.

This has had a major impact on the lives of all involved and to all role players on "both-sides-of-the-horn".

For those living in the reserves and responsible for the protection of all our now highly targeted species, the impact on them emotionally and physically has been extreme. Where they once had time to worry about things like the health of vegetation, population densities, carrying capacities, erosion control, bush clearing, and even road maintenance, now the focus is purely on poaching, poaching and of course, poaching. Keeping yourself, your rhino and your staff safe are all one has the time or ability to worry about. Khaki-clad rangers have now had to become camo-clad militarists.

In my more recent years, from around 2001, I became involved in the filming industry, particularly the production of wildlife documentaries, with the BBC being a primary client. One of the analogies I have used with many of the film crews in the area, when trying to explain the changes and the stresses that have occurred over the last few years, and that are now facing those working in the bush is as follows:

In the early days, in order to do this job, all one needed was a khaki uniform, velskoens (a traditional type of shoe made from suede animal hide), a floppy hat, a single shot rifle and a bird book and you were all set. Nowadays, the same people need camouflage gear, military boots, a bulletproof vest, a semi-automatic or similar high-powered weapon and military tactics to do the same job.

It is the equivalent of taking a nursery-school teacher and sending them off to war. They are two worlds apart.

And this, quite literally is no exaggeration. It is not the job our khaki-clad rangers signed up for and not the passion that they sought; in fact, it is quite the opposite in every way imaginable. However, in order to protect themselves and all that they love, they have been forced to adapt and change. It is a matter of survival. And so it is with most South Africans, we have had to adapt just to survive.

On the flip-side-of-the-horn, Poaching has also had an immense impact on the rural villages and villagers themselves – both on the Mozambican side with the original poachers and now on the South African side as well. As these poachers started having access to large amounts of available cash, so too have their needs changed. This easily available cash, is spent on alcohol, drugs, cars and girls. Life in the rural villages rapidly changed.

Youngsters also look up to the newly affluent and aspire to copy them and to be them. This helps breed an entirely new generation of youngsters looking for any opportunity for quick cash. On the fringes, supporting markets to supply the alcohol, drugs, cars and girls to this newly affluent and spend-thrift community, have developed in turn, all of which has led to an increase in a culture of crime and criminal mind-sets within what was once a rural, laid-back and tribal based community. Tribal values are no longer respected, and elders have little control over this new and powerful "elite".

This mind-set in itself has helped contribute towards the occurrence of other major crimes in the area. The majority of criminals or poachers that we catch are all involved in various types of crimes, from armed robberies, to ATM bombings to cash-in-transit heists, cable theft and of course, poaching.

Further to this, and as the battle continues and the rangers and reserves start having more and more successes through the numerous arrests of poachers, or even more extreme, where poachers have been killed, this then leaves large numbers of families behind, now without a "breadwinner" and without a father head in the family, and we can once again turn to our social causes of youngsters growing up without father figures and the contributions this may have to the future development of criminals. It is a self-feeding and self-continuing problem creating more criminals, encouraging more criminals, and inspiring more criminals.

Once again, major focus and development is required both socially within the communities and nationally within our government to bring this crisis down with a crash.

Where To From Here

"If you wrote a novel in South Africa which didn't concern the central issues, it wouldn't be worth publishing.
To give up the task of reforming society is to give up one's responsibility as a free man."

Alan Paton, Cry the Beloved Country

To date, I have looked at and brought to the fore many of the concerns, issues and failures in our systems that are leading to, contributing to and even supporting crime, while also preventing the successful mitigation of crime in this beloved country of ours. Most of them we have stumbled across and experienced in our story alone, and others I have discovered in all the work I have undertaken thereafter. All of these various issues need to be addressed and mitigated. The horrifying reality is that everything that has been encompassed in this book by no means covers it all. There are many other focus areas and issues that could still be included and that exist in our country. However we have to start somewhere and all the aspects outlined so far, can help create a strong base and starting point.

Those that have been outlined in this book may seem totally exasperating, and may make the entire situation look hopeless and helpless. However, if you break them down into their smaller components, there is no reason why, without the correct attention and commitment, South Africa could not get on top of, and totally combat crime within a few short years.

The reality, however, is that for this to be achieved, not only will it take a change of attitude from each and every one of us as citizens, but more importantly the government would need to truly step up and come to the party. This is where the greatest challenge lies.

The government would need to take a serious look at national budgets and the reallocation of vital and necessary funds towards improving basic resources, physical structures, and relevant technology to all departments involved in the identification, apprehension, conviction and finally long-term housing of the criminals in South Africa, from the police stations to the courts. Fixing the many issues that have been allowed to develop over the last few decades is going to take an incredible commitment through re-allocation of budget amongst other focus areas. it will not be cheap, but certainly will have a massive impact. I only shudder to think of the R19,6 billion that Eskom lost in 2018 due to "irregular spending" and just what a difference that could have made if correctly spent on the safety and security of our citizens.

In addition we need to give better focus to our prisons and improve their abilities to potentially reform criminals as much as is possible.

It is my core belief that until we sort out crime and criminals in our country, all other social and fiscal development endeavours will continue to fail. Crime and all its consequences will continue to erode away at any positive ever achieved in this country.

So where do we start?

Staffing of police stations and the resourcing of these with, if not advanced, at least basic technological equipment needs to be addressed with urgency.

Apart from improving computer technology and software, every police station should have a basic fingerprint reader; a tool that would overcome the challenges of immediate re-identification of suspects and criminals daily. One would think this would be expected in a police station, however, surprisingly there are very few that have and use this basic piece of equipment to immediately identify any arrested suspects.

The minute a suspect is brought into the station, his fingerprint should be read in order to access a revised CAS system that will automatically bring up a single profile on who he is, what names he may have been given previously, what he has been arrested for or what cases he may have been linked to, and of course should contain a photo of the suspect that can be updated as he ages and changes.

Our banks have similar systems, many of the country's security companies run similar systems on all the staff entering into gated estates or premises and even businesses run the same systems for their staff where necessary. There is no given reason why SAPS should not be set up with similar systems. The technology is certainly available, and the laws are in place through the implementation of the new fingerprint law to allow for and enable this. All that is needed is our government's support and commitment through properly equipping and resourcing all stations to do so, and a true desire from the very top towards combatting and mitigating crime.

Re-staffing of our stations also needs to be addressed and can also be achieved initially through a fairly simple and quickly implemented process that will not create an excessive budget demand on the state.

Throughout time SAPS has had a system in place known as Police or SAPS Reservists. Police Reservists consist of volunteers who are put through a week or two of police training and thereafter avail themselves to their local police station on a voluntary basis for a set number of hours a week. They're fully uniformed and have access to relevant or available police resources. Reservists are a fantastic way to bolster numbers in the police force at no continual cost to the state, apart from their initial training and the supply of uniforms.

Five years ago, 36 men from the Hoedspruit Farmwatch Reaction unit applied to be reservists, and there is a good chance that today, we could easily double that number. These 36 alone will almost treble the staff compliment at Hoedspruit Police Station. However, for a still unexplained reason, SAPS at a national level has been dragging its feet on enlisting any new reservists and the entire process has been stagnant for years.

Not only that, but there are many existing reservists whose contracts have been allowed to lapse as their senior officers "forgot" to submit their contracts for renewal. So not only have no new reservists been enlisted in the last five to 10 years, but even the existing reservists are no longer legally enrolled and we have lost this valuable resource in many of the stations around the country.

This is an issue that the Hoedspruit Farmwatch feel strongly about and use every opportunity to bring up the issue in meetings or SAPS-orientated platforms. So far, we have still not been given any constructive feedback or promise in this regard.

A number of the potential solutions to the issues I have discussed to date may require exceedingly great expectations and demands from government and as a result we may feel that all is hopeless as we will never get this input. However, looking at the more socially based issues discussed, there is a large amount that we as citizens can do. Apart from assisting our local police where possible, there is also plenty citizens can do to prevent the "creation" of criminals in the first place and we too need to take on the responsibility of addressing these issues and not just wait for government to deliver.

"Charity starts at home," so they say. So does the creation of a secure and stable society. Until we realise that and do all that we can, not just within our own homes, but in others around us, we will continue to be subject to the social ills currently influencing the crime rate amongst us.

Issues such as reviewing company policies about staff and our workforces and changing principles to allow for, enable and encourage family unity and family support are crucial. Some of the most successful companies in the world such as Netflix, Google and IBM have policies and structures built around encouraging the combination of families and work and allowing for working men and women to play active and involved roles within their children's upbringing, regardless of whether they're a low wage employee or a top level director.

We, as average South Africans employing staff in any kind of field that stay on premises, can take this on board and see what can be done to encourage family unity and lessen the number of disrupted families countrywide from tourism, to agriculture, to the corporate world. There is room for improvement in every sphere.

Further to creating family unity, anyone, whether you are a farmer, the owner of an industrial workshop or a white-collar corporate industry, that employs any number of people, has the opportunity to reach out and assist with improving family and parental skills (and may pick up on something beneficial themselves). The chances are high that the majority of your workforce are either parents or will become parents at some time in the future. Consequently, additional support and advice on how to be a supportive parent, to enable positive discipline and respect, and how to encourage self-confident and productive children is always helpful and welcome to many, and quite frankly, just needed for others.

This may seem like a distant objective when considering the fight against crime, however offering of basic parenting advice and skills workshops for your employees can in fact go a long way in contributing to a better society of individuals and families. It can contribute towards increasing general knowledge on how to raise better children and create a more stable and secure society. This is something that is much needed if we are to move South Africa into a brighter and safer tomorrow. This factor relates to all levels of society and all cultures within our country.

As we have also discussed, the presence of EQ also has a remarkable affect in preventing the need or desire to turn to crime in response to negative life situations. In addition to general parenting skills, businesses can also look at implementing EQ workshops amongst all their staff. EQ in the work environment has been proven time and again, to result in higher turnovers, greater creativity and less absenteeism.

Further to that, EQ has been implemented in many prisons around the world and here too, it has had remarkable results. Released inmates who had previously undergone EQ workshops while incarcerated showed exceptionally low to non-existent rates of recidivism (repeat offending). On learning EQ skills, they were endowed with the emotional and social skills to prevent the need or desire to turn to crime once again and subsequently were endowed with the self-confidence to create goals and objectives in life and to make something of themselves thereafter.

The amazing thing about EQ is that it can be learnt, and it should be learnt by all, regardless of age or educational level.

Within schools, families and the home structures, EQ has also proven to have extensive benefits. It should be built into school curriculums. Teachers and pupils alike, should be encouraged to explore the benefits and skills of an increased EQ.

There are pages and pages of resources available on the Internet on this subject, whether you are a mother who wants to build your child's EQ, or a boss that wants to implement EQ within the workforce.

As an emotional species, it is highly surprising that we give so very little attention and focus to this part of who we are when it affects so much about what we do and what we are able to achieve. Increasing the EQ of the nation will have a dramatic effect on many of the ills we have to deal with daily in South Africa and will contribute towards stemming the tears in this beloved country of ours.

∽

As a last solution to be discussed; a good practice would be to look elsewhere in the world, where the successful reduction of crime may have already been achieved and just how this was in fact done.

One of the best living examples of the overnight reduction of crime, is New York City in the late 90s.

During his time in office Mayor Giuliani, the 107th mayor in New York from 1994 to 2001, took on the focus of cleaning up the streets of New York and did everything possible to win the city back from the criminals. New York at the time was wracked with crime – from murder to car thefts, from armed robbery to drugs. The parks were not safe for the children to play in, the streets not safe for the elderly to walk - it was overrun and controlled by the criminally minded. Much like the South Africa of today.

New York's subsequent drop in crime thereafter was unquestioningly astonishing. Within his term of service, Mayor Giuliani was able to turn the crime in New York, entirely on its head.

South Africa can learn a thing or three from Mayor Giuliani and all that was done to defeat crime in New York and to bring about this astonishing decline. Some of the theories applied, were considered literally "out-of-the-box" but yet proved to be significantly successful. The turnaround was categorically linked to positive growth aspects such as improving the economy, changing the drug use and implementing demographic changes, however, the one that he is most famous for, and is the primary strategy that has been credited with the success of New York's crashing crime rate is what is known as the "Broken Window Theory"

Broken Window Theory suggests that those that live in a broken neighbourhood tend to leave it broken, therefore leaving the neighbourhood open for crime to move in and take over. On a governance level, it also creates the understanding, that if an area cannot deal with its "little issues" such as maintaining basic infrastructure or dealing with petty crime such as graffiti, then it most certainly will not be able to deal with bigger crime and thus enables a mindset leading towards the easy perpetration of bigger crimes. On a social and individual level, it also creates a mindset that if one's value is equal to that of the environment in which they are living, they will then only live up to the expectations allotted with such an environment. In other words, give them a better environment to live in and chances are far greater that they will raise their self-expectations and live up to the value of the environment in which they are living and behave accordingly.

Putting this theory into infrastructure terms, part of the New York reform process involved, as the name suggests, quite literally fixing all the broken windows within the city and immediately repairing any that were subsequently broken thereafter – with the intention of showing that the area was cared for and miscreant behaviour is no longer acceptable. There is obviously always a grey-area phase while the community is adapting to the new environment in which old behaviours still exist, but within a matter of time, these are replaced by behaviours equivalent to the environment around them and suddenly the numbers of recurring broken windows reduced dramatically to close to zero.

In addition to replacing of broken windows, they also focused on getting rid of any and all graffiti in the city and subways and immediately removing it should it return. These seemingly simple steps were implemented, together with more complex strategies such as environmental design to create safer areas like streetlights, cleaning of alleys and dark areas and any other identified aspects whereby the simple vision and indication of a "dodgy location" exists and is duly mitigated.

One of the challenges in implementing this is that we would in turn need to rely to a certain extent on local government.

Once again, expecting government, specifically local government, to come to the party in this regard would be a huge challenge specifically, based on a report in March 2018, that only as few as 7% of our local governments (municipalities) in South Africa are actually functioning well. The rest are in different degrees of function, with 31% being almost dysfunctional and 31% being totally dysfunctional and the remaining 31% at a push could be considered reasonably functioning.

If we cannot even rely on our municipalities to offer basic services such as sufficiently supplying water to its constituents, then I guess expecting higher level activities from them, such as replacing broken windows, or heaven forbid, implementing environmental design to mitigate dangerous areas, could be considered a little hopeful.

However, as private individuals, we most certainly can do our bit to implement the Broken Window Theory within the realms of our own influence.

Communities themselves can get together and clean up streets, tidy up parks, and take responsibility for improving the physical environment within their immediate surroundings.

Further to that, situations such as on farms, reserves or lodges, can also go a long way by looking into the condition of existing accommodation and staff villages in which their staff are accommodated.

I have to be honest here and state, that I have been absolutely horrified when I have seen the state of some of the staff accommodation facilities on farms and reserves in the area. Many with broken windows (see the immediate opportunity here?), with doors that don't open or close properly, without proper lighting inside, and are all in desperate need of a couple of layers of paint.

Building better communities and living environments for people around us is something relatively small that many of us can do.

∽

On a different level, there are many people who feel the need to "do something" or find a way to contribute towards fighting crime but are too scared to get directly involved and fight crime head on. There is, however, a solution.

As so much of this early childhood development, that can contribute towards a self-aware, self-confident and stable individual, is missing in many of the homes and communities in general, in South Africa, the development of organisations to facilitate this in townships and rural communities is vital towards mitigating crime.

For these individuals who feel the need to do something positive in this country and want to do all they can to mitigate the scourge of crime, yet they themselves are too fearful to take on the dangerous world that fighting crime directly may involve, initiating or supporting community projects focused on the development of our children is one of the arenas where they can get involved in compassionate, caring and positive work that will in fact go a long way to changing the criminal future and the criminal potential of South Africa in years to come.

This kind of input is crucial towards helping to create a country of positive and productive citizens and I honour and thank all those that are already committed to this and give of themselves tirelessly with the intention of simply improving someone else's life. This is the South African attitude that will lead us into a new tomorrow, a tomorrow free from crime and a tomorrow that sees the production of a generation of strong, stable and emotionally secure citizens.

There is much to be done by both citizens and government. Whether we want to prevent the development of future criminals or lessen the perpetration of current criminals, it's only with everyone working together and towards the same goal, that we will succeed. It has successfully been achieved in other countries and cities around the world. There is no reason why South Africa cannot do the same.

I am also of the very strong opinion that crime and the consequences of crime are prime role players in all negative and destructive processes in our country and until such time as we sort out crime first, all other positive processes implemented will merely be like blossoms in the wind, some may hold and some may survive but most will continue to blow away. Thus we need to give urgent and focused attention towards the mitigation of crime first if we are to move forward as a country in any way possible

Those of us still in this country are clearly the ones who have chosen to stay. We obviously love, and are committed to this Beloved Country we call home. As such, it is up to each and every one of us to do something in some small way to get control back from the criminals and to do all we can to create a self-confident, secure and responsible society.

Epilogue – Final Thoughts

> *Who indeed knows the secret of the earthly pilgrimage? Who knows for what we live, and struggle, and die? Who knows what keeps us living and struggling, while all things break about us? Who knows why the warm flesh of a child is such comfort, when one's own child is lost and cannot be recovered? Wise men write many books, in words too hard to understand. But this, the purpose of our lives, the end of all our struggle, is beyond all human wisdom.*
>
> **Alan Paton, Cry the Beloved Country**

As I have tried to outline in my very unskilled and unlearned way, but sadly self-experienced way, there are many different aspects within the processes involved in the South African systems, that need to be reviewed, corrected and, quite frankly, totally overhauled. A large number of these can be improved and counteracted through simple but committed actions, not just from government level, but from us all as passionate South African citizens as well.

One of the first, and possibly the most challenging will be to restore integrity and honesty as an expected culture within South African society. Until such time as crime in South Africa is mitigated and balance is restored, I truly believe that anyone involved in any field related to anything described herein, should go through regular integrity testing to make sure that we employ those with morals worthy of a positive and growth orientated society. This is a standard procedure in the anti-poaching world and should be within all other similar arenas as well. This statement alone will be met with contradiction. However, the reality is that the only person who would object to such activities, is generally the same person that has something to hide.

Government really needs to come to the party and to open its eyes and see what an effect crime is having on all of its citizens.

South Africa is a country whose citizens are trying hard to move on and move away from all the legacies of our past, and I see evidence of this constantly in so many avenues of life. However, so often government seems to be responsible for keeping negativity alive. Additionally, the continual threat of crime on its own is a strong contributor towards its further continuation. A small and seemingly inconsequential example that I think of daily is visible on the many long roads one travels in the rural areas of South Africa. We all know that public transport is severely lacking, particularly in farming and rural areas of our country. The many citizens without their own transport have to rely heavily either on taxis or simply hitching a lift with a passing vehicle, an action that is becoming more and more dangerous for all concerned.

Every day I drive past people and feel guilty as I am in a car alone and could easily give them a lift. Sadly, there have been far too many incidents, including a friend of mine from town, where picking up a hitchhiker has resulted in a hijacking or rape. Thus, I don't pick up anyone and I avert my eyes, swallow my guilt and drive past the poor souls who may just be wanting to get home to see their children.

The potential threat is so great that the need to protect myself, is far greater than the need to assist another.

On the other side of the coin, I can only image the evil thoughts they must have at me as I come past, on my own, in my car, seemingly not caring, and leave them standing on the streets alone. I certainly would be as bitter as anything if it were me and would curse the culture that seems so indifferent to my needs.

Crime has increased to such an extent that for these poor commuters too, the threat of the "Samaritan in disguise" that stops to give a lift is just as concerning for them. I have often had to go and assist both women and men at the police station who were given a lift and robbed. Even more horrifying, a few years ago, there was a scare in the Lowveld area where mothers with babies were being targeted and given lifts. Once in the car, they were offered a bottle of water to drink that contained a sedative. Hours later, the mother would wake up somewhere along the road and her baby would be missing. How does a mother ever deal with that?

Earlier this year, there was another such incident that to this day makes my stomach turn when I think of it.

A middle-aged woman – I guess in her 40s or 50s, but it was difficult to tell with her subsequent injuries, was hitch-hiking to get back to work on one of the nearby farms. She was picked up by two black men in a single cab bakkie who told her to climb into the back. As they neared the entrance to the farm where she worked, she knocked on the back of the window to tell them that this is where she wants to stop and get out. The passenger in the vehicle turned around to face her through the rear window and laughing at her, shook his head and moved his hand across his throat to indicate they were going to kill her. The poor woman was so frightened that she threw herself off the back of the speeding vehicle. By the time we got to her on the side of the road to assist, she had taken a flight across the tar and into the bushes on the side, and apart from general injuries to her body, she had lost the majority of her face, from landing nose-first on the tar.

I see her in her agony as she tries to talk to us and tell us what happened through what little is left of her lips and cheeks, and my heart just cries. How can our government not want to do something to stop all of this?

Crime has just become too common, too easy and is just an accepted culture now, that quite literally no one is safe anywhere anymore.

This is not just a political problem. This is a national problem that involves political issues, social issues, historical issues, infrastructure issues and ethical issues. This is a national problem that is affecting ALL and there are far too many of the citizens in this beloved country crying, and the only way to stop this is for government to step up and lead the way and for citizens to take responsibility themselves.

∞

Crime is so rampant and so common that close to every single one of our 56-million people have been exposed somehow and somewhere. These days it is near impossible to find a single South African citizen who has not been directly affected by, not just crime, but SERIOUS crime in one way or another. It needs to stop; we have all had enough!

My Beloved Country, please hear me, we have all had ENOUGH!

We know that expecting government to bring its end of the bargain is a big ask and an unrealistic expectation. However, it's important that as citizens, if we truly feel that we want this to come to an end, all take on one little aspect, whether discussed in this book or not, and commit to it and to improving one other person's life.

If each and every person does something, with or without the government, we will make some kind of a difference and hopefully prevent at least one little girl from being raped, or if we can prevent at least one other family from going through what we, the Patersons and the Redmonds have had to go through, or if we can prevent at least one other child from having to watch their father die. For these reasons and these reasons alone, it would be worth every ounce of effort.

We're near the end of our journey, you and I. But, before you leave this book, there's one more story I'd like to share with you. It's a horrific story and is a stark reminder of just what threat we live under day-to-day!

It's a story that I have wanted to fit into the book somewhere, but it has been so intense I have battled to find the right place to include it. This is a story of what life in South Africa has been reduced to and this is a story of what extent community members are prepared to go to protect each other. This is a story that I hope very few have to experience.

In the first quarter of 2018, through the various means available to us, we got wind of a potential farm attack in our area in which there was the intended use of high-powered weapons – AK47s to be exact. This could only mean that the criminals intend to use extreme aggression. Initially, we were only able to pick up on small threads of information. However, using this, we started putting together a potential list of targets. In doing so, I had to take a deep breath as one of my very closest and best friends and her husband, filled all known criteria at the time and had made their way onto our initial "potential targets" list.

As if it would have an effect, I desperately kept trying to skew information thereafter towards an alternative option and potential victim, but sadly, this would only have been fooling myself. Dealing with all of this is one thing, but with this kind of a threat against someone so close to me, was an entirely different ball game.

After a little more digging around the next thread that came through stopped me in my tracks and made my heart go cold. There was no doubt and no denying it. They were definitely the intended target. Our small management team dealing with the information at the time, could immediately see the effect this information had on me. Suddenly I wasn't just dealing with the protection of our community in general. Suddenly we were needing to protect one of my best friends, someone that I have shared 18 years of friendship, thousands of adventures and a million laughs with, someone who is central and critical in my day-to-day journeys through life.

For the purposes of this story and to protect their identities, I've referred to her as the "Jam Donut" and her husband the "Fine Doctor". Both being euphemisms we have been known to throw around in the past.

Once we were 100% certain that they were the target of the attack we had to break the news to them. We broke the news to them on the worst timed day ever; the Jam Donut's birthday. In a 20 minute conversation we turned their world upside down.

As we needed the incident to go ahead so we could hopefully arrest the syndicate and prevent this kind of activity in the future, we all entered into what has to have been one of the most tense and trickiest times ever. Everything the Jam Donut and the Fine Doctor did from there onwards had to be extremely alert and careful, while at the same time, not giving any external indication that we were aware of an impending attack.

We knew that one of the staff on their farm was involved yet could not give away any indication as to just what we did in fact know. Needless to say, the Jam Donut and the Fine Doctor entered into a phase of sleeping with one eye open. Every noise sent adrenaline rushing through them. However, despite this, they had to pretend to go back to work as normal, life as normal and all normality that the situation can allow.

Thankfully, there was nothing normal about their lives, so normal was not necessarily normal at all.

As they had so little routine in their day-to-day activities, it was a lot easier to hide any potential changes in activities without being too obvious. Nonetheless, none of us wanted the Jam Donut anywhere near harm's way. So, we moved her off the farm at night and she temporarily moved in with me. She would, however, occasionally go back to the farm and work in the office by day.

The Fine Doctor, on the other hand, had to stay on the farm and act as if everything was normal so that he could lure the attackers out. Every evening, after eating a meal with us at my house, we would send him off back to the farm, sometimes on his own, and occasionally with an armed cohort hidden in his car. I cannot explain to you the emotions one feels when you have to watch him and the rest of our team head off towards known danger and the level of threat that we knew was waiting for them, and not being able to do too much about it. The stress and depth of emotions it brought about is indescribable.

Every evening when he left, we sent him off with the ritual departing words of, "We'll see you tomorrow." However, knowing what he was potentially facing and the potential outcomes that may or may not occur, these simple words were exaggerated and expressed as … we WILL see you tomorrow!

The Jam Donut has always been a special little cupcake, however, throughout all of this, she has totally blown my mind. Although the stress and concern was always so clear, there was never any panic, drama, or excessive emotion.

One of the trickier things at this time, is that we could not talk to anyone else or let anyone else know what was going on; it was all still too sensitive, and all information gleaned so far, needed to be protected. As a release, the Jam Donut and I talked to each other every night. We had many conversations that friends shouldn't have. We had to talk through aspects such as what she needs to do, or how she needs to cope with outcomes and threats, should they still catch her by surprise and arrive at the house while she's there during the day and working in the office.

We discussed rape in detail and how to best deal with it, or even prevent it if possible. We discussed the possibility of torture if the deviants couldn't get what they want or suspected there was more to be had. Remember how George had tortured Bronwyn Patterson because he believed that there was a firearm in her house.

We discussed the need for her to know exactly where the keys to the safe are, where to keep any valuables that are easy for them to get to and retrieve. All this was aimed at keeping the attackers' anger, frustration and aggression in check.

The rest of the Farmwatch management was doing its best to ensure that these kinds of outcomes would never ever happen, and they were all going through their own stresses and sleepless nights. The reality, is that it is impossible for us to be fully in control of the situation and entirely on top of things 24/7 and thus there were potential gaps where things could catch us off-guard and end in disaster. Thus, I had to make sure that the Jam Donut was as prepared as possible to come out of it as best as she possibly could. The Jam Donut was a target and I had to do all I could to keep her safe or prepare her for all eventualities if this were not possible.

Obviously, we discussed and prepared for the eventuality that we least liked to think of yet remained a constant possibility whenever the Fine Doctor headed off back to the farm. What if it all went down, and he was killed? It was not an easy time and they were certainly not easy conversations, and not the kind friends should ever have to have night after night.

In the first few weeks of the ordeal, the Jam Donut and I had to release the pressure. We found this through humour, specifically the humour of the comedy king, Trevor Noah. I'm without doubt, a fan and have all his DVDs in my collection. As the majority of his material is about the state of South Africa, the crime, and the differences between all of our cultures and many of the subjects I have covered within this book alone, it was exactly what we needed to keep our minds positive through all of this and to try and keep a sense of looking at the "brighter side" of the situation we were currently experiencing.

This ritual of evening laughter and giggles meant so much to us and made such a difference in keeping our spirits up, instead of sitting in constant morbid worry. "Trevor, from the bottom of our hearts we say thank you for getting us through a tense and difficult first few weeks. Without your humour, the forces of darkness and despair would have overwhelmed us."

When Trevor's comedy wasn't helping us, we would find some way to help ourselves. Every evening before turning to the television and the Trevor Noah session, we would sit on my deck with a cup of tea in hand, and watch the sun setting on the incredible mountain in front of us. I live at the foothills of the Mariepskop Mountain, one of the pillar heads leading into the Blyde River Canyon. It's a majestic sight to behold and I'm thankful for it every day.

One evening we were browsing through our respective Facebook accounts for something different to do and see what the rest of the world was up to whilst we were waiting for potential impending disaster. I came across a post with a link to an article discussing whether it was healthier to sleep with pyjamas on, or to sleep naked. I start giggling out loud, and the Jam Donut looks at me questioningly. I show her the article and she starts giggling too. This is clearly an article from another country we exclaim. In South Africa, you have to decide whether to sleep in your most non-revealing-in-case-someone-breaks-into-your-home-at-night-pyjamas or you sleep in a bullet proof vest, just as the Fine Doctor was doing each night!

"Imagine the freedom of being able to sleep naked," we giggle, "What a wondrous thought! Perhaps, one day," we sigh.

The other really difficult thing we had to deal with was the anticipation and uncertainty. We had no idea exactly when the attack was going to take place.

The first indication of potential attack coincided with a grand reunion at my old school, Bryanston High. It was the school's 50th Anniversary and my own class's 30-year reunion. We were combining it all into a spectacular event. I, however, could not bring myself to leave the Jam

Donut all by herself, and should anything have gone down that weekend, it would have destroyed me to know that I was not there to help her with whatever outcome may have transpired.

We discussed the option of her coming up to Johannesburg with me and tagging along to the reunion. However, there were a few other details that prevented this and thus in the end, we both opted to stay in Hoedspruit and face whatever awaited us here. However, as can be expected with African Time, "their" plans seemed to change once more, and we found ourselves back in the waiting game. It has been a seesaw of patience, emotions and tension as we seem to repetitively move from a "waiting phase" to an "seemingly eminent phase" and then back to a "waiting phase" once more.

Waiting for an imminent attack is beyond stressful for everyone. I was amazed at how both the Jam Donut and the Fine Doctor faced the whole situation with a continual positive attitude. Imagine knowing that you will be attacked and possibly injured or killed, all the while having to continue with your day-to-day life. The stress is inconceivable.

As it was all starting to drag on for so long, the Jam Donut found herself a little flat to rent a stone's throw from my home. This at least allowed her to claim back some independence, some routine and of course, her own space. There was no kitchen in the flat, just a tiny little semi-functional kitchenette, so she continued to share my kitchen and a large number of main meals were created and shared here, before she would head to the flat and the Fine Doctor back to the farm.

Things seem to be settling down and it has been a few months since we last picked up any relevance to an impending attack; so much so, that we presumed all planning had fallen flat and that the attack was halted. The Jam Donut even started contemplating giving up her rent on the flat so they could think about settling back into their home on the farm once more. No sooner had we started discussing this option than indications were received once again that the suspects were back in the area, and in fact, everything indicated that it was to happen that very night.

This indication sent everyone into action. As we had been through this so many times in the months previous, both the Jam Donut and I commented on how this just felt like something we had done before, this was almost becoming the new normal; a normal that sucked!

Just to give you a glimpse at what they have gone through and are still going through, as I write this, it has now been almost five months since we first sat them down and delivered the crappiest birthday gift ever. Throughout this time, we have swayed in and out of at least four "imminent phases" and each time, just as we are all on the edge of our seats and the tip of our nerves, something interrupts "their" planning and we pick-up indications that it's delayed once again and we pick up signals that the gang have left the area once more.

In each of these "imminent phases" things have been so close, our core team has been able to record the syndicate's movements onto and off the farm itself, they have monitored their movements in and around the town, so much so, that there has been no doubt that it's about to go down.

There is nothing worse than waiting for the inevitable and the unknown. Waiting for an enemy that we all fear to finally show its face and reveal itself to you. We know that it's definitely going to happen, and that the syndicate won't give up until they have achieved whatever it is, they want to achieve. But heaven only knows for how much longer we have to wait, and heaven only knows for how much longer the Jam Donut and the Fine Doctor can keep up their strength in waiting. They're both definitely taking strain.

Now is probably a good time to talk about the astounding commitment and input from the men in our Farmwatch Reaction Unit. This is one thing that both the Jam Donut and the Fine Doctor have been absolutely blown away with. Both were confirmed farming recluses, prior to all of this, and loved nothing more than being as far away from everyone as possible. However, overnight, they have become confirmed advocates of community support, community interactions and community living.

To see how this group of incredible men, both young and old, have put their lives on the line, night-after-night, week-after-week, the hours and hours assessing all they could to gain intelligence in trying to stay one step ahead of these criminals, has warmed the very depth of their hearts. It has been an enlightening experience for them to see to what extent of threat these ordinary farmers, fathers and husbands are prepared to face to protect each other, to protect our community and to protect the morality of our nation and of course, to protect the Jam Donut and the Fine Doctor.

Once again, I have to state, and this time I know without a shadow of a doubt that the Jam Donut and the Fine Doctor join me in my sentiments, these men are true South African heroes. Whether you are white or black, whether you are young or old, whether you are a resident or a visitor, I have seen these men give of themselves and stay up all night trying to protect another, regardless of who they might be, where they're from, or what culture or creed they represent. A soul is a soul and any soul in need, is a soul worth saving. These men are true heroes and I honour and respect them in every way possible.

What the Jam Donut and the Fine Doctor are going through is not the sort of thing that an average citizen should have to face or deal with. I doubt that there are many countries in the world where citizens need to go to these extremes. However, in South Africa it's a necessity for survival and has almost become as normal as breakfast in the mornings.

Through this "new normal", we are exceptionally fortunate that all our hard work as an organised Farmwatch unit over the years, has created the platforms through which we can be informed in advance and hopefully prepared for this kind of threat, instead of the alternative, where the first we may of heard of it, would have been a desperate plea for help from that Jam Donut after whatever may have transpired. This is where we are getting to as a community, a proactive community who take responsibility in the control of their own safety and security, where we can hopefully be one step ahead of the criminals where possible, and take all necessary precautions to protect everyone living within.

We have experienced many frustrations over this time period. However, the reality, is that we are simply trying to adapt to the challenges that life in South Africa is throwing at us, this "new normal". We are doing our best to adapt in a proactive and responsible manner, but at the same time, not allowing these criminals to take over and rule this country that we all love so much. This story is a summary of all that life in South Africa entails for many. The trials, the challenges, the threat of crime and of course the everyday heroes involved in keeping it all at bay.

I know that many of you are sitting there shouting at me and wondering in frustration that if we can monitor the movements of the syndicate in the area, then why do we not just go and pick them up and arrest them. Hopefully, having reached the end of this book, that answer may be clear to you already. If nothing else, then hopefully everything I have shared with you has given you a little more insight into just what the reality is as regards our policing, and our judicial systems, and how often the only time any of this is dealt with, is when it turns to the extreme.

If we were to arrest them early, then what do we charge them with? There is little focus and attention put towards "minor crimes" and in fact they will probably get off with little more than a slap on the wrist. We may even have a challenge to get them charged with anything at all. However, if we can arrest them in the middle of an armed robbery, then we have a far greater chance of securing a proper and long-term sentence and a far better chance of removing them from society, for a while at least. Thus, we need this event to happen and we need to keep sending the Fine Doctor off to the farm to draw them out. Although we are prepared to see this to its end, after this extended period of waiting, we do all agree, that it just needs to end soon. The emotional strength and ability to keep this up is definitely waning. It's becoming tougher and tougher each day.

But as with so much that so many people have had to deal with on the plains and savannahs of this beloved land, all we can do is take one day at a time and just keeping doing all that we have to do.

∽

Throughout this difficult time, I am sent a Facebook post that further helps restore my faith in South Africa and the future potential out there.

The original post is dated 22 November 2017 and is posted by a man named Sipho Simelane. In his post he acknowledges and honours a white Afrikaans man who is a retired policeman in the Gauteng area.

Sipho's post reads:

Johan Scott, a retired policeman from Heidelberg, South Africa started the vegetable garden on his pavement after his cauliflowers were stolen. He realised that there were people that are hungry in his neighbourhood so he decided to cultivate an even bigger garden on his pavement in order to feed more people.

"It makes my heart happy when I see people wanting my vegetables."

"That is why I planted this, because the people are hungry, they need this."

Scott decided to plant beans, tomatoes, eggplants and beetroot for the local community to help themselves to free produce. He hoped that this garden would change how many hungry people there are in his town.

His act of kindness has sparked a warming in our hearts, and we are not alone! Facebook users have been sharing their love for this act of kindness and some even stated how much they respect Johan. The hope is that this selfless and generous act will inspire more people in the town and around South Africa to become proactive in the fight to prevent hunger.

There are many places around South Africa that have vegetable gardens for the homeless, these offer a form of employment and a food source for people actively working to change their circumstances.

What a difference this changed mindset can make. Instead of building bigger walls and preventing his cauliflowers from being stolen again, he chose rather to look at the root cause behind why his cauliflowers were being stolen and to do something instead to fix that and prevent the need for theft.

This single story sums up a large part of what I want to achieve with this book. I want South Africans to truly know and understand what lies behind this issue that affects us daily and in doing so, to find the right solution that is built on positivity and built on growth for us all as a nation. I want us to find a solution that builds a better and more positive society and not one built on further destruction, or breaking down of others, or through the construction of bigger fences, higher walls and greater divides. To move this country forward, we all need to focus on understanding our world around us and on supporting one another's lives and not on creating greater divides and bigger walls. With that, we will go nowhere.

There are so many wonderful stories in this country of individuals and situations where on a private basis, there is peace and prosperity and individuals are working hard to improve the lives of others and to build bridges between cultures, societies and individuals. Sadly, on a general basis and a mass expectation of one group towards another, negativity thrives. As long as this is kept alive and promulgated and until such time as this is corrected and we can stop living in fear of each other, South Africa will never truly be able to move forward to a world of true peace and acceptance. Sadly, the racial barriers will always remain.

To truly become a rainbow nation, we have to destroy the fears that are keeping us apart, and crime is one of the greatest threats responsible for this. We need to bring crime to a crashing halt. This is my Beloved Country, and I will do everything I can to stop crying myself and prevent others from crying with me. Isn't it time that we all start to smile and like the Jam Donut, put aside all our fears and to laugh together instead?

References & Additional Reading

Books And Reports

BURGESS, A. (2018). Heist!. Cape Town, South Africa: Penguin Random House.

GIULLIANI, R. (2003). Leadership. London: Time Warner Paperbacks.

GOLEMAN, D. (1996). Emotional Intelligence. London: Bloomsbury Publishing.

GOLEMAN, D. (1998). Working with emotional intelligence. London: Bloomsbury Publishing.

GOLEMAN, D. and THE DALAI LAMA (2003). Destructive Emotions and how we can overcome them. London: Bloomsburty Publishing.

HUSCHKA, D. and MAU, S. (2005). Social Anomie and Racial Segregation in South Africa. Social Indicators Research, 76(3), pp.467-498.

THOBANE, M. (2014). The criminal career of armed robbers with specific reference to cash-intransit robberies,. University of South Africa, Pretoria. [online] Available at: http://hdl.handle.net/10500/18353

WALTON, S. (2004). Humanity: an Emotional History. London: Atlantic Books.

ZINN, R. (2010). Home invasion. Cape Town: Tafelberg.

Online Resources

Razor Gang Articles

ELISEEV, A. (2008). 'Gang of robbers behind brutal robberies' | IOL News. [online] Iol.co.za. Available at: https://www.iol.co.za/news/south-africa/gang-of-robbers-behind-brutal-robberies-385135

ELISEEV, A. (2009). Notorious 'Razor Gang' part of jail break | IOL News. [online] Iol.co.za. Available at: https://www.iol.co.za/news/south-africa/notorious-razor-gang-part-of-jail-break-458241

ELISEEV, A. and SMILLIE, S. (2011). Razor Gang boss jailed | IOL News. [online] Iol.co.za. Available at: https://www.iol.co.za/news/razor-gang-boss-jailed-1165806

NEWS24. (2009). 'Razor' gang member rearrested. [online] Available at: https://www.news24.com/SouthAfrica/News/Razor-gang-member-rearrested-20091113

NEWS24. (2009). Razor gang kingpin not in court. [online] Available at: https://www.news24.com/southafrica/news/razor-gang-kingpin-not-in-court-20091119

LINDEQUE, M. (2015). Widow of Razor Gang victim calls for justice 8 years on. [online] Ewn.co.za. Available at: http://ewn.co.za/2016/02/15/Plettenberg-Bay-widow-wants-to-see-justice-doneafter-8-years

SECURITY.CO.ZA. (2009). Lawyer delays 'Razor' trial. [online] Available at: https://www.security.co.za/news/13033
SOUTH-AFRICA-PIG.BLOGSPOT.COM. (2009). Hero Cop nails 'Razor' rat. [online] Available at: http://south-africa-pig.blogspot.com/2009/11/herocop-nails-rat.html

Sandton Knife Gang Articles

ELISEEV, A. (2006). Cops smash 'Sandton Knife Gang' | IOL News. [online] Iol.co.za. Available at: https://www.iol.co.za/news/south-africa/cops-smash-sandton-knife-gang-286919

ELISEEV, A. (2006). Knife-gang leader nailed | IOL News. [online] Iol.co.za. Available at: https://www.iol.co.za/news/south-africa/knife-gang-leader-nailed-292343

STAFF REPORTER (2006). 'Knife-gang' man says he burgled Phumzile's home. [online] The M&G Online. Available at: https://mg.co.za/article/2006-09-08-knifegang-man-says-he-burgledphumziles-home

ELISEEV, A. (2006). 'I'm not Knife Gang mastermind' | IOL News. [online] Iol.co.za. Available at: https://www.iol.co.za/news/south-africa/im-not-knife-gang-mastermind-292668

Rolex Gang Articles

SOUTH-AFRICA-PIG.BLOGSPOT.COM. (2009). Gauteng's most wanted criminal finally nabbed. [online] Available at: http://south-africa-pig.blogspot.com/2009/11/gauteng-most-wantedcriminal-finally.html

DU PREEZ, Y. (2011). Freed 'Rolex Gang' back in dock | IOL News. [online] Iol.co.za. Available at: https://www.iol.co.za/news/freed-rolex-gang-back-in-dock-1093662

Crime in SA, Social Theories & Causes Behind Violence

AMATO, B. (2017). What turns some children into criminals? A look into the effects of emotional trauma. [online] News24. Available at: https://www.news24.com/SouthAfrica/News/what-turnssome-children-into-criminals-a-look-into-the-effects-of-emotional-trauma-20171127

ANDERSEN, N. (2018). Shocking stats reveal 41% of rapes in SA are against children. [online] The South African. Available at: https://www.thesouthafrican.com/rape-statistics-41-children/

STAFF WRITER (2017). The shocking truth about rape in South Africa. [online] Businesstech.co.za. Available at: https://businesstech.co.za/news/general/163503/the-shocking-truth-about-rape-insouth-africa/

WILKINSON, K. (2016). GUIDE: Rape statistics in South Africa

| Africa Check. [online] Africa Check. Available at: https://africacheck.org/factsheets/guide-rape-statistics-in-south-africa/.

AFRICA CHECK (2017). FACTSHEET: South Africa's crime statistics for 2016/17 | Africa Check. [online] Africa Check. Available at: https://africacheck.org/factsheets/south-africas-crime-statistics-201617/

STAFF WRITER (2017). South Africa crime stats 2017: everything you need to know. [online] Businesstech.co.za. Available at: https://businesstech.co.za/news/lifestyle/207087/south-africacrime-stats-2017-everything-you-need-to-know/

PIJOOS, I. (2017). Crime Stats: Political interference in police is the cause of poor leadership - ISS. [online] News24. Available at:https://www.news24.com/SouthAfrica/News/crime-stats-politicalinterference-in-police-is-the-cause-of-poor-leadership-iss-20171025

GERBER, J. (2017). Crime Stats: SABRIC remains concerned about cash-in-transit heists. [online] Fin24. Available at: https://www.fin24.com/Economy/crime-stats-sabric-remains-concerned-about-cashin-transit-heists-20171024

WILLIAMS, C. (2015). Worried about crime? Here's how to keep yourself and your home safe. [online] W24.co.za. Available at: https://www.w24.co.za/Home/Interior-design/Worried-about-the-crimestats-Heres-how-to-keep-yourself-and-your-home-safe-20150929

SHAH, S. (2017). Social Disorganization: Meaning, Characteristics and Causes. [online] Sociology Discussion - Discuss Anything About Sociology. Available at: http://www.sociologydiscussion.com/society/social-disorganization-meaning-characteristics-andcauses/2360

SITES.GOOGLE.COM. (n.d.). Applications of the Strain Theory - Strain Theory: Basics, Theorists, and Applications. [online] Available at: https://sites.google.com/site/rlarue23x/applications-of-thestrain-theory

BRUSCHER, B. (2016). 'Rhino poaching is out of control!' Violence, race and the politics of hysteria in online conservation. [online] Brambuscher.files.wordpress.com. Available at:https://

brambuscher.files.wordpress.com/2011/01/bucc88scher-rhino-online-violenceepa2016.pdf

PIJOOS, I. (2017). Crime Stats: Political interference in police is the cause of poor leadership - ISS. [online] News24. Available at:https://www.news24.com/SouthAfrica/News/crime-stats-politicalinterference-in-police-is-the-cause-of-poor-leadership-iss-20171025

PELSER, E. and RAUCH, J. (2001). South Africa's Criminal Justice System: Policy and Priorities. [online] Csvr.org.za. Available at: http://www.csvr.org.za/docs/policing/southafricascriminal.pdf

Psychological Effects Of Boredom And Inactivity As Well As Low-Self Esteem

ABOUTZOOS.INFO. (2012). Captive animals show signs of boredom, study finds | About Zoos. [online] Available at: http://aboutzoos.info/zoos/news-zoos/466-captive-animals-show-signs-ofboredom-study-finds

BERGLAND, C. (2012). The Brain Drain of Inactivity. [online] Psychology Today. Available at: https://www.psychologytoday.com/us/blog/the-athletes-way/201212/the-brain-drain-inactivity

HARRIS, M. (2018). The relationship between physical inactivity and mental wellbeing: Findings from a gamification-based community-wide physical activity intervention. [online] Health Psychology Open. Available at: https://www.ncbi.nlm.nih.gov/pmc/articles/PMC5774736/

HEDRICK, M. (2018). Boredom Can Be Dangerous for Mental Illness. [online] World of Psychology. Available at: https://psychcentral.com/blog/boredom-can-be-dangerous-for-mental-illness/

LACHMANN PSY.D, S. (2013). 10 Sources of Low Self-Esteem. [online] Psychology Today. Available at: https://www.psychologytoday.com/us/blog/me-we/201312/10-sources-low-self-esteem

MCLEOD, S. (2012). Low Self Esteem. [online] Simplypsychology.org. Available at: https://www.simplypsychology.org/self-esteem.html

TARTAKOVSKY, M. (2018). When You Feel Worthless. [online] World of Psychology. Available at: https://psychcentral.com/blog/when-you-feel-worthless/

Emotional Intelligence

GODWIN, J. (2018). What is EQ?. [online] Just Being. Available at: https://justbeing.life/blog/whatis-eq/
LOVEJOY, D. (2013). What is EQ? Emotional Intelligence in the Workplace. [online] Workology.com. Available at: https://workology.com/what-is-eq-emotional-intelligence-in-the-workplace/

Dr. PAWLIW-FRY, J. (2014). What is EQ? - IHHP. [online] IHHP. Available at: https://www.ihhp.com/what-is-eq/

RESEARCH GATE. (2015). The relation between emotional intelligence and criminal behavior: A study among convicted criminals. [online] Available at: https://www.researchgate.net/publication/280865308_The_relation_between_emotional_intelligence_and_criminal_behavior_A_study_among_convicted_criminals[

WILSON, R. (2017). What Aspects of Emotional Intelligence Help Former Prisoners Make Decisions to Desist Crime?. [online] Fisherpub.sjfc.edu. Available at: https://fisherpub.sjfc.edu/cgi/viewcontent.cgi?article=1336&context=education_etd

SHARMA, N., PRAKASH, O., SENGAR, K., CHAUDHURYS, S. and SINGH, A. (2015). The relation between emotional intelligence and criminal behavior: A study among convicted criminals. [online] The Industrial Psychology Journal. Available at: https://www.ncbi.nlm.nih.gov/pmc/articles/PMC4525433/

IHHP. (2017). Test Your Emotional Intelligence, Free EQ Quiz, EI Test. [online] Available at: https://www.ihhp.com/free-eq-quiz/

Childhood Development, Community Development And The Importance Of Family

NIKKI BUSH. (n.d.). Nikki Bush Speaker and Author | Nikki Bush. [online] Available at: https://nikkibush.com
NIKKI BUSH. (n.d.). Parenting Scorecard FREE Report | Nikki Bush. [online] Available at: https://nikkibush.com/parentingsurvey/

BRAINBOOSTERS. (n.d.). ECD Solutions. [online] Available at: https://www.brainboosters.co.za

LUSA. (n.d.). Restoring Hope - Transforming Lives. [online] Available at: http://www.lusa.co.za

FERNANDES, P. (2016). Support Your Employees by Creating a Family-Friendly Workplace. [online] Business News Daily. Available at: https://www.businessnewsdaily.com/9614-family-friendlyworkplace.html

BARNEY, A. (n.d.). 16 Companies With Innovative Parent-Friendly Policies. [online] Explore Parents. Available at: https://www.parents.com/parenting/work/parent-friendly-companies/

SHENFELD, H. (2017). Companies Supporting Families. [online] PEOPLE.com. Available at: https://people.com/human-interest/companies-supporting-families/

MEDIUM. (2018). Supporting Working Parents: A Guide for Companies and Coworkers. [online] Available at: https://medium.com/taking-note/supporting-working-parents-a-guide-forcompanies-and-coworkers-49f1ef3506c

HEALY, S. (2018). What the 10 Best Companies to Work For Offer for Family-Friendly Benefits. [online] Workplace.care.com. Available at: http://workplace.care.com/best-companies-family-friendlybenefits

FAST COMPANY. (2016). How These Companies Have Created Kid-Friendly Offices For Working Parents. [online] Available at: https://www.fastcompany.com/3056417/how-these-companieshave-created-kid-friendly-offices-for-working-parents

FAST COMPANY. (2018). How Companies Can Really Make Their Workplaces Family-Friendly. [online] Available at: https://www.fastcompany.com/40525237/how-companies-can-really-make-theirworkplaces-family-friendly

Dept. Of Correctional Services and Dept Of Justice

ISS Africa. (1998). Correcting Corrections Prospects for South Africa's Prisons - ISS Africa. [online] Available at: https://issafrica.org/research/monographs/monograph-29-correctingcorrectionsprospects-for-south-africas-prisons

AFRICA CHECK (2017). FACTSHEET: South Africa's crime statistics for 2016/17 | Africa Check. [online] Africa Check. Available at: https://africacheck.org/factsheets/south-africas-crime-statistics- 201617/

WITS.AC.ZA. (2017). Overcrowding, disease and torture - Wits University. [online] Available at: https://www.wits.ac.za/news/latest-news/research-news/2017/2017-07/overcrowding-diseaseand-torture.html

SANEWS. (2012). Reading for Redemption campaign taken to correctional centres. [online] Available at: https://www.sanews.gov.za/south-africa/reading-redemption-campaign-taken-correctionalcentres

VUKUZENZELE. (2012). Reading redeems offenders | Vuk'uzenzele. [online] Available at: https://www.vukuzenzele.gov.za/reading-redeems-offenders

DEPT OF JUSTICE, (n.d.). Restorative Justice. [online] Available at: http://www.justice.gov.za/rj/rj.html

MASHABA, S. (2018). Inhumane conditions in jail blamed | Saturday Star. [online] Iol.co.za. Available at: https://www.iol.co.za/saturday-star/news/inhumane-conditions-in-jail-blamed-14373794

MZANTSI, S. (2016). Pollsmoor Prison conditions declared unconstitutional | Cape Times. [online]

Iol.co.za. Available at: https://www.iol.co.za/capetimes/news/pollsmoor-prison-conditionsdeclared-unconstitutional-2095712

RAPHAELY, C. (2017). The hell that is life in SA's jails | IOL News. [online] Iol.co.za. Available at: https://www.iol.co.za/news/the-hell-that-is-life-in-sas-jails-8065928

HLATI, O. (2017). Understaffing issue in prisons puts wardens at risk | IOL News. [online] Iol.co.za. Available at: https://www.iol.co.za/news/understaffing-issue-in-prisons-puts-wardens-at-risk-8949399

MAKOU, G. (2017). FACTSHEET: The state of South African prisons. [online] Africa Check. Available at: https://africacheck.org/factsheets/factsheet-the-state-of-south-africas-prisons/

DISSEL, A. (1996). South Africa's Prison Conditions: The inmates talk.. [online] Csvr.org.za. Available at: http://www.csvr.org.za/publications/1364-south-africas-prison-conditions-the-inmatestalk.html

THE YOUNG INDEPENDENTS. (2018). 9 of The Worst Prisons in SA | The Young Independents. [online] Available at: https://www.tyi.co.za/news/international/9-of-the-worst-prisons-in-sa/

MAKOU, G., SKOSANA, I. and HOPKINS, R. (2017). Fact sheet: The state of South Africa's prisons. [online] Daily Maverick. Available at: https://www.dailymaverick.co.za/article/2017-07-18-factsheet-the-state-of-south-africas-prisons/

SEFALI, P. (2014). How I was raped in prison. [online] GroundUp News. Available at: https://www.groundup.org.za/article/how-i-was-raped-prison_1765/

Special Assignment - Prisons. (2014). [video] https://www.youtube.com/watch?v=tbberUWq-Pk: SPECIAL ASSIGNMENT - YOU TUBE.

STREET TALK TV (2016). The Pollsmoor Sessions Pt.1. [video] Available at: https://www.youtube.com/watch?v=B8-kZBz5nW8

STREET TALK TV (2016). The Pollsmoor Sessions Pt.2. [video] Available at: https://www.youtube.com/watch?v=m3SyAN9bxag

PRISONER (2011). Thinking Back. [Blog] Diaries of a prisoner. Available at: http://diariesofaprisoner.blogspot.com

Farm Attacks

WILKINSON, K. (2017). FACTSHEET: Statistics on farm attacks and murders in South Africa. [online] Africa Check. Available at: https://africacheck.org/factsheets/factsheet-statistics-farm-attacksmurders-sa/

KILLALEA, D. (2016). South Africans reveal brutality of crime taking place. [online] NewsComAu. Available at: https://www.

news.com.au/finance/economy/world-economy/south-africa-farmattacks- brutal-crimes-landowners-face/news-story/dfaabafca743056b6d6656ea1fff49eb

ABDULLA, M. (2017). South Africa's farm murder statistics are more political than accurate. [online] The M&G Online. Available at:https://mg.co.za/article/2017-10-30-south-africas-farm-murderstatistics- are-more-political-than-accurate

SOUTH AFRICA TODAY - Media. (2017). Farm Murders – 'Terror' Lekota getting very angry in Parliament - video | South Africa Today - Media. [online] Available at: https://southafricatoday.net/media/south-africa-video/farm-attack-videos/farm-murders-terrorlekota-getting-very-angry-in-parliament-video/

FREE WEST MEDIA. (2017). Questions in Dutch parliament after citizen is killed in farm attack | Free West Media. [online] Available at: http://freewestmedia.com/2017/04/11/questions-in-dutchparliament-after-citizen-is-killed-in-farm-attack/

GUMBI, C. (2017). Farm attacks – an evil within. [online] Polokwane Observer. Available at:http://www.observer.co.za/farm-attacks-an-evil-within/

Rhino Poaching

VALOI, E. (n.d.). Oxpeckers | Mozambique's poaching castles are crumbling. [online] Oxpeckers.org. Available at: https://oxpeckers.org/2017/03/mozambiques-poaching-castles-crumbling/

TOTLAND, M. (n.d.). Oxpeckers | The uphill battle to save rhinos in Mozambique. [online] Oxpeckers.org. Available at: https://oxpeckers.org/2016/06/2811/

SMILLIE, S. (2012). The evolution of a rhino poacher | IOL News. [online] Iol.co.za. Available at: https://www.iol.co.za/news/the-evolution-of-a-rhino-poacher-1442771

www.ingramcontent.com/pod-product-compliance
Lightning Source LLC
Chambersburg PA
CBHW032147080426
42735CB00008B/609